# LITERATURE, LANGUAGE AND CHANGE

## From Chaucer to the Present

How did the rise of polite society change the language of literature? What was the effect of Romanticism on poetic word order? How does knowing the answers to these questions alter the meaning of a text for us?

Reading literature is a quest for sense, involving us in a need to grasp both how meaning is produced by the words on the page and how history, culture and ideology have influenced the choice of those words. Literary English changes from period to period as it reflects variations in the society and culture in which it is produced – variations in the ways writers construct images of their world, shifts in the relationships between readers, texts and writers, and linguistic change.

*Literature, Language and Change* offers an historical perspective on literary English, from the mid-fourteenth century to the present day. Through detailed analyses of individual texts and comparisons with texts from different periods, Stephens and Waterhouse build up a picture of the important and distinctive characteristics of each period and of the changes between them.

At the end of each chapter the authors provide the opportunity to put theory into practice through exercises giving suggestions for further thought. Terms which may be unfamiliar to the student are defined and explained in a glossary, and the bibliography gives useful pointers for supplementary reading.

John Stephens and Ruth Waterhouse are Associate Professors in English at Macquarie University, Australia.

**The INTERFACE Series**

'A linguist deaf to the poetic function of language and a literary scholar indifferent to linguistic problems and unconversant with linguistic methods, are equally flagrant anachronisms.' – Roman Jakobson

This statement, made over twenty-five years ago, is no less relevant today, and 'flagrant anachronisms' still abound. The aim of the INTERFACE series is to examine topics at the 'interface' of language studies and literary criticism and in so doing to build bridges between these traditionally divided disciplines.

**The Series Editor**

Ronald Carter is Senior Lecturer in English Studies and Director of the Centre for English Language Education at the University of Nottingham. He is Chair of the Poetics and Linguistics Association (PALA).

Already published in the series:

David Birch: *Language, Literature and Critical Practice: Ways of analysing text*

Alan Durant and Nigel Fabb: *Literary Studies in Action*

Michael J. Toolan: *Narrative: A critical linguistic introduction*

Walter Nash: *Language in Popular Fiction*

# LITERATURE, LANGUAGE AND CHANGE

## From Chaucer to the Present

**JOHN STEPHENS and
RUTH WATERHOUSE**

**London and New York**

First published 1990
by Routledge
11 New Fetter Lane, London EC4P 4EE

Simultaneously published in the USA and Canada
by Routledge
a division of Routledge, Chapman and Hall, Inc.
29 West 35th Street, New York, NY 10001

Disc conversion by Columns Ltd
Printed in Great Britain by Cox & Wyman Ltd

*British Library Cataloguing in Publication Data*
Stephens, John
    Literature, language and change: from Chaucer to the
    present – (The Interface series, ISSN 0955–730X)
    1. English literature. Language. Cultural aspects
    I. Title    II. Series
    820.9

*Library of Congress Cataloging in Publication Data*
Stephens, John.
    Literature, language and change : from Chaucer to the present /
    John Stephens and Ruth Waterhouse.
        p.    cm. — (The Interface series)
    Includes bibliographical references.
    1. English language—Style.    2. English literature—History and
criticism.    I. Waterhouse, Ruth.    II. Title.    III. Series:
Interface (London, England)
PE1421.S674    1990
820.9—dc20        89–10956

ISBN 0–415–03087–0
        0–415–03088–9 pbk

# Contents

# Series editor's introduction to the Interface series

There have been many books published this century which have been devoted to the interface of language and literary studies. This is the first *series* of books devoted to this area commissioned by a major international publisher; it is the first time a *group* of writers have addressed themselves to issues at the interface of language and literature; and it is the first time an international professional association has worked closely with a publisher to establish such a venture. It is the purpose of this general introduction to the series to outline some of the main guiding principles underlying the books in the series.

The first principle adopted is one of not foreclosing on the many possibilities for the integration of language and literature studies. There are many ways in which the study of language and literature can be combined and many different theoretical, practical and curricular objectives to be realized. Obviously, a close relationship with the aims and methods of descriptive linguistics will play a prominent part, so readers will encounter some detailed analysis of language in places. In keeping with a goal of much work in this field, writers will try to make their analysis sufficiently replicable for other analysts to see how they have arrived at the interpretive decisions they have reached and to allow others to reproduce their methods on the same or on other texts. But linguistic science does not have a monopoly in methodology and description any more than linguists can have sole possession of insights into language and its workings. Some contributors to this series adopt quite rigorous linguistic procedures; others proceed less rigorously but no less revealingly. All are, however, united by a belief that detailed scrutiny of the role of language in literary texts can be mutually enriching to language and literary studies.

Series of books are usually written to an overall formula or design. In the case of the Interface series this was considered to be not entirely appropriate. This is for the reasons given above, but also because, as the first series of its kind, it would be wrong to suggest that there are formulaic modes by which integration can be achieved. The fact that all the books address themselves to the integration of language and literature in any case imparts a natural and organic unity to the series. Thus, some of the books in this series will provide descriptive overviews; others will offer detailed case studies of a particular topic; others will involve single author studies; and some will be more pedagogically oriented.

This variety of design and procedure means that a wide variety of audiences is envisaged for the series as a whole, though, of course, individual books are necessarily quite specifically targeted. The general level of exposition presumes quite advanced students of language and literature. Approximately, this level covers students of English language and literature (though not exclusively English) at senior high-school/upper sixth form level to university students in their first or second year of study. Many of the books in the series are designed to be *used by students*. Some may serve as course books – these will normally contain exercises and suggestions for further work as well as glossaries and graded bibliographies which point the student towards further reading. Some books are also designed to be used by teachers for their own reading and updating, and to supplement courses; in some cases, specific questions of pedagogic theory, teaching procedure, and methodology at the interface of language and literature are addressed.

From a pedagogic point of view it is the case in many parts of the world that students focus on literary texts, especially in the mother tongue, before undertaking any formal study of the language. With this fact in mind, contributors to the series have attempted to gloss all new technical terms and to assume on the part of their readers little or no previous knowledge of linguistics or formal language studies. They see no merit in not being detailed and explicit about what they describe in the linguistic properties of texts, but they recognize that formal language study can seem forbidding if it is not properly introduced.

A further characteristic of the series is that the authors engage in a direct relationship with their readers. The overall style of writing is informal and there is above all an attempt to lighten the usual style of academic discourse. In some cases this extends to the way in which notes and guidance for further work are presented. In all cases, the style adopted by authors is judged to be that most appropriate to the mediation of their chosen subject matter.

We now come to two major points of principle which underlie the conceptual scheme for the series. One is that the term 'literature' cannot be defined in isolation from an expression of ideology. In fact, no academic study, and certainly no description of the language of texts, can be neutral and objective, for the socio-cultural positioning of the analyst will mean that the description is unavoidably political. Contributors to the series recognize and, in so far as this accords with the aims of each book, attempt to explore the role of ideology at the interface of language and literature. Secondly, most writers also prefer the term 'literatures' to a singular notion of literature. Some replace 'literature' altogether with the term 'text'. It is for this reason that readers will not find exclusive discussion of the literary language of canonical literary texts; instead, the linguistic heterogeneity of literature and the permeation of many discourses with what is conventionally thought of as poetic or literary language will be a focus. This means that in places as much space can be devoted to examples of word play in jokes, newspaper editorials, advertisements, historical writing or a popular thriller as to a sonnet by Shakespeare or a passage from Jane Austen. It is also important to stress how the term 'literature' itself is historically variable and how different social and cultural assumptions can condition what is regarded as literature. In this respect the role of linguistic and literary theory is vital. It is an aim of the series to be constantly alert to new developments in the description and theory of texts.

Finally, as series editor, I have to underline the partnership and co-operation of the whole enterprise of the Interface series and acknowledge the advice and assistance received at many stages from the PALA Committee and from Wendy Morris at Routledge. In turn, we are all fortunate to have the benefit of three associate editors with considerable collective depth of experience in this field in different parts of the world: Professor Roger Fowler, Professor Mary Louise Pratt, Professor Michael Halliday. In spite of their own individual orientations, I am sure that all concerned with the series would want to endorse the statement by Roman Jakobson made over twenty-five years ago but which is no less relevant today.

A linguist deaf to the poetic function of language and a literary scholar indifferent to linguistic problems and unconversant with linguistic methods, are equally flagrant anachronisms.

In their contribution to this series Ruth Waterhouse and John Stephens provide a necessary and often neglected historical perspective on literary language which is simultaneously attentive to linguistic and literary issues. They do so by means of a theoretical framework grounded in a distinction between syntagmatic and paradigmatic features of language organization – a framework which is clear and enabling and allows systematic appraisal of the evolution of literary language(s) from Chaucer to the present day. The language focus is not however predominant and in a range of examples the authors demonstrate the interrelationship between views of language, language change and historical and cultural context. Additionally, Ruth Waterhouse and John Stephens are continually alert to recent developments in literary theory. Their study is thus more than a survey, however useful a survey it is. They have provided a modern textbook which is of equal service to the interests of students of language and literature as to the growing body of scholars who would use the evidence of this book to demonstrate that there are no easy divisions between the two.

Ronald Carter

# Acknowledgements

A book such as this may have a long germination, and we wish to thank Associate Professor Elizabeth Liggins for planting the seed, and the many students of English in our 'Literary Discourse' units for their patience in bearing with us as we tried out various ideas on them. We also wish to thank Macquarie University for some periods of study leave during which much of the book was written.

We owe a more direct debt to Ron Carter for his critical comments which have helped bring the book to its present shape. Finally, we are especially grateful to Margaret Bartholomew, who has cheerfully contributed her time and energy far beyond what could be reasonably expected.

We are grateful to the following for permission to reproduce copyright material:

Ammons, A. R.: 'Pet Panther' is reprinted from *Lake Effect Country*, Poems by A. R. Ammons, by permission of W. W. Norton & Company, Inc. Copyright © 1983 by A. R. Ammons.

Ash, John: Excerpt from 'In the Street' is reprinted from *Disbelief*, 1987 edition, by permission of Carcanet Press Ltd.

Ashbery, John: From 'Grand Galop', *Selected Poems* by John Ashbery. Copyright © John Ashbery, 1985. All rights reserved. Reprinted by permission of Viking Penguin, a division of Penguin Books USA, Inc. Also reprinted by permission of Carcanet Press Ltd, 1986 edition.

Atwood, Margaret: 'You Fit Into Me' is reprinted from *Power Politics* by permission of Stoddart Publishing Company. Copyright © Margaret Atwood, 1971.

Duncan, Robert: Excerpts from 'At the Loom' and 'The Moon', from *Bending The Bow*. Copyright © 1968 by Robert Duncan. Reprinted by permission of New Directions Publishing Corporation.

Eliot, T. S.: Excerpts from *Collected Poems 1909–1962* by T. S. Eliot, copyright 1936 by Harcourt Brace Jovanovich, Inc., copyright © 1964, 1963 by T. S. Eliot, reprinted by permission of the publisher. Also reprinted by permission of Faber and Faber Ltd from *Collected Poems 1909–1962* by T. S. Eliot.

Jarrell, Randall: Excerpt from 'A Girl in a Library', from *The Complete Poems* by Randall Jarrell. Copyright © 1951 and renewal copyright © 1968, 1969 by Mrs Randall Jarrell. Reprinted by permission of Farrar, Straus and Giroux, Inc. Also reprinted by permission of Faber and Faber Ltd.

Larkin, Philip: 'A Study of Reading Habits', reprinted by permission of Faber and Faber Ltd from *The Whitsun Weddings* by Philip Larkin.

Nemerov, Howard: Excerpt from 'The Blue Swallows', from *The Collected Poems of Howard Nemerov*, University of Chicago Press, 1977. Reprinted by permission of the author.

Pound, Ezra: 'In a Station of the Metro' and excerpts from 'Hugh Selwyn Mauberley', reprinted by permission of Faber and Faber Ltd from *Collected Shorter Poems* by Ezra Pound. *Personae*, copyright 1926 by Ezra Pound, reprinted by permission of New Directions Publishing Corporation.

Reed, Henry: Excerpt from 'Judging Distances' reprinted by permission of J. Tydeman, Literary Executor of the Henry Reed Estate, from *A Map Of Verona* by Henry Reed.

Rich, Adrienne: 'A Valediction Forbidding Mourning' is reprinted from *Poems, Selected and New, 1950–1974*, by Adrienne Rich, by permission of the author and W. W. Norton & Company, Inc. Copyright © 1975, 1973, 1971, 1969, 1966 by W. W. Norton & Company, Inc. Copyright © 1967, 1963, 1962, 1961, 1960, 1959, 1958, 1957, 1956, 1955, 1954, 1953, 1952, 1951 by Adrienne Rich.

Stevens, Wallace: Excerpts from 'The Snow Man' and 'The Emperor of Ice Cream' reprinted by permission of Faber and Faber Ltd from *The Collected Poems of Wallace Stevens*. Also reprinted by permission of Alfred A. Knopf, Inc. Copyright 1923 and renewed 1951 by Wallace Stevens.

Thomas, Dylan: Excerpts from 'A Refusal to Mourn the Death,

by Fire, of a Child in London' and 'The Force that through the Green Fuse' from *Poems of Dylan Thomas*. Copyright 1939 by New Directions Publishing Corporation. Reprinted by permission of New Directions Publishing Corporation. And from *Collected Poems 1934–1952* by Dylan Thomas. Reprinted by permission of David Higham Associates Ltd.

Wilbur, Richard: Excerpt from 'Praise in Summer' reprinted by permission of Faber and Faber Ltd from *Poems 1943–1956* by Richard Wilbur. Excerpt from 'Praise in Summer' in *The Beautiful Changes*, copyright 1947 and renewed 1975 by Richard Wilbur, reprinted by permission of Harcourt Brace Jovanovich, Inc.

Williams, William Carlos: 'Poem', from *Collected Poems 1909–1939,* Vol. I (1986). Copyright 1938 by New Directions Publishing Corporation. 'Poem' reprinted by permission of New Directions Publishing Corporation. Also reprinted by permission of Carcanet Press Ltd.

Yeats, William Butler: Excerpt from 'Easter 1916' reprinted by permission of Macmillan Publishing Company from *The Poems of W. B. Yeats: A New Edition*, edited by Richard J. Finneran. Copyright 1924 by Macmillan Publishing Company, renewed by Bertha Georgie Yeats. Also reprinted with permission of A. P. Watt Ltd on behalf of Michael B. Yeats and Macmillan London Ltd.

While every effort has been made to secure permission, we may have failed in a few cases to trace the copyright holder. We apologize for any apparent negligence.

# 1 Approaches to decoding the language of literature

My two fears are distortion and inaccuracy, or rather the kind of inaccuracy produced by too dogmatic a generality and too positivistic a localized focus.

(Edward W. Said, *Orientalism*, p. 8)

## Introduction

In the context of the recent proliferation of theories about culture, about literature, and about textuality, it has become increasingly difficult to write an account of the language of literature in the last six hundred years. When the hegemony of the white, middle-class male critic created the illusion of a monolithic literary culture, it was possible to approach a given text, or group of texts, in a spirit of empiricism, describing 'what was there' and then drawing conclusions from the description with which any educated reader might be expected, in general, to concur. This is no longer possible. Even approaches which are explicitly textualist – that is, which are concerned to ground interpretation in the linguistic structures of the text – now differ widely in their understandings of what constitutes textuality.

An immediate challenge to 'merely textualist' approaches issues from the conjunction of two important tenets widespread in late twentieth-century literary critical discourse: on the one hand, there is substantial doubt that empiricist textual studies can achieve a very high level of general validity (see, for example, Carroll, 1975); on the other hand, it has been extensively argued by poststructuralist and feminist critics that the concept of a literary 'canon' is a localized socio-historical phenomenon, so that any grouping of texts as 'central' or 'important' is ultimately an *ad hoc* grouping made, consciously or not, to serve or reflect the purposes of a particular sub-culture in a particular time and place.

Any attempt to present a detailed and practical account of the differences in the nature of texts between periods and between authors can no longer make easy assumptions about which texts are representative, and it would seem an act of folly to propose any texts as essential. It is for these reasons that we have quoted Said's warning to himself as the epigraph for this chapter. The fabric of literary discourse is thick and rich, and any study of it which pretends to include detailed analyses of specific texts will be compelled to inspect that fabric at certain points and to try to suggest how these relate to the whole. Our approach, however, is not empiricist, and we hope that its underpinning method will avoid the pitfalls both of dogmatic generalization and of positivism. While concentrating our discussion on the analysis of particular texts, we will be using a methodology which incorporates many elements: a theory of how texts signify; an awareness of the socio-linguistic dimension of signification; a sense of the importance of intertextuality in literary meaning. We will also from time to time draw examples from authors who, from some points of view, might seem 'minor', or 'regional', or 'marginal'. The aim of this first chapter is to describe the elements of our method.

Any undertaking to offer an historical overview of texts from the time of Chaucer to the present must face the problem that there is a plurality of theories of meaning, since the history that gets written will already be predetermined by the writer's presuppositions and assumptions about culture and language. Implicit in most contemporary theories is the assumption that, given the arbitrary relationship between verbal sign and referent, an important aspect of signification lies in what happens in the space between sign and thing. To one theory, the very arbitrariness of the relationship questions the possibility of any stable meaning; to others, the covert attitudes which culture implants within the transaction between sign and thing are the proper focus of attention, so that to read a text is to examine the culture which produced that text. The role of the author (and in another way, the role of the reader) in the transaction has become problematized, since s/he must use (or receive) a language already culturally coded and one which can therefore be analysed from perspectives possibly inimical to the author's own assumptions about what s/he was doing. Culture becomes an implicit co-author and co-reader of the text.

## Language, culture and the determination of meaning

To begin to illustrate this problem of language we will consider the opening lines of a poem by Randall Jarrell, in which the problem takes four forms:

### A Girl in a Library

An object among dreams, you sit here with your shoes off
And curl your legs up under you; your eyes
Close for a moment, your face moves toward sleep . . .
You are very human.

First, the male speaker's framing of the description in terms of an implicit 'I' and an explicit 'you', the fundamental indicators of Selfhood and Otherness, can be regarded by some readers as immediately encoding within the text not merely differentness but also subordination within a power relationship. This may be consciously or unconsciously exploited — here it seems overtly reinforced by the initial choice of 'object' to denote the student, since to reify people, to turn them into things, is to assert power over them.

Secondly, the choice of *girl* in the title to signify a female person entails an ambiguity of attitude. It emerges later in the poem (line 64) that this 'girl' is 19: the transition from the state signified by *girl* {+ female, + child} to that signified by *woman* {+ female, + adult} is culturally determined (and indeterminate), but to apply the former where the latter would be more appropriate can be patronizing or pejorative, and can be seen as another form of power appropriation. (The usage goes beyond establishing a quasi adult–child relationship, since from the seventeenth century *girl* has also denoted 'a servant' — a usage still implicit in such collocations as 'shop-girl' or 'office-girl', or in expressions such as 'I'll give it to the girl to type'.) The age of the young female in Jarrell's poem may make her eligible to be a *girl*, but this may also be largely a male point of view. This word, then, presents the student of textuality with a diachronic problem, in that a feminist today would probably eschew even Jarrell's use of *girl*, whereas the assumptions which the term masks would have passed unobtrusively when the poem appeared in 1951.

The third feature of the text we wish to comment on is similar to the second: this is the use of the word *human*, which clearly signifies more than an organic species. It is not usual to define *human* as 'a female person who falls asleep in a library', but this, in effect, is what Jarrell has done, marking the term *sexually* by its object's femaleness and vulnerability, and *socially* by the library location, markings sanctioned by synchronic mid-twentieth-century humanist values, and so liable to diachronic distortion.

These second and third features offer small examples of how the modes of thought which dominate a culture may appropriate the significances of words which have an important function in the structuring of relationships between individuals, and between individuals and their world. When such words enter literary texts, whether at the point of production or of consumption, they are thus already heavily marked. In chapters 2 to 5 we will attempt to locate our discussions within an awareness of such dominant modes of thought.

Finally, a textualist approach to *A Girl in a Library*, which is quite different from those emphasizing the cultural coding of sign/thing relationships, might choose instead to focus on the indeterminacy of the signification of the phrase 'among dreams', posing such questions as: whose dreams are they, those of the 'I' or the 'you'? does the term *dreams* denote 'images perceived during sleep', 'reveries', 'vain fancies', 'aspirations'? or does the interaction with *object* suggest that *dreams* refers to 'persons of unbelievable beauty' (other women in the library, as contrasted with this one)? or does it even refer to the surrounding books, or their contents? To what extent is the meaning of 'an object among dreams' affected by its structural similarity with such phrases as 'a man among men'? With the failure of the sign to point to a determinable meaning, the very first phrase of the poem offers a deconstructive critic an obvious loose thread with which to begin unravelling the text.[1] This fourth textual problem raises the question of the extent to which, and the ways in which, context can either determine or discourage the achieving of textual meaning. We will argue below and in later chapters that it is capable of both.

The ideologies and emphases distinguishing the fourth of the above mini-analyses from the other three show something of the problems we faced in embarking upon any kind of history of textuality, because, while all the observations we made can be supported by particular features in the text, their presuppositions and objectives tend to be incompatible. A feminist approach to the text would clearly benefit from applying deconstructive strategies to *girl*, but would not (nor wish to) conclude that the meaning is indeterminable, since the main purpose of such an analysis is likely to be to demonstrate how culture determines meaning. A marxist analysis of the link between *human*, *library*, and the implied concept of 'vulnerability' operates within the same parameters.

## A pluralistic approach

The major problem that faced us in co-authoring a book on the language of literature was whether we should attempt to work within a single ideological position, accepting that the limitations inherent in any one position would render our history partial, or whether we should attempt to generate a more pluralistic approach, drawing upon the strengths and potential of several different theories, and accepting the risk that the exponents of such theories would regard our endeavour as merely eclectic, or incoherent, or lacking an ideological centre. In the event, the prospect of writing a collaborative work committed us to a pluralist position, for the text that one of us reads is not the text that the other of us reads. The text/reader interaction is affected by our differing cultural and societal backgrounds and environments, differing attitudes and patterns of belief, and by the fact that one of us is female and the other male: the result is that we do not bring the same presuppositions and assumptions to texts; we have different expectations of what a text will be and do. And we share with all readers the simple condition that neither of us can read a text in the same way twice: at the very least, the text itself becomes part of the textual background for its own re-reading, and this changed circumstance is further complemented in that other texts, and other cultural and personal experiences, occur between readings of the 'same' text. To return to our earlier example, 'A Girl in a Library' becomes a different text after the implications of *girl*, for example, have been considered. A reader might decide that to articulate those implications would be semantically anachronistic, but this would be to ignore the force of that observation as a comment on the cultures within which the text is situated, whether for writer or reader.

Despite those factors which preclude the two of us from reading a text in the same way, we do share some basic assumptions, one of the most fundamental of which is that the study of the language of a literary text constitutes a common jumping-off point for all critical approaches. We also share a belief that twentieth-century linguistic studies have much to offer the processes of literary criticism, at both the conceptual and analytical levels, and we draw quite heavily upon them as a basis for much of our own analyses. In what follows we have striven to develop what we imagine all analysers of texts hope to acquire, a reading methodology which in its efficacy is both powerful and flexible.

## The primary textual distinction: *story* and *discourse*

The problem of *how* to begin interpreting a literary text faces all readers. Whether consciously or not, the most 'innocent' reader will bring to a new text expectations and interpretive practices formulated from past reading experiences; the more experienced reader may apply various techniques of analysis acquired from contact with some kind of critical discourse; the 'fallen' reader may attempt to schematize these techniques into some sort of model or grid against which to measure the text, and this can easily lead to the temptation to make the text fit the model, with the consequence that the reader may fail to become aware of other facets of signification. Current critical practices can rarely be accused of schematizing to that extent, but the recurrence of particular presuppositions about texts often implies underlying critical models.

Because it is merely inefficient to operate on the basis of an undisciplined, and covertly subjective, empiricism, some kind of critical methodology is necessary, but it is equally necessary to remain conscious of the parameters of such a methodology. These need to be clear enough to facilitate communication of observations on texts, and sufficiently multi-faceted to enable texts to be examined from a multiplicity of perspectives. An important element of the methodology employed in this book is derived from the structuralist linguistics originating in the work of de Saussure, but it has needed to be modified in many ways. Much of the critical discourse influenced by Structuralism has tended to depend implicitly or explicitly upon systems of binary opposition, such as langue/parole, signifier/signified, syntagm/paradigm and synchronic/diachronic, and from here binary oppositions have become a feature of much narratology in such distinctions as story/discourse, narrator/narratee, acteur/actant, and the like. Such convenient short-hand descriptors need to be used carefully, however, since their analytical elegance may actually conceal textual relationships which are not binary, but rather ternary or even quaternary. It has been our constant concern to prevent our methodology from becoming locked into any such oversimplification.

Perhaps *the* primary literary distinction is that between *story* and *discourse*, or, to put it in somewhat simplistic terms, the distinction between *what* the text depicts and *how* it depicts it (Chatman, 1978, 19). The particular terms tend to be associated with narrative forms, but the distinction is basic to literature of any kind, and is the primary analytical distinction to be made when one embarks upon textual interpretation. It is an oversimplification, which owes its origin partly to a frustration with readers who are dominated by what Salman Rushdie has called 'what-happens-nextism' (1982, 39), and partly to the attempt to side-step arguments earlier this century over the status of form and content (because 'discourse' comprises both). The functional importance of the distinction can be seen in a discourse such as the following extract from a poem, in which the speaker describes a scene containing some buildings, some trees, and two people:

> There to the west,
> On the fields of summer the sun and the shadows bestow
>     Vestments of purple and gold.
>
> The still white dwellings are like a mirage in the heat,
> And under the swaying elms a man and a woman
> Lie gently together. Which is, perhaps, only to say
> That there is a row of houses to the left of arc,
> And that under some poplars a pair of what appear
>     to be humans
>   Appear to be loving.
>                     (Henry Reed, 'Judging Distances', 52–60)

The lines describe 'the same thing' (the 'story') twice, but inscribe the landscape and the figures within it in different discourses, as the transitional cliché 'Which is . . . only to say' foregrounds. The reader can easily abstract and even rephrase the shared referents from each discourse, but the obvious point of the passage lies in the attitudes to those referents indicated in the very disparate types of language selected (the first, for example, is rich in adjectives and adverbs, and in figurative language, but the second has none of these; the first is also distinguished by slightly strange, rather formal grammatical constructions, such as 'fields of summer', and by an archaism like 'bestow'. The simplest way to describe the contrast between the two discourses is to say that they are in different *registers* (Leech, 1969, 9–12).

## THE TERNARY STRUCTURE OF TEXTS

However if a wider signification of meaning (such as that drawn from the clash of registers and what it implies about the speaker) can be inferred from discourse in the same way as 'story' is, it would follow that a merely binary opposition of discourse and story is a misrepresentation of the nature of textuality.[2] Another piece, a complete, simple narrative, shows clearly that the actual structure of a text is ternary, not binary:

> The itsy bitsy spider climbed up the water spout
> Down came the rain and washed the spider out
> Out came the sun and dried up all the rain
> And the itsy bitsy spider climbed up the spout again.

Here is presented a series of events, set out in a chronological time sequence, and involving a protagonist located in a particularized space. The story is abstracted from the discourse in much the same way that a referent is deduced from a verbal sign; just as, above, we asked, 'What does the term "dreams" denote?', so a stretch of text can be asked the question, 'What is the discourse about?' If the import of that question is 'What happened to whom when and where?', the paraphrase answer will point to the 'story'. But the 'story' about the spider's experiences is only one type of abstraction that can be drawn from the discourse. If the question is directed rather towards what can be called the *hypersignification*, asking, for example, 'What deeper signification lies behind the discourse? What is the theme? What does the interaction of "story" and discourse further signify?', then the answer here will be thematic, perhaps 'persistence in the face of adversity'.

Instead of a binary opposition, then, the text operates through three elements, which can be represented as in Figure

1.1 (though properly the plane should be presented so as to show how the 'story' and the 'hypersignification' lie behind the actual 'discourse' on the page; the two-dimensionality of a printed book does not permit this):

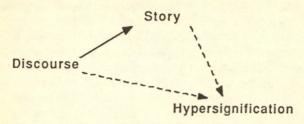

Figure 1.1

The secondary abstraction, the hypersignification, is derived from both the primary abstraction, the story, and the actual discourse which encodes it. Readers (and this probably includes most literary critics) who progress from the primary to the secondary level of abstraction do so usually by intuitive inference. But to analyse exactly *how* the discourse encodes this secondary level of abstraction, the reader must enter into the area of interface between linguistics and literary criticism.

A way into this particular text is offered by a pattern of three interlocked verbal oppositions: first, the directional pair, 'up:down', also reversed as 'down:up'; second, the weather pair, 'rain:sun', with the immediate corollaries of 'wet:dry', and then the more abstract culturally loaded overtones of 'sorrow:joy'; and third, the implied opposition 'small:large' (the 'itsy bitsy' spider and the forces of nature). The iterative 'itsy bitsy' foregrounds the fact of smallness, doing so by selecting from a colloquial register carrying overtones of affection for small things (the regional variants, 'insey winsey' and 'ipsey wipsey', are precisely equivalent realizations of the same signified). The events described are chronologically linear, but the last is a re-enactment of the first, expressed in almost the same words, but now reinforced by 'again'.

In these ways, a pattern is imposed upon the concepts which are signified by the patterning of the language used to represent them and by interrelationship of the signifiers within the discourse. The pairs of oppositions themselves and their interaction with the other pairs complicates signifier–signified relationships so that the signifiers chosen to represent the 'story' evoke further signifieds for which there are no overt signifiers in the discourse. Even the simple pair 'up:down' is thus re-encoded to signify struggle and defeat, as the narrative discloses the theme that lies behind the discourse surface and the simple 'story' decoding.

The discourse/story/hypersignification triad is, however, only one aspect of textuality; it is perhaps the aspect of most interest to literary critics because its essential emphasis is on the end product(s) of the text, the final decoding. Our analysis moved quickly from such encoding details as 'up/down' or 'rain/sun' to this end, but the constituents of the discourse itself – the only member of the triad which actually appears as words on the page – are, or should be, a prior consideration.

## Foregrounding and textual interrelationships

Any description of a text is a selection from a myriad of details and an infinity of interrelationships, and the best one can hope to achieve is a selection of such aspects as appear to have been placed in the foreground of the text itself; this seems immediately to lock the reader into the hermeneutic circle of interpretation, depending on the whole to indicate how emphases fall amongst the parts, yet selecting and stressing various partial elements in order to construct the whole. In practice, though, this poses few problems for the reader, since it must be expected that any moment in a text beyond the immediate beginning and close must be read both prospectively and retrospectively. Moreover, the constant interplay at any given moment between openness of meaning and strategies of foregrounding is a vital aspect of textuality – indeed, probably the main thing that persuades readers to continue reading the text. Beginnings, for example, even beginnings of a seemingly innocuous kind, will tend both to be open and to indicate significant emphases. This is readily apparent in the opening lines of Elizabeth Jolley's *The Well*:

> One night Miss Hester Harper and Katherine are driving home from a celebration, a party at the hotel in town, to which Miss Harper has been an unwilling guest. Katherine had wanted very much to go to the party.

There is immediately much the reader does not know: who are

these characters, what is their relationship, what was the 'party' for and why was it a 'celebration', why did one character wish to go but not the other? On the other hand, the modes of naming (the full, formal 'Miss Hester Harper' as opposed to the less formal and less informative 'Katherine') differentiate the status of the two protagonists, and they are further differentiated by the opposition between 'unwilling guest' and 'wanted very much to go'. The verb tenses recede one by one into the past ('are driving . . . has been . . . had wanted'), neatly inverting text-order and 'story'-order and suggesting a sequence of conflicts prior to the imprecise but present-time opening temporal, 'one night'.

Such details both begin to unfold discourse towards story and hypersignification and also suggest further questions and even mysteries. The choice of an impersonal third person but present tense narrative voice, with its potential for discord between omniscience and the uninterpretable present, further signals that, like the verb tenses of its first three clauses, the novel's larger discourse will move back to a previous point of time to (attempt to) explain this present moment. A phrase such as 'the hotel in town' not only indicates that the characters live outside a one-hotel town, but also suggests an idiom or register within which the narrating voice might be located.

## The elements of textuality

It would be possible to continue examining this small Elizabeth Jolley extract, but enough has been pointed out to illustrate how complex are the possible relationships between the signifiers selected (the *paradigmatic axis*), the ways they are combined (the *syntagmatic axis*), certain generic features characteristic of novels (narrator, narrative voice), and factors determining how the available range of language choices is encoded and decoded (cultural intertextuality). Some of the multifarious elements of which a text is constituted are set out in Figure 1.2, though as with Figure 1.1, only some elements are present in the text while others lie on a plane behind it. The proportion of ternary relationships (as against binary ones) should also be noted, as well as those relationships on each side of the discourse which are isomorphic.[3]

If discourse is considered to be, in some sense, the site on which an author/text/reader transaction occurs, it is a site both

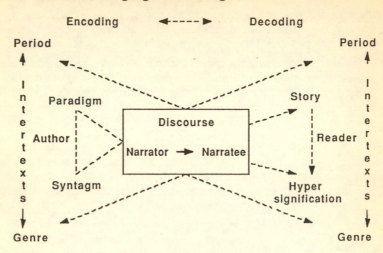

Figure 1.2   Elements of Textuality

heavily preconditioned and innately complicated. The author's production of the text is preconditioned by the cultural milieu of the period in which s/he lives and works – by, for example, dominant ideologies to be reflected or resisted (silently or otherwise), by literary traditions to be absorbed and modified, by constraints imposed by the state of the language, its available lexicon (already culturally coded) and conventions of grammar; it is also preconditioned by the genre which the author chooses to work within, whether the large, loosely conceived 'genres' of novel, poetry or drama, or more narrowly conceived (sub-) genres such as tragedy, comedy, lyric, fantasy, and so on, for all place inherent constraints on the language of the discourse.

The reader's reception of the text is isomorphically conditioned by similar factors: any synchronic or diachronic differences between the reader's milieu and the author's will affect the process of decoding and re-encoding the discourse; the initial recognition of genre will arouse expectations which may be fulfilled or defeated by the discourse as it unfolds, in another version of simultaneous openness and foregrounding; and the reader's assumptions about any and all of these features will only approximate to the writer's.

Notions of genre and period involve processes of synchronic selection along a diachronic axis; as such, they are broadly analogous to the immediate processes by which the text is encoded – paradigmatic selection along a syntagmatic axis. Perhaps the simplest way to describe the interaction we are referring to is to compare it with a chain, stressing that a chain is made up of a series of links: the *syntagmatic axis* refers to the horizontal, linear progression of the text (the process of linking), whereas the *paradigmatic axis* refers to what happens at each of the links, that is, the process of selection which occurs at each place or slot along the syntagmatic axis. In making the syntagm/paradigm relationship the basis for our account of the language of literature, we have found it necessary both to modify and to expand the concept; we do this by expounding first the complications of the paradigm and second the complexities of syntagmatic linking. The concept can also be extended to describe larger stretches of a text's discourse, yielding the concepts of the hypersyntagm and hyperparadigm, which are particularly useful in discussion of narrative.

## The complications of the paradigm

### THE SIGNIFIER/SIGNIFIED RELATIONSHIP

A limitation inherent in a simple model of interacting horizontal syntagm and vertical paradigm is that it reduces signification to two dimensions, whereas an adequate account of the significa- tion of meaning requires a three-dimensional model which incorporates the further concept of the signifier–signified relationship. Every verbal sign can be said to consist of a *signifier* (made up of acoustic and/or graphological features) and a *signified*, a concept, thing, or meaning to which the signifier points. The connection between the two is never straightforward, since every signifier has a range of possible signifieds to which it can point, and every signified can be more or less encoded by a range of signifiers.

The signifier/signified relationship within the sign is focused or defined or even subverted by the paradigm/syntagm relationship within which it is located. Thus discourse consists of a paradigmatic axis, comprising signifiers selected from a range of possibilities, filling the series of slots along the syntagmatic chain. An author has a number of more or less synonymous signifiers available to express a particular signified, and from these one (or more) will be selected for any one or more of a variety of reasons: its register, its overtones, its sound, its ability to rhyme with another already chosen, its concreteness or abstractness, and so on. As soon as the selection is made (or when one term is substituted for another), the influence of the syntagm comes into operation by giving the signifier a context. Even then, the words not chosen can still hover round it, partly because a word is always to some extent defined by what it is not, and partly by reason of semantic relationships or sound similarity or some other association, cultural or individual, so that a core of meaning is surrounded by a penumbra of associations. Saussure ignored the denotation/connotation differentiation of words, especially the extent to which no two readers will conjure up exactly the same signified in response to the signifier chosen, but his point that signifiers still remain potentially available even when not actually selected for a paradigmatic slot has important implications for literary texts.

THE RANGE OF SIGNIFIERS

Apart from its syntagmatic context, then, the paradigmatic slot has other potentialities, and it is these which bring out the limitation of the two dimensions implied by a model structured as two intersecting axes. For example, the heading 'horse' in *The Macquarie Thesaurus* (1984, 261.7) is followed by seventy-five signifiers (apart from others for teams of horses); there is an enormous paradigm of horse terms. But they function in different ways. Just a few of them are:

> bronco, brumby, cob, colt, dobbin, gee-gee, jade, neddy, palfrey, pony, stallion, steed, thoroughbred.

Around the core of 'meaning', each has a penumbra of associations or overtones, which are qualitative or descriptive, some culturally coded, some individually influenced for the particular reader, and each signifier then fits certain registers and contexts: for instance, 'gee-gee' is a child's term, and suggests a much more colloquial context than 'horse'; on the other hand 'steed' suggests a more formal context, 'palfrey' conjures up a mount for a medieval lady, and 'stallion' does not. In linguistic parlance, the term 'horse' is neutral or unmarked, while the others are marked in some way by the associations or overtones that they carry. So while the set of signifiers points to the same very general signified (a particular type of solid-hoofed quadruped), the choice of one rather than another (and the displacement of one by another) for a paradigmatic slot will alter the impact even before taking into account the syntagmatic influence, and then the individual response of the reader.

The signifier/signified relationship which interacts with the syntagm/paradigm relationship functions on a different plane from that of the two-dimensional axes, and entails a third dimension lying behind the other two, as the signifier in its paradigmatic slot directs the reader back to the signified, indeterminate as that signified may be in some respects. Figure 1.3 suggests one way of presenting this three-dimensional model:

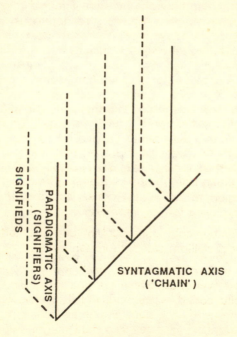

Figure 1.3

This third dimensional relationship is a shifting one, in several ways. For one thing, it can direct more attention to either the signifier or the signified, as 'horse' probably persuades us to consider the signified, while 'gee-gee' may well alert us to the signifier as much as or more than to the signified. An analogy can be drawn here with an idea expressed by William Blake, when he was talking about his vision of the Last Judgment:

> I question not my Corporeal or Vegetative Eye any more than I would Question a Window concerning a Sight. I look thro' it & not with it.

A signifier may also be like a window, in that it can indeed be transparent, unobtruding; this seems to be generally the case with prose, whereas in verse cultural convention and long tradition encourage readers to perceive the signified with the signifier more consciously in mind. Even within verse, however, the relative weighting of one as against the other can minimize or maximize the gap between the two. Though it can never go beyond a certain point in directing reader focus, a relatively unmarked signifier which points to a concrete signified, apprehended through the senses, such as a horse, is more likely to function like the window through which most readers will perceive roughly that same signified than, for instance, the term 'palfrey', which focuses attention much more on the signifier itself. Furthermore, another important consideration is the extent to which the penumbra involves the intellectual and/or the sensory and/or the emotive appeal of the signified. If, for instance, a signifier makes its appeal to something concrete with sensory appeal, the text exercises more control over the response of a greater number of readers than it will be able to achieve through the use of an abstract signifier. The term 'glory', for example, carries an emotive penumbra which will vary from reader to reader, so that the signified tends to drift away from the signifier in directions which vary from one individual reader to another, as well as being heavily influenced by the syntagmatic pressure of its context (Stephens and Waterhouse, 1987).

DISPLACING THE SIGNIFIED

So far, we have concentrated on the function of the syntagm/paradigm interaction to determine signifier/signified relationships, but it is also able to float the signifier away from the signified to which, through normal coding, it is conventionally if arbitrarily related. This floating is different from the controlled displacement which occurs frequently in jokes (which may be especially dependent upon the aural representation of words) when, with two signifieds lying behind the one signifier, the syntagmatic context displaces the initially perceived signified with the second signified. This may involve repeating the signifier, as in the following exchange from *Twelfth Night* (II.iii.9–12):

> *Sir Toby* Does not our life *consist of* the four elements?
> *Sir Andrew* Faith, so they say; but I think it rather *consists of* eating and drinking.

Displacement may also be retrospective, as in Pope's 'And sleepless lovers just at twelve awake' (*Rape of the Lock*, I.16), where the syntagmatic context retrospectively displaces the initial signified of 'sleepless' when the last word of the line is reached, and returns attention to the signifier, as the reader, mentally searching for some sort of congruity between the signifier and the signified, perceives the signifier as referring to a (literary) convention of behaviour rather than to a physiological state. The floating of the signifier occurs when the context detaches the conventionally coded signified from the signifier, and leaves indeterminate the signified that the whole context seems to demand; this can happen particularly easily with abstracts, such as the terms 'glory' and 'Lie', juxtaposed by Owen at the conclusion of 'Dulce et Decorum Est':

> My friend, you would not tell with such high zest
> To children ardent for some desperate glory,
> The old Lie: Dulce et decorum est
>    Pro patria mori.

Here the frame of reference is a gas attack, so the hypersyntagm has a pervasive effect upon the penumbra of all paradigmatic choices. In the phrase 'The old Lie', the definite deictic, in accordance with its normal function, preceding the dismissive adjective, limits the range of possible signifieds for the abstract; but the juxtapositions of 'Lie' both with 'glory' and with the quotation from Horace function to float both abstracts. The word 'glory', moreover, in association with its modifier 'desperate', is forced away from its more usual core signified (itself surrounded by a penumbra of connotations), and is thus left floating indeterminately.

So far, then, we have dealt with a continuum from a minimal to a maximum gap between signifier and signified, as well as a displacement of the signified in some contexts, and its drifting or floating in others. The extent to which, within the dimension of intersecting syntagm/paradigm axes, the syntagmatic context throws emphasis upon syntagm or paradigm further complicates the paradigmatic signifier/signified relationship. Since, to state the obvious, paradigmatic choices must in part be determined by the syntagmatic string of which they are to be constituents, and the syntagmatic axis is partly determined by the words selected to fill the paradigmatic slots, the analytic process of exploring the complications of the paradigm goes on as a continual dialectic with the synthesizing process of the syntagm. Another important factor which complicates the paradigm is figurative signification, and we will return to an extensive discussion of this in chapter 6.

## Syntagm, syntax and cohesion

The grammatical chaining together of paradigmatic choices within a single clause is largely self-evident, though the importance of the syntagm is made immediately obvious when some device such as inversion occurs, as in the Pope line already cited; the disrupted S[ubject]–A[djunct]–V[erb] ordering of the line creates more comic social satire than the normal prose order of S–V–A, *'And sleepless lovers awake just at twelve', where the closer proximity of the contradictory terms 'sleepless' and 'awake' lessens the surprise achieved by Pope's inversion. Throughout this book we will use the term *syntax* to refer to such small-scale syntagmatic elements as whether a clause deviates from, or includes some modification to, the subject–verb–object norm. Other elements of syntax are: whether a sentence is simple, or compound (having more than one principal clause), or complex (having at least one subordinate clause); and what kinds of modality options have been exercised.

A crucial aspect of the syntagmatic axis is the forging of cohesive links between elements that do not occur in the same clause, or even the same sentence. This is done in two main ways. First, connections are made by formal syntactic devices generally functioning within the sentence, such as subordination

---

* Here, and throughout the book, an asterisk preceding a quotation indicates that what follows is our own rewriting.

which explicitly relates clauses in a particular way signalled by the opening subordinator, and which, by organizing the information they carry into various hierarchies, provides by the subordinate clause's relative position within the syntagm an additional perspective upon the clausal relationships. The second kind of connection is that made less overtly by what has come to be known as 'cohesion', which, to put it simply, is an important range of mechanisms (including substitutions and deletions) which interconnect segments of various sizes along the syntagmatic axis, functioning both within the structural unit of the sentence and within larger stretches of text. These mechanisms are generally known as *cohesive ties*,[4] and are distinct from the syntactic hierarchical subordinators which point to the temporal, spatial, conditional, concessive, etc., relationships between clauses. Since both types of linking device function along the syntagmatic axis, and since both have important implications for signification, any discussion of texts will examine them in close conjunction. This will be especially important when we relate them to the broader concepts of congruence and coherence.

Since readers tend to take the syntagmatic axis for granted, it is not surprising that both syntactic subordination and cohesion as an aspect of the syntagm generally function below the level of attention. However the importance of subordination stems from whether it precedes or follows the principal clause (as when a conditional clause, for instance, can precede or follow its principal clause), with considerable difference of effect. The importance of cohesion stems not only from the intra-sentence relationship it builds up between pieces of information, but also from the ability of cohesive ties to make links between sentences; this is why linguists are more interested in how cohesion operates beyond the confines of a single sentence. Within the sentence, linking functions are carried out primarily by syntactic elements in conjunction with cohesive substitutions (as in 'If I want a *cake*, I'll bake *one*'), which are more or less obligatory, whereas between sentences they are more subject to discretion. Where choice operates more freely, as in deviation from normal extra-sentence cohesive ties, or in placement of the subordinate clause relative to its principal, both grammatical subordination and cohesion begin to have stylistic and literary effects, especially as a foregrounding device.

Further, cohesion is an aspect of literary language which

shows gradual diachronic change: as Leech and Short point out, 'in the history of fiction writing, there has been a progressive tendency, over the past three hundred years, to dispense with such logical connections [as subordinators which spell out relationships, and other conjunctions and linking adverbials], and to rely instead upon inferred connections' (1981, 249). Readers usually assume that contiguous clauses and sentences make interrelationships, and hence try to find links if they are not explicitly there. Different degrees of cohesion therefore involve readers with the text in different ways. A heavy and explicit use of cohesion may contribute towards consigning the reader to a passively receptive role, whereas the use of more implicit cohesive ties can encourage a more active and imaginative engagement with the text. One of the special narrative uses of cohesion is thus to situate the reader in relation to the discourse. For example, it sometimes functions at the opening of texts to imply that discourse has begun encoding story after some indefinite period of story-time has already elapsed, as in the opening of Katherine Mansfield's *The Garden Party*: 'And after all the weather was ideal.' Because the discourse commences with cohesive ties – the connective 'and' and the temporal qualifier 'after all' – the reader is immediately presupposed to assume a preceding discourse expressing concern about 'the weather'.

As always, however, cohesion is not by itself responsible for such effects, but as one feature of the syntagmatic axis functions in conjunction with other aspects of the text. As we will argue, particularly in chapter 3, the concept of cohesion is of great importance to the analysis of syntagm/paradigm relations in prose fiction. Cohesion operates (hyper-)syntagmatically in conjunction with two other, perhaps less explicitly definable, concepts, *congruence* and *coherence*. By *congruence* (and its opposite, *incongruity*) we mean the relationships between *paradigmatic* choices at various places along the syntagmatic axis; it subsumes such concepts as lexical set and register (thereby including register-shift and register-mixing). The wry comedy of the following extract comes from the incongruity derived from register-shifting at both the paradigmatic and the syntagmatic levels:

He was . . . of that ancient type – as ancient as the human race, or certainly as human war – the Roman comedians dubbed the *miles gloriosus*; the military boaster, or eternal bag of bullshit.

(John Fowles, *A Maggot*, 1986, 35)

Lastly, we will describe such an effect as that achieved here as a breaking of *coherence*, a term we use to refer to a (hyper-) syntagmatic concord of cohesion and/or congruence.


## The foci of subsequent chapters

The central focus of our study is diachronic shift as perceived in literary uses of English. Literary texts in various ways embody human temporal experiences, and their own existence is subject to crucial temporal states and constraints. It is a truism that readers experience texts linearly – that the syntagmatic axis moves in Time and there are only minimal (and, it might be said, marginal) strategies available to writers to escape this linearity. Texts also exist within Time in other ways, especially as whole texts within the stretch of human chronological history, when inevitably they interrelate with a vast complex of factors working, on the one hand, to limit and constrain meaning and, on the other hand, to liberate meaning from the tyranny of Time.

Our strategy in the following chapters is to explore diachronic movements in literary English from the last quarter of the fourteenth century to the present day by focusing attention on the relationships of the syntagmatic and paradigmatic axes. We will find that both axes are subject to constraints imposed by particular periods. The syntagmatic axis reveals, in individual writers and in whole periods, preferences for special types of structural and grammatical options which may be of little or no significance in other periods. At times such options are scarcely a matter of choice at all, even though they are theoretically always possible. This is also to be seen in the matter of paradigmatic choice. For its user, the writer, a word may have a penumbra, or a newness, or a strangeness, which will always remain beyond the *emotional*, if not the intellectual, grasp of a later reader. The best we can do is to attempt to reconstruct its denotative/connotative ranges and to filter out anachronistic associations – unless, of course, we choose to argue that because texts are unstable anyway semantic change can only contribute to their richness and complexity. The latter view is not accepted for the purposes of this study. Rather, we consider that temporal constraints on the production of meaning are as important as the atemporal constraints imposed on the paradigmatic axis by the syntagmatic. Ultimately, indeed, the two are inextricable.

Another important temporal factor which has a bearing on the syntagm/paradigm relationship is intertextuality, especially, but not exclusively, as it affects paradigmatic choices. The relationship with pre-texts and intertexts is perhaps one of the primary features which distinguishes literary language from other kinds of language because of the vast extension to the penumbra of a word which it makes possible.

What follows in this book, then, is an account of literary discourse in terms of the description of textuality outlined in this chapter. Chapters 2 to 5 will proceed more or less chronologically: chapter 2 considers texts composed between the times of Chaucer and Donne; chapter 3 the Augustans and Romantics, with some discussion of earlier prose; chapter 4 the Romantics and Victorians; and chapter 5 the twentieth century. Chapter 6 examines figurative language between Chaucer and the present.[5]

## Notes and further reading

1   This metaphor for the reading process is J. Hillis Miller's (1976, 341).
2   For a brief discussion of the advantages and problems inhering in binarism, see Culler (1975, 14–16).
3   'The word "isomorphism" applies when two complex structures can be mapped on to each other, in such a way that to each part of one structure there is a corresponding part in the other structure, where "corresponding" means that the two parts play similar roles in their respective structures.' (Hofstadter, 1979, 49).
4   The definitive account of cohesion is Halliday and Hasan (1976); a convenient, more summary account was prepared by the same authors in 1985; for literary applications of cohesion see Gutwinski (1976) and Leech and Short (1981, 243–54).
5   For further reading concerning issues raised in this chapter, see: Culler (1975) for literary applications of structuralism; Toolan (1988) for story and discourse and the elements of

narrative. For discussion of texts in a social and historical context, see Carter and Simpson (1989) for papers on discourse stylistics, and Barrell (1988) for an approach firmly grounded in cultural materialism.

## Exercises

1   What sorts of problems for the determination of meaning does the first stanza of T. S. Eliot's 'The Love Song of J. Alfred Prufrock' pose?

2   Examine how the story is encoded in the discourse of the ballad 'Edward, Edward', and go on to analyse how it also encodes the hypersignification.

3   Examine what is foregrounded and how in this version of the opening to one of Grimm's Fairy Tales:

> Hansel one day took his sister Grettel by the hand, and said: 'Since our poor mother died we have had no happy days; for our new mother beats us all day long and when we go near her, she pushes us away. We have nothing but hard crusts to eat; and the little dog that lies by the fire is better off than we; for he sometimes has a nice piece of meat thrown to him. Heaven have mercy upon us!'

4   Examine the displacement of signifieds in *Much Ado about Nothing* I.i.49–61 ('He hath done good service . . . we are all mortal'). What dramatic function does the play with the signifieds have in this context?

5   Analyse the syntagmatic axis, paying particular attention to the cohesive ties, of W. S. Merwin's poem 'Odysseus' to bring out their relationship to the signification of meaning. Then go on to look at the extent to which paradigmatic congruence is also an important part of the poem's coherence.

# 2 Syntagm and paradigm from Chaucer to Milton

'My little body is aweary of this great world.'
(*The Merchant of Venice*, I.ii.1–2)

## Analogical thought

For the first three centuries of 'modern' English literature –
from, roughly, the middle of the fourteenth century to the
Restoration – the dominant frame within which significant
relationships between people and the world were constructed
was that of microcosm and macrocosm.[1] This theory entailed an
intricate set of isomorphic relationships whereby the cosmos,
the State, the family and the individual were perceived as
analogous, within a descending hierarchy, with each entity
having its own inner hierarchy (governed, respectively, by God,
the ruler, the husband/father, and the reason). Inevitably, this
important cultural concept informed the language used to
express ideas about aspects of existence, whether those ideas
were affirming or questioning the status quo. The continuing
pervasiveness of the model is reflected in the epigraph to this
chapter, the first words spoken by Portia in *The Merchant of
Venice* (I.ii), in which the joke depends on the audience readily
perceiving the double significations of '*little* body' (Portia as
physical self and as microcosm) set against '*great* world' (the
society in which Portia lives and the macrocosm). Throughout
this chapter, we will observe how this tenet of social context
acts as an important predetermining factor for some aspects of
the language choices – especially paradigmatic choices –
available to writers throughout these centuries. It does not,
however, seem to have a consistent impact on whether writers
lean more towards a syntagmatic or paradigmatic style.

# Chaucer and fourteenth-century style

At the beginning of the period, in the writings of Chaucer and Gower, there exists a period style which, because of its relative weighting of the two axes, can be described as predominantly syntagmatic. Chaucer, like his great contemporaries Gower and Langland, does not have a poetic diction, in the sense of a language cultivated exclusively for use in poetry. Where this does exist, in the alliterative verse of Chaucer's northern and western contemporaries (which, in retrospect, can be seen as outside the main stream of English literature), it is part of a mainly paradigmatic style, a style which flaunts a large range of paradigmatic choice through the development of a specialized diction (Stephens, 1988). This is not to suggest that Chaucer's own lexicon lacks inventiveness – on the contrary, it shows substantial innovation, but as part of a general fourteenth-century expansion of the vernacular vocabulary, rather than a purely poetic one.

Chaucer's work, indeed, has something in common with literary English of the twentieth century, something which, as we shall see, is an important general principle in the diachronic study of lexis, namely, that in some periods literary language (and particularly that of poetry) is co-extensive with the language of the day, in the sense that nothing seems to be considered either unfit or especially apt for use in poetry, while in other periods literary texts restrict in particular ways what can be chosen for the paradigmatic axis, so that its lexis becomes specialized.

Such a shift within mainstream English poetry had already taken place within a generation of Chaucer's death, and is probably to be attributed to a baroque decadence within the decaying International Gothic style which coincides with, and partly causes, the first impulses in English writers to enlarge paradigmatic choice by borrowing 'elevated' terms from Latin and the Romance languages. The rise in the status of the English language during the fourteenth century has been well documented (Cottle, 1969; Leith, 1983), but Latin remained the language of intellectual and scholarly discourse. Chaucer himself evolved a subtly varied discourse by augmenting his native English with borrowings from his Latin and Romance pre-texts (Boethius, Boccaccio, etc.), but throughout the following century his writings were valued for such lexical innovations as enabled a heightening of register by accumulating Romance terms. What the imitators of this style all too often could not see, let alone reproduce, was Chaucer's mastery of the paradigmatic effects of register-shift both into and out of such moments of heightening, a mastery which interacts with and in the final analysis depends on the kinds of syntagmatic control evident in the following extract.

CHAUCER'S *TROILUS AND CRISEYDE* (1380s)

Therwith he gan hire faste in armes take,
And wel an hondred tymes gan he syke,
Naught swiche sorwfull sikes as men make
For wo, or elles when that folk ben sike,
But esy sykes, swiche as ben to like,
That shewed his affeccioun withinne;
Of swiche sikes koude he nought bilynne.

Soone after this they spake of sondry thynges,
As fel to purpos of this aventure,
And pleyinge entrechaungeden hire rynges,
Of whiche I kan nought tellen no scripture;
But wel I woot, a broche, gold and asure,
In which a ruby set was lik an herte,
Criseyde hym yaf, and stak it on his sherte.

Lord, trowe ye a coveytous or a wrecche,
That blameth love, and halt of it despit,
That of tho pens that he kan mokre and krecche
Was evere yit yyeven hym swich delit
As is in love, in o poynt, in som plit?
Nay, douteles, for also God me save,
So perfit joie may no nygard have.

(*Troilus and Criseyde*, III.1359–79)

There are two kinds of discourse here, a narrative segment and an exclamatory digression by the narrator. What the two have in common is the nature of the analogies employed, in that the beauty of the lovers' individual experience is to be described not by attempting some means of defining its innate uniqueness, but by finding points of opposition with other aspects of human life. That is, individual experience is shown to acquire its meaning when it is set in a larger social context. There are, on the other hand, some obvious lexical differences between the two kinds of discourse, in keeping with the differences in subject, and a comparison offers a clear example of three interrelated textual implications of paradigmatic choice: first, it is never neutral, but always implies an attitude; second, the pressure of the syntagmatic context ordinarily determines which signifieds are selected; and third, the creation of a narrating persona within the text is largely a consequence of paradigmatic choice.

The first point is obviously illustrated by the lexical set associated with love's materialistic detractors: 'coveytous, wrecche, blameth, despit, nygard' (and the set is sustained beyond the end of our extract). Substantial doubling within a paradigmatic slot ('coveytous/wrecche') reinforces the effect. The second point is particularly important in Middle English, in which commonly occurring signifiers may point to a large number of diverse signifieds, so it is the syntagm that must narrow the range of both denotative and connotative possibilities. Thus an attitude towards *pens*, for example, is largely determined by the previous references to avarice and by the pejorative language of its modifying clause, in that 'mokre and krecche' are 'low', barnyard terms [*mokre*, 'to heap up dung']. The result is that 'pens' is drawn into the ambience of the pejorative 'coveytous' set. Thirdly, the lexical set which establishes an attitude towards the detractors at the same time discloses something about the narrator who selects that language. This disclosure is also shown by his attitude towards the sighs in the opening stanza, conveyed by the setting up of oppositional terms (such as 'sorwfull:esy') with the term he downgrades located within a strongly negative syntagmatic frame ('Naught swiche . . . But').

But with the shift from narrative to exclamation the narrator loses control of this contrastive technique, and syntagmatic hiatus then helps to emphasize discourse at the expense of story: the narrator himself moves into the foreground. The first two stanzas are carefully constructed, with elements of balance, firm cohesion, and a mixing of co-ordination and hypotaxis in a way that generates a strong flow along the syntagmatic chain. By contrast, the third stanza lacks this effective organization. The doublets in the first three lines create an illusion of pattern and order, but the grammar is a hypotactic shambles as clauses are piled upon, or embedded within, one another. One sentence seems to extend over the first five lines, but it cannot be determined whether its grammatical subject is 'a coveytous or a wrecche' or 'swich delit'; either way, the apparent, but false, parallel between lines 2 and 3 ('That . . . That. . .') constitutes a difficulty. The obvious disruption comes with the indirect object 'hym' in line 4, but perhaps line 2 ends with an anacoluthon.[2] The passage is not difficult to follow, however. It functions as part of the dramatic representation of the narrator in *Troilus and Criseyde*, in that his urgent wish to pour scorn on the straw man he sets up has resulted in an agrammaticality which we might take as an imitation of outraged speech. In combination with his set of paradigmatic choices, his syntagmatic disorder betrays his biased over-involvement with the characters and events of his story, and also functions as a foregrounding device, drawing attention to the events themselves: Criseyde does give brooches to her lovers, and later in the poem this is how Troilus will discover her unfaithfulness.

## Gower's syntagmatic art (*c.* 1390)

The syntagmatic axis can be manipulated as heavily by John Gower as by Chaucer, though usually for different ends. The following extract consists of two long and elaborate sentences in marked syntagmatic contrast to one another:

1   And so it fell hem ate last,
    That this Machaire with Canace
    When they were in a prive place,
    Cupide bad hem ferst to kesse,
    And after she which is Maistresse
    In kinde and techeth every lif
    Withoute lawe positif,
    Of which she takth no maner charge,
    But kepth hire lawes all at large,
    Nature, tok hem into lore
    And tawht hem so, that overmore
    She hath hem in such wise daunted,
    That they were, as who seith, enchaunted.

2   And as the blinde another ledeth
    And til they falle nothing dredeth,
    Riht so they hadde non insihte;

But as the bridd which wole alihte
And seth the mete and noght the net,
Which in deceit of him is set,
These yonge folk no peril sihe,
But that was likinge in here yhe,
So that they fell upon the chance
Where wit hath lore his remembrance.

(*Confessio Amantis*, III.166–88)

In (1) the syntagmatic axis seems utterly chaotic; in (2) it is clear and reinforced by patterning of various kinds. The syntagm here is being manipulated to reflect the moral attitude: the story is concerned with brother–sister incest, placed in this passage within the context of the general moral problem of the conflict between natural affection and cultural taboo. Instead of using the macrocosm/microcosm relationship to legitimate the period's conventional attitudes towards deviancy, Gower shows a strong awareness that such notions are not transcendent universals, but are culturally determined; and this awareness leads to some interesting strategies in the way he handles his material. The business of the first sentence is obfuscation. Its frame is:

| | |
|---|---|
| main clause | it fell hem. . . |
| dependent clause 1 | that. . .Cupide bad hem ferst to kesse, |
| dependent clause 2 | and after she . . . Nature . . . tawt hem so . . . |
| dependent on 2 | that they were . . . enchaunted |

But this frame is obscured by another example of anacoluthon and by heavy embedding of subordinate units (indicated in the frame by ellipses). Thus the grammatical function of 'this Machaire with Canace' is uncertain: it initially appears to be the subject of a *that*-clause beginning in line 2 and interrupted by an embedded temporal clause, but this construction dissolves into anacoluthon at the end of line 3, and a new subject, 'Cupide' is introduced. Secondly, dependent clause 2 has four clauses embedded between the subject 'she' and its restatement as 'Nature'. This embedding teases the audience as to the identity of 'she', since the usual collocation with Cupid would be Venus, but more importantly it defines the educational principles of this 'she' before her identification as Nature. Such a deferral is another way in which syntagmatic context can prospectively *and* retrospectively limit the range of associations of a paradigmatic choice, in this case forcing us to see it in the narrator's terms and from his point of view. The effect of the complex syntagmatic structuring of sentence (1) is to mirror moral ambiguity and uncertainty, culminating in the final word of the sentence – made ambiguous because of its isolation, when placed at the end of the syntagmatic string and cut off from its auxiliary by the embedded (non-)qualifier 'as who seith' – *enchaunted*: 'bewitched; held spellbound; deluded'.

The second sentence retrospectively defines the appropriate signified for 'enchaunted' as pejorative, and now develops a firm moral stance. The sentence begins with two large co-ordinate structures built on the same pattern, analogy → conclusion, with the conclusions paralleling one another:

> as the blinde . . . Riht so they hadde non insihte
> as the bridd . . . These yonge folk no peril sihe.

As in the Chaucer passage, the analogies serve to define individual experience by making connections with other kinds of experience, in this case represented by biblical and moralized intertexts. The polyptoton ('in*sihte/sihe*'), in conjunction with the repeated negation ('non/no'), emphasizes the notion of seeing (and especially the shift from perceptual to conceptual 'seeing') in relationship to self-deception. Immediate moral focus also comes exophorically from the biblical intertext: 'Let them [the Pharisees] alone: they are blind leaders of the blind. And if the blind lead the blind, both shall fall into the ditch' (Matt. 15:14). A final effect stems from a pleasing, if slight, syntagmatic ambiguity within the sentence as the concluding clauses re-echo, through eyes and falling, the analogies: the line, 'But that was likinge in here yhe' hovers between 'peril' and 'sihe' for its antecedent, thus stressing the danger of pursuing an object of desire without regard for contingent circumstances.

## The fifteenth-century weakening of the syntagm: Lydgate (*c.* 1370–*c.* 1450)

Gower carries his reader through moral ambiguity to moral certainty by means of a superb syntagmatic control which, as we have suggested, is characteristic of much of the best writing of this period. An important reason for the fifteenth-century decline in literary quality was a failure to comprehend the importance of the syntagm. John Lydgate, the most notable example, seems to have perceived that within the works of

Chaucer and Gower neologisms and complex sentences were responsible for striking effects, and then, somewhat naïvely, he attempted to make them the backbone of his own poetic. The result is all too often a proliferation of signifiers which achieve at best minimal signification. Sufficient attention has already been paid to the so-called 'Aureate Diction' of the fifteenth century (for example, Pearsall, 1970, 262–3 and 268–74), however, so we will confine ourselves here to some brief remarks on the syntagm. Lydgate attempted the long, periodic sentences handled so well by his forebears, but with consequences of two kinds. The first of these is illustrated by the following sentence (in which we have designated the sentence frame by italics):

> [*I biheld*]
> How that there knelid *a lady* in my sight
> Tofore the goddess, *which* right as the sonne
> Passeth the sterres and doth hir stremes donne,
> And Lucifer to voide the nyghtes sorow
> In clerenes passeth erli by the morow,
> And so as May hath the sovereinte
> Of every moneth of fairness and beaute,
> And as the rose in swetnes and odour
> Surmounteth floures, and baume of al licour
> Haveth the pris, and as the ruby bright
> Of al stones in beaute and in sight
> (As it is know) hath the regalie:
> Right so this lady with hir goodlie *eye*
> And with the stremes of hir loke so bright
> *Surmounteth al thurugh beaute* in my sight.
>
> (*The Temple of Glass*, 247–64)

The main amplification here has been of the *which* (= 'who'); as often happens in left-branching structures of this kind, even at times in Chaucer, it has become so elaborate that the subject 'lady' has to be repeated when the main part of the clause is about to be reached (and even here there are two further 'with' qualifications). Lydgate's attempt to achieve a high style demands heavy subordination and extensive paradigmatic expansion, but the subordinated elements here are actually serialized. The string of analogies does more or less descend down the great chain of being from macrocosm to microcosm, from the sun to minerals, thus situating the described lady within a pattern of hierarchies within hierarchies, but the effect is at best cumulative, falling far short of Gower's climactic and retrospective complexity. Even the parallelism is illusory, as the repetition in the main clause of previously occurring items exemplifies. The recurrence of the 'bright/sight' rhyme after only one intervening couplet seems merely tired; it is 'surmounteth' which is most revealing. This was still an unusual word (first used, it seems, by Chaucer), and hence is doubly foregrounded. The repetition should suggest shape and pattern, but the initial use is only a variation in the series *passeth*, *hath sovereinte*, *haveth the pris*, etc., whereas the second use is summative. The two do not effectively connect, and what has really happened is that their co-presence is an accident. The first turns out to be a reworking of a passage from Chaucer's *Legend of Good Women* (123–4) and the second of a passage from *The Book of the Duchess* (825–6). The result is the worst kind of intertextuality – imitative pastiche which has habitualized rather than defamiliarized both its pre-texts and its informing ideology.[3]

As this passage continues, the second, and more disastrous, effect of Lydgate's syntagmatic ineptitude emerges (the sentence runs on for seventeen lines – we will only consider the first half of it):

| | |
|---|---:|
| For to tell hir gret semelines, | 265 |
| Hir womanhed, hir port, and hir fairnes, | |
| It was a mervaile how ever that Nature | |
| Coud in hir werkis make a creature | |
| So aungellike, so goodli on to se, | 269 |
| So femynyn or passing of beaute, | |
| Whose sonnysh here brighter than gold were, | |
| Like Phebus bemys shyning in his spere, | |
| The goodlihed eke of her fresshli face . . . . | 273 |

The anacoluthon which breaks off the list at the end of 266 appears to capture the sense of excitement characteristic of this rhetorical device, but when the next list collapses into incoherent agrammaticality after 270 it would seem a misreading to perceive any syntagmatic control in this verse: there is simply a complete failure to resume the syntagmatic chain after the analogy embedded in line 272 within a dependent clause (signalled by 'Whose'), the verb of which never eventuates. The new direction in 273 itself will turn out to be a grammatical subject whose verb is forever deferred.

For another century, the Lydgatean misreading of Chaucer

and Gower was to dominate English verse, until Wyatt's careful re-reading of Chaucer and of Petrarch resulted in the reinstatement of the syntagm.

## The recovery of the syntagm: Wyatt (1503–42)

And one is left sitting in the yard
To try to write poetry
Using what Wyatt and Surrey left around,
Took up and put down again
Like so much gorgeous raw material . . . .
(John Ashbery, 'Grand Galop')

These lines by a modern poet reflect a common view of the sixteenth century as ushering in an age of 'gorgeous' writing; the term 'gorgeous' itself begins to be applied to writing in the 1560s,[4] though compared with the Latinate lexical excesses of the preceding century (such as those of Lydgate) the expansion of sixteenth-century lexis is selective and restrained. It is, indeed, another age in which the lexical possibilities of poetry are co-extensive with those of other kinds of discourse. In addition, in the works of a poet such as Wyatt there is a return to a poetic highly conscious of the functions of the syntagm in constructing meaning, a movement which was to be reinforced during the following century by the developments of fluency and variety in the drama, and by the active debate about the aesthetics and practicalities of prose style (Croll, 1921; Trimpi, 1962; Williamson, 1951). In Wyatt's lyrics, deviance within the syntagmatic axis becomes primarily a foregrounding device, as is suggested in the following example (addressed to the cruel lady) by the contrast between units approximating speech-order and heavily inverted units:

What rage is this? what furour of what kynd?
What powre, what plage, doth wery thus my mynd?
Within my bons to rancle is assind
    What poyson, plesant swete?

Lo, se myn iyes swell with contynuall terys;
The body still away sleples it weris;
My fode nothing my faintyng strength reperis,
    Nor doth my lyms sustayne.

In diepe wid wound the dedly strok doth torne
To curid skarre that never shalle retorne.
Go to, tryumphe, rejoyse thy goodly torne,
    Thy frend thou dost opresse.

The opening interrogatives have normal speech order, though
the interplay within the double subject, *powre/plage*, helps
draw attention to the patterning behind the first two lines: the
two halves of line 1 are strongly cohesive, both with each other,
and with the next line, whether the second half is interpreted as
an extension of the subject, parallel with *rage*, or as a new
sentence which has elided *{is this} in re-posing the original
question. It can also be taken as an anticipatory subject of line
2's 'doth wery', with its repetition of 'What' parallel to the
double 'What' of that line. There is probably an upwards
register-shift in *rage → furour* – the terms, the only ones in the
line with any semantic weight, share a common signified, but
the second was a relatively recent borrowing (first used by
Caxton in the late 1470s), and, though it never achieved wide
currency, its newness would have enhanced its claim to
'gorgeousness'. Finally, the semantic density is increased in line
2, by the tightening of the syntagmatic axis so that its two
subjects are in apposition and because the line contains twice as
many words with semantic loading ('powre, plage, wery,
mynd'), despite the slight redundancy involved in using the
otiose auxiliary 'doth'.[5] There is also an extension of semantic
overtones here as 'powre' and 'plage' invest the speaker's
experience with macrocosmic scope. Wyatt's poems are often
suspected of being more about politics than about love, and an
important effect of such semantic extensions from the personal
to the public sphere is to create that very possibility. It also
represents an important inversion of the isomorphic theory, as
individual and personal experience can be used to interrogate
the macrocosmic.

The next two lines of the poem contrast with its initial orderly
structure and patterning. Considered at phrase level, the
sentence reverses normal speech order: *'what poyson/ plesant
swete/ is assind/ to rancle/ within my bons.' Wyatt's order does
more than make it strange; it gets 'mynd' and 'bons' close
together to stress the comprehensiveness of the assault on the
speaker's faculties;[6] and it places 'plesant swete' in the position
of end focus, setting up, by its combination with 'poyson', a

Petrarchan paradox that shifts 'poyson' from literal to figurative and thus retrospectively loosens all signifier–signified relationships in the preceding stretch of text.

An even more radical use of transposition to make the text strange occurs in the first two lines of the third stanza, where the adjuncts 'In diepe wid wound' and, more confusingly, what the wound will never become, the negated 'To curid skarre', begin their respective clauses rather than following their verbs. The effect is to foreground the contrastive emotive elements, wound and scar, and to set up the rhyme, with its witty interplay of word classes and meanings. (Eat your heart out, Dylan Thomas!)

The second stanza proceeds in a manner similar to the first, in that after the speech-order of the original line all the remaining lines have some order inversion. Perhaps the exigencies of the stanza's rhyme-form dictate the inversion of object and verb in the third line, but the reason for repeating this order in the fourth, where there is no such constraint, must be a desire to maintain a parallel between the two negative clauses depending on 'fode'. In the midst of this, the second line is grammatically loose: the verbal group 'weris away' has been inverted and separated by a modifier belonging to the subject and by a pronoun which is apparently a restatement of the subject. This broken grammar might be taken as an attempt to enact the speaker's emotional state, but it also places some of its key terms in a chiastic configuration with synonyms and antonyms in the preceding line, introducing an almost playful conceit:

> swell . . . contynuall . . . / . . . still . . . away weris

playful, because it is a play of signifiers, not of signifieds, and so a pointer to the extent to which the whole poem is more a game than a personal plea. In each of the three stanzas considered, we have found the lover's suffering undermined by this element of linguistic play, and perhaps this also functions as a means to redirect the poem's meaning from personal to political relationships.

Wyatt does not always have recourse to extreme syntagmatic inversions of the kind seen here, and they probably did not serve as models for later poets (who, anyway, knew his work in the smoothed versions printed in *Tottel's Miscellany*). The major culmination of the sixteenth-century search for the gorgeousness of expressive style comes with the work of Sidney and Spenser.

## Petrarchism and the politics of love: Sidney (1554–86)

After Chaucer and Wyatt, Philip Sidney is the next great master of register-shift. His language extends across several functional varieties, and from its basis in good 'conversational' English readily moves into quiet irony, anger, sorrow or praise, modulating almost imperceptibly from one to another. The sonnet discussed below, from the *Astrophil and Stella* sequence, makes for an interesting comparison with the Wyatt example in its handling of 'Petrarchan' themes and of the unresolvable conflict between speaker and beloved. Even more than with Wyatt, though, Sidney's love sonnets are a vehicle for the poet's social, political and economic concerns. Arthur Marotti has argued that the fictionalized love represented in *Astrophil and Stella* functions as a figure for ambition, and hence 'erotic desire for the sexual favors of a Petrarchan mistress (whose conditions for loving explicitly forbid such yielding) is the amorous analogue of the poet's political wilfulness' (1982, 404). The possibility of such a figurative reading has as important implications for signification in, for example, Sidney's Sonnet 48 (where there are no explicit political references) as those that Marotti (1982, 410–12) and Barrell (1988) have perceived in Shakespeare's Sonnet 29:

> Soule's joy, bend not those morning starres from me,
>> Where Vertue is made strong by Beautie's might,
>> Where Love is chastnesse, Paine doth learne delight,
> And Humblenesse growes one with Majestie.
> What ever may ensue, O let me be
>> Copartner of the riches of that sight:
>> Let not mine eyes be hel-driv'n from that light:
> O look, O shine, O let me die and see.
>> For though I oft my selfe of them bemone,
>> That through my heart their beamie darts be gone,
> Whose curelesse wounds even now most freshly bleed:
>> Yet since my death-wound is already got,
>> Deare Killer, spare not thy sweet cruell shot:
> A kind of grace it is to slay with speed.
>> > > (*Astrophil and Stella*, Sonnet 48)

If Barrell (1988, 24) is right in suggesting that the signifier 'love' in the sixteenth century frequently signifies the patron–client relationship, it could link here with the 'Humblenesse–Majestie' union and 'Copartner' to suggest that the love sonnet masks a plea to 'Majestie' for preferment. Nevertheless, it is constructed as a love sonnet and, as such, based almost entirely on antitheses and paradoxes, is one of the more apparently Petrarchan sonnets in the sequence. In other sonnets, Sidney mocked the paradoxes, oxymorons and hyperboles associated with the name of Petrarch. As David Kalstone has pointed out, 'Petrarch' and 'Petrarchan' signify different things in the sixteenth century (1965, 105–15). The language of this sonnet is characteristic of the sequence: some words belong to the diction of Petrarchan love poetry, though in themselves they may be quite unobtrusive; indeed, there is nothing in the lexis here which would be out of place in prose, and Sidney neither borrowed from other languages (despite his fluency in Greek, Latin, French and Italian) nor did he resort to archaisms as did other sixteenth-century poets (Wyatt, Sackville, Spenser). There are perhaps eight or ten archaisms in the whole sequence – 'bemone' in line 9 is an example, but we will argue a special reason for this. Inherent in what Sidney doesn't do with lexis is an attitude reflected in what he does do, that is, he widens the range of both signifiers and signifieds which can be made available to poetry, in such examples as 'copartner, killer, shot'. One effect of adulterating the conventional Petrarchan lexicon in this way is to alert readers to how the conventions of love poetry may be used to express the socio-political context within which an economically and politically ambitious poet wrote in the sixteenth century.

SEMANTIC DENSITY AND SYNTAGM/PARADIGM RELATIONSHIPS

Another characteristic of Sidney's style, and of late sixteenth-century style generally, is the relative density of various lexical categories. In this sonnet there are 10 adjectives/adverbs and 26 nouns to 18 verbs, which is a typical Sidney distribution; in a Wyatt sonnet there are more typically 13 adjectives, 13 nouns and 19 verbs. (For a more extensive statistical study of these relativities, see Miles, 1965.) In the later poetry, the syntagmatic axis is rendered by a grammar which enables a greater compression by decreasing the number of function words (conjunctions, pronouns, prepositions, intensives). The major grammatical expedients for doing this are: loading the basic sentence frame with modifying phrases; using apposition rather than co-ordination/subordination; avoiding paradigmatic doublings (especially doublets), which were common in the age of Wyatt; linking nouns by means of the possessive inflection ('Beautie's might' instead of 'the might of Beautie'); generating compounds (simple ones such as 'hel-driv'n'; more complex examples, as 'long-with-love-acquainted' in Sonnet 31). These stylistic choices have implications for semantic intensity as well as density, concepts we will take up in more detail with reference to Spenser.

Sidney's handling of syntagm/paradigm relationships is more subtle and assured than Wyatt's. The paradox with which Sonnet 48 begins – that the speaker's subjugation of desire, which makes him a better person, depends on the presence of his beloved – is expressed mainly through abstract signifiers such as 'soule's joy', partly through the hyperbolic and macrocosmic conceit of the beloved's eyes as 'morning starres', and generally through the syntagmatic patterning of these elements into oxymoronic relationships, creating pseudo-binary oppositions out of 'Vertue:Beautie', 'Love:chastnesse', 'Paine: delight' and 'Humblenesse:Majestie'. Stella is thus reified (and so more readily can figure ambition), and Astrophil's renunciation remains intellectual rather than felt. The syntax is patterned as heavily as in the Wyatt example, but perhaps more delicately because of its stronger conformity to speech order. The five clauses in the first quatrain all adhere to the one simple pattern:

| Subject | Verb | Object/complement | Adjunct [optional] |
|---|---|---|---|
| Soule's joy | bend not | those morning starres | from me |
| [where] Vertue | is made | strong | by Beautie's might |
| [where] Love | is | chastnesse | — |
| Paine | doth learne | delight | — |
| [and] Humblenesse | growes | one | with Majestie |

Further, clause-boundaries always coincide with line-ends, and each of the clauses in line 3 occupies exactly half the line. It could be argued that this is a recipe for dullness (though the rhythm and the optional adjuncts provide variety), but the parallelism is emphasized so that it can obviously break down at the grammatical level. That is, the repetition of 'where' at the beginning of lines 2 and 3 suggests that they are variations on one another, and the reader has to remake the clause relationships when s/he realizes that the second is subordinated to the clause that follows, so that the first two lines are about Stella, and the next two about Astrophil. Once this point is reached, the *where*-clauses come back into logical relationship, since her virtue (strengthened because her beauty makes her macrocosmically inaccessible) guarantees the chasteness of his love. Once again, syntagmatic organization is making a subtly powerful contribution to meaning, as the lines imply the point that there is no compensation in the personal world of sexual love for socio-political rejection.

PETRARCHISM DECONSTRUCTED

Where Sidney does obviously deviate from speech order, in lines 9–11 and 14, it becomes an indication of how much the Petrarchan language of Wyatt has now become an object for deconstruction. Lines 9–10, in particular, exemplify a deliberate, mock-Petrarchan badness Sidney cultivates here and there in his sequence (it is a way of distancing himself from Astrophil and confirming that the poems are about something other than love). The preceding quatrain had been rhetorically passionate – four *O*s, the conceits of 'copartner' and 'hel-driv'n from that light', and the religious implications of the order 'die and see'. The last is worth pausing over, for it rather nicely raises the question of syntagmatic constraints on the free play of meaning. It would be easy, especially reading back from the end of the sonnet, to see a sexual pun in *die*, and, once proposed, difficult to show it is *not* there: it would be paradigmatically incongruent, and convention strongly links this dying to the dart of love shot from the eye, but, on the other hand, one of the poem's strategies is to deconstruct this convention anyway.

Perhaps the octet–sestet division is a crucial aspect of the syntagm here, since the deconstruction takes place in the sestet rather than in the octet. For what the sonnet is building up to is the shattering of the Petrarchan mode in the final two lines. After the turgidity of lines 9–11, line 12 seems a comfortable expression of a convention, but is transformed into mock-innocence by the extraordinary register-shift of 'Deare Killer': it is another oxymoron, like 'sweet cruell' later in the line, but it deviates markedly from the Petrarchan lexicon and is further emphasized by its remarkable rhythmic deviation,

<pre>
      /      / ×        /       /
   deare killer / / spare not
</pre>

since such a grouping of stresses is a very unusual onset to an iambic pentameter. Moreover, the conventional *dart* of line 10 (a convention insisted on by the internal stock rhyme *heart/dart*) is transformed into 'shot', giving the conceit a contemporary military immediacy. Finally, there are for the final two lines clear pre-texts in Petrarch: *il dolce amaro/ colpo* 'the sweet bitter blow' (*Rime* 296:3–4); by the sixteenth century *colpo* had also come to denote 'shot', which possibly influenced what Sidney did with it) and *et fia . . . un modo di pietate occider tosto* 'it will be a kind of pity to kill quickly' (*Rime* 207:88). Sidney's choice of register has allowed him at once to echo Petrarch and to destroy the Petrarchan mode.

## The relationship of semantic density and semantic intensity

The brief contrasts made between Wyatt and Sidney point to some of the influences exerted by period on the way that a writer of lyrics manipulates paradigmatic and syntagmatic choices. Mode of writing is another important culturally-influenced factor, and we will now turn our attention to the other genres employed by English Renaissance writers – narrative poetry, various types of prose, and drama. There are differences within each genre, especially in terms of semantic density and semantic intensity: the density points to the relative numbers within the word classes, at the level of the signifiers themselves, especially the proportion of adjectives to nouns (and by implication verbs); while the intensity points to the signifieds, rather than the signifiers, the extent to which adjectives give information which differs from that of the nouns they modify, and whether they direct attention to their denotation, or whether it is the penumbra of associations they evoke which is their main function. Within the work of one writer (and so synchronically) there can be a large variation between one text and another, and even within one text. In addition, there are different types of variation in the diachronic progression from one writer to another, and from one period to another.

# Spenser (1552?–99)

One of the most varied poets writing in this period was Edmund Spenser; considered diachronically he is also one of the most important poets in the history of English poetry, because of his influence on later writers. Up to and including Spenser, poets look back to Chaucer (and, to a lesser extent, to his contemporaries, Gower and Lydgate) as a standard, and Chaucer's influence upon Spenser is apparent in various ways, such as in the deliberate use of archaisms, or of elaborate, 'aureate' terms. From Spenser's time on, poets look back to Spenser himself, and there are reminiscences of him in a wide variety of poets, including Milton, the later Augustans, Keats, Tennyson, and Hopkins. His diachronic influence is great, then, and the range of differences amongst the poets just listed is so wide as to suggest in itself something of the variety within Spenser's own use of language. His best known poems – the long narrative poem, *The Faerie Queene*, the sonnet sequence *Amoretti*, and the two bridal poems, *Prothalamion* and *Epithalamion* – readily display the remarkable variety of his writing.

SPENSERIAN LYRIC POETRY

In the shorter poems, Spenser's use of lexis and grammar is similar to that of the other lyric poets of his age. An informative example is the *Epithalamion*, where lyric celebration is situated within a type of narrative framework, in that the poem describes the bride's procession in her first public appearance on her bridal day:

> Loe where she comes along with portly pace
> Lyke Phoebe from her chamber of the East,
> Arysing forth to run her mighty race,
> Clad all in white, that seemes a virgin best.
> So well it her beseemes that ye would weene
> Some angell she had beene.
> Her long loose yellow locks lyke golden wyre,
> Sprinckled with perle, and perling flowres a tweene,
> Doe lyke a golden mantle her attyre,
> And being crowned with a girland greene,
> Seeme lyke some mayden Queene.
> Her modest eyes abashed to behold

So many gazers, as on her do stare,
Vpon the lowly ground affixed are.

(148–61)

The ordering of the syntagmatic axis plays a key role in representing the shifting point of view of the narrator, with both temporal and spatial aspects being suggested as he draws the attention of the narratees to the bride's general bearing and the way she moves, then to her white attire (without any details); as she comes closer, her hair attracts his attention, as he makes three references to its colour, and compares it to golden wire (a cliché originated by Lydgate in the extract on p. 32, though used here in a much more controlled syntagmatic context). But the signification moves outwards as well: just as the ideal gentleman constructed within *The Faerie Queene* embodies the culture's major symbolic matrices (Miller, 1986, 171), so the bride here is invested with value by the poet's choice of analogies germane to Elizabethan culture, analogies which integrate the bride's individual self with elements of higher standing in the hierarchies of being (moon and angels) and of society (Queen). The controlled syntagm within which these analogies occur ensures that they are functional (as a very similar group in Lydgate's *The Temple of Glass*, 265–73, cited on p. 32, is not), and form part of the way the narrator's point of view, the physical perception, is also being used to convey an attitude. This is further evident in the identification of the moon as Phoebe, in the reference to dress, and in the comparison of the golden hair to a mantle, which together suggest that she is attired both royally and like the goddess of chastity (as the white overtly symbolizes), and appears, indeed, as an isomorph of Queen Elizabeth herself. Finally, in the last lines of the extract the narrator attributes the quality of modesty to the bride, and this explicitly signals the shift in point of view from the visual to the attitudinal and moral.

In retrospect, however, this moral attitude permeates most of the paradigmatic choices. If Spenser's celebratory nuptial discourse is considered in the context of the sixteenth century Puritan idealization of marriage as both a spiritual union and the basis of an ordered society (Rose, 1984), both the larger analogies and the collocation of the epithets of power ('portly', 'mighty', 'Queene') with those of humility ('modest', 'abashed', 'lowly') serve to load these signifiers with a greater semantic weight than each might carry individually.

The lines proceed by accumulation, so the syntactic structure is fairly simple, with some left- and some right-branching in most sentences. The texture is semantically dense, with fifteen adjectives to seventeen nouns; there are, for instance, three adjectives for her hair, in 'her long loose yellow locks', where each signifies a different aspect, but 'golden' appears twice shortly after; Spenser's paradigmatic choices are not as varied as, say, Sidney's, and the repetition and synonymy make for a lesser intensity. There is also an element of specialization in Spenser's choice of register in his paradigmatic selections. He is writing in the pastoral mode, for one thing, and so his use of archaisms can suggest the idealized golden age of the past. But it is important to distinguish between what was archaic for his contemporary audience and what is archaic for the twentieth century; for instance, the word *portly* survives in the meaning of 'stately' until the nineteenth century, and is not at all archaic for Spenser; and neither 'beseemes' nor 'weene' is archaic in the sixteenth century. But in the stanza which follows (line 173), he has used the word 'rudded', a revival from the fourteenth-century lexicon which doesn't long survive his attempt to bring it back into currency.

SPENSERIAN NARRATIVE

As might be expected, *The Faerie Queene* displays a greater range of textures, since a long poem can't remain constantly on an intellectually demanding level without losing audience attention. It has to vary its style and its pacing, and one way of varying the pace is by altering the semantic density *and* intensity. Where both are thin, forward movement along the syntagm and hypersyntagm can be rapid, without need to pause too long over either the signifiers or the signifieds. This is often a characteristic of transitions, and of the representation of more marginal aspects of story events:

> at length nigh to the sea they drew;
> By which as they did trauell on a day,
> They saw before them, far as they could vew,
> Full many people gathered in a crew;
> Whose great assembly they did much admire.
> For neuer there the like resort they knew.

> So towardes them they coasted, to enquire
> What thing so many nations met, did there desire.
>
>                                        (Book V, Canto II, 29)

This stanza begins a new segment of the narrative by
introducing what Artegall and Talus see. The semantic density is
very thin; there are only four modified nouns – 'full many
people, great assembly, the like resort, and so many nations' –
and all make more or less the same point, that there were a lot
of people there. So after the first adjective/noun combination,
the later phrases add little to the signified already given; further,
the semantic loading of the adjectives is small (they are scarcely
more than intensives), and since there are altogether only eight
nouns in the extract, the semantic density remains very slight.
There is some hypotaxis, with six subordinate clauses in all, but
none of it is very complex, and the stanza as a whole merely
creates a pause before the next main incident is introduced.
Thus neither signifiers, nor signified concepts, nor syntagmatic
order, impedes comprehension, and the reader can coast
through the stanza at low pressure.

A contrasting kind of language is found a little later in the
same Canto (stanza 50):

> Like as a ship, whom cruell tempest driues
>     Vpon a rocke with horrible dismay,
>     Her shattered ribs in thousand peeces riues,
>     And spoyling all her geares and goodly ray,
>     Does make her selfe misfortunes piteous pray[,]
>     So downe the cliffe the wretched Gyant tumbled;
>     His battred ballances in peeces lay,
>     His timbered bones all broken rudely rumbled,
> So was the high aspyring with huge ruine humbled.

This is an epic simile, structured round the syntactic left-
branching 'Like as . . . So' framework. The semantic density
couldn't be more different, with sixteen nouns, and (if the noun
that modifies 'piteous pray' is included) there are thirteen
modifiers. Reading must be slowed, just to take in the
comparison, with each part, the vehicle and the tenor, being
heavily nominal and with lots of modification. The semantic
intensity, however, is not especially marked, for 'cruell' to
modify 'tempest' is fairly predictable, and 'horrible' for 'dismay'
similarly expresses an attitude without adding a great deal of

new information; this is true of most of the modifiers, in that they reinforce the signified of the noun, rather than bringing a new signified into contact with it. There is also some redundancy in 'her geares and goodly ray'. So, although pace and pressure have been varied from stanza 29, the stanza is not making for the sort of pressure that the Sidney sonnet, for example, exerts, where both signifiers and signifieds, and especially their combination, slow the reader's comprehension. However there are other climactic segments in the poem which rival the *Epithalamion* extract in their density and intensity, and it is their hypersyntagmatic functioning as part of a larger overtly narrative framework that differentiates them from the lyric stanzas and sonnets, where even the sequences only imply a narrative.

## Varieties of prose writing

In a narrative poem the forward progress is paramount, and is only delayed here and there, as in the description of the Giant's destruction; in this respect, such a text may have as many affinities with prose as with other kinds of poetic discourse, though prose itself is as varied in style and purpose as is verse. Narrative verse is rarely as simple and direct as 'artless' narrative prose may be.

HAKLUYT'S SPEECH-BASED PROSE

Hakluyt's prose, for example, in *Voyages and Documents*, suggests such a concentration on 'story' as to leave discourse to take care of itself; it is speech-based, using mainly right-branching sentences and a rather loose, cumulative co-ordination:

> Immediatly tokens were given unto the Delight, to cast about to seaward, which, being the greater ship, and of burden 120 tunnes, was yet formost upon the breach, keeping so ill watch, that they knew not the danger, before they felt the same, too late to recover it: for presently the Admirall strooke a ground, and had soone after her sterne and hinder partes beaten in pieces: whereupon the rest (that is to say, the Frigat in which was the Generall and the Golden Hinde) cast about Eastsoutheast, bearing to the south, even for our lives into the

> *windes eye*, because that way caried us to the seaward.
>
> (*The Voyage of Sir Humphrey Gilbert* (1583),
> in Hakluyt, 1958 edn, 270)

Information is presented in small units, generally in chronological order; the detail about the size of the *Delight* is embedded by means of a present participial link and is then expanded by a simple co-ordination. No attempt is made to impart shape or balance to the discourse, nor to increase its dramatic impact by means of heightening paradigmatic choices. Rather, the signifiers are drawn largely from a nautical register, and point directly to specific signifieds ('cast about', 'strooke a ground'). Even the one piece of figurative language – 'bearing . . . into the windes eye' – is a dead metaphor, nautical jargon for sailing in the direction from which the wind is blowing. Prose of this kind might be termed 'naïve realism' because of its simple underlying assumption of a direct and uncomplicated relationship between signifiers and signifieds, and comparable examples can appear whenever story and signified take precedence over discourse and signifier. Bunyan is a later obvious example.

BACON'S LATIN-BASED PROSE

Between the sixteenth and nineteenth centuries, especially, the main stream of English prose writing swung back and forth between speech-based styles and various versions of an Anglicized classical, specifically Latin-based, style. The rise of Romanticism, coinciding and interacting with major developments in prose fiction, was ultimately to be responsible for the virtual demise of the Latin influence, though classical rhetoric shaped certain kinds of non-fiction discourse well into the twentieth century. An early, staple Latin-based style is well exemplified by the writings of Francis Bacon; it seems overpatterned and ornate to a modern reader, but is in fact a relatively sparse 'Latin' style. One complex sentence will suffice to illustrate this:

> Lastly, leauing the vulgar arguments, that by learning, man excelleth man in that, wherein man excelleth beasts; that by learning man ascendeth to the heauens and their motions; where in bodie he cannot come; and the like; let vs conclude with the dignitie and excellency of knowledge and learning, in that whereunto mans nature doth most aspire; which is

immortalitie or continuance; for to this tendeth generation, and raysing of houses and families; to this buildings, foundations, and monuments; to this tendeth the desire of memorie, fame, and celebration; and in effect, the strength of all other humane desires; wee see then how farre the monuments of wit and learning, are more durable, than the monuments of power, or of hands.

> (*The Aduancement of Learning* (1605),
> in Muir, 1956, 62)

This is a heavily nominal style, with thirty-nine nouns to only three adjectives in the sentence; there is a substantial sprinkling of abstract and Latinate terms, made more overt by their occurrence in doublets (as 'dignitie and excellency' or 'immortalitie or continuance', where the signifiers point to very similar signifieds and diminish semantic intensity). Lexis thus contributes to the formal effect imparted by the overall symmetry of the syntagmatic patterning, in turn made obvious by the repetition both of grammatical structures and of key words, and by the apparent multiplication of paradigmatic elements at similar places in similar clauses. The essence of the style, however, is a broad repetition of syntagmatic units which allows for a lot of grammatical and paradigmatic variation. The clauses expanding 'vulgar arguments' illustrate one aspect of this:

[1]   that by learning man excelleth man in that

[2]                              wherein man excelleth beastes

[3]   that by learning man ascendeth to ‖ the heauens   ‖
                              and ‖ their motions ‖

[4]                              where in bodie he cannot come

Clauses [1] and [3] are identical as far as the verbs, and these fall generally within one semantic field, but have different grammatical functions within the predicate; the object/complement slots then contrast in two ways, placing the simple, microcosmic 'man' against the paradigmatically doubled, macrocosmic 'heavens . . . their motions'. Clauses [2] and [4] effect a syntagmatic balance only in the broad sense that they are subordinated to [1] and [3] respectively, and are approximately the same length; but this creates a rhythmic pattern only, the clauses being otherwise unrelated, and the very different grammatical functions of 'wherein' and 'where in' neatly exemplify the interplay of difference and sameness. This interplay is still more obvious in the three clauses expanding the doublet 'immortalitie or continuance': the verb 'tendeth' occurs in the first and the third, and is implied by ellipsis in the second; in each clause the subject follows the verb, but then the list which is being presented is built up in a different way in each clause – in the first the subject slot is filled by a doublet with the second element extended by a unit consisting of a further doublet, in the second by a triplet, and in the third by a single term extended by a triplet. This allows the writer to create the impression that a large body of evidence is amassed within his argument, thus furthering his aim of rhetorical persuasion.

## An extended example: Donne (1624)

Powerful rhetoric of a more speech-based kind is employed by Donne in his sermons. We will make here an extended analysis of an extract from the *Sermon Preached at Pauls upon Christmas Day, 1624*, which we have set out to show the syntagmatic/paradigmatic structuring and to bring out other features which are perhaps less obvious in a normal prose format (we have numbered the clauses, capitalized the principal clauses and subordinating conjunctions, and printed some of the patterning devices in bold-face):

```
1a  IF some King of the earth have
         so large an extent of Dominion,                      in North, and South,
2         AS THAT he hath Winter and Summer                    together
                    in his Dominions,
1b    so large an  extent                                      East and West
3         AS THAT he hath day     and night                    together
                    in his Dominions,
4     MUCH MORE    HATH GOD
                   MERCY AND JUDGEMENT TOGETHER:
5     HE BROUGHT    LIGHT OUT OF DARKNESSE,
                  not out of a lesser light;
6     HE CAN BRING THY SUMMER OUT OF WINTER,
7          THOUGH thou have no Spring;
8          THOUGH in the wayes of ‖ fortune,
                            or    ‖ understanding
                            or    ‖ conscience,
            thou have been ‖ benighted                         till now
                           ‖ wintred and frozen,
                           ‖ clouded and eclypsed,
                           ‖ damped and benummed,
                           ‖ smothered and stupefied           till now
```

9                                                              **NOW**

GOD COMES TO THEE,
    **NOT** as in the dawning  of the day,
    **NOT** as in the bud      of the spring,
    BUT as    the Sun    at noon
      to illustrate all    shadowes,
      as   the sheaves  in harvest,
      to fill    all     penuries,
10                  ALL   OCCASIONS INVITE HIS MERCIES,
11          and ALL   TIMES     ARE   HIS SEASONS.

This is a very heavily patterned prose. The repetitions and parallelism function on both a syntactic and a semantic level, and, despite the dependence of the argument on a conventional analogy, point to contrast as strongly as to comparison. There are two major left-branching syntactic units, the first being formally conditional with the opening 'If', though functioning like a concessive, and the second (clause 8, following) formally concessive; both units give climactic force to the principal clause when it finally arrives after such postponement. The climax is also reinforced by a change in rhythmic stressing. The second syntactic unit continues after the principal clause (9) with further right-branching units, balancing negative against positive in the lead-up to the final pair of summative principal clauses.

The analogy upon which the argument is built makes overt use of the theory of macrocosm/microcosm isomorphism. The opening 'If' clause gives the ground for the analogy, with binary oppositions emphasizing the sheer extent of the King's dominions, first with the compass points, and then with the seasons as units of measurement. The strategy is to build up a space–time dimension which overrides the seeming oppositions by encompassing them, so paving the way for the non-paradoxical paradox of 'mercy and judgement'. Then within the larger-scale balanced structures, there is further balance. Syntagmatically, the opening clause designates a King of the earth which already implies its opposite, the King of Heaven, and the repeated phrase 'so large an extent' foregrounds the aspect that Donne wishes to focus on: size. This, together with the binary opposition of the compass points in two directions, suggests a spatial focus, but since all the major ways of measuring *time* are incorporated within the seasonal terms and the day/night opposition, the space/time dimensions of power are conflated. The way is thus prepared for the next contrast. The indefinite deictic 'some' leaves the 'King' unspecified, and has slightly dismissive overtones, in contrast to the following principal clause with its four adjacent stresses on 'Much more hath God'. The comparative adverb foregrounded by the inversion which gives it initial position in the principal clause marks the move from the unidentified King to the heavenly King of Kings. In the paradigmatic slot following the verb 'have/hath', the abstracts 'mercy and judgement' parallel the earlier space/time oppositions (with 'dominion(s)' shifting its signified from abstract to concrete); since the earlier emphasis has been on the linking of oppositions, so the seemingly opposed 'mercy' and 'judgement' are linked, as the parallel repeated 'together' makes clear.

The verb form throughout the first sentence is the present tense of the neutral verb 'to have'; in the two following principal clauses Donne switches to the active verb 'to bring', and also alters tense, from past to future, contrasting the original creation of the macrocosm with the microcosm of the singular addressee, 'thou', in an important deictic pointer which governs the next section of the excerpt. 'Light' and 'darkness' become non-sensory, vehicles for a metaphor, a shift probably promoted as much by the intertextual allusion to Genesis 1 and to Isaiah 9.2, since it also alludes to the initial act of redemption, as by the preceding abstracts 'mercy' and 'judgement'. So when the nouns of clauses 5 and 6 repeat major concepts from the preceding subordinate clauses, what is foregrounded are the differences: the components of the binary opposition 'day/night' are replaced with their key attributes 'light/darkness', which are also figurative and suggest in turn figurative senses for summer and winter, in their now inverted order; the third, hitherto unmentioned, seasonal term 'spring' is then added, and is fraught with significance, both because of the immediate figurative context and because of the larger context, in that the sermon is written for delivery on Christmas Day.

The second left-branching sentence picks up the preceding concessive, and from syntactic parallels moves to the strategy of cumulation, with three abstract nouns, followed by a series of participles, all passive in form, as 'thou' becomes the one acted upon by the winter conditions. The paradigmatic selection works to build up rhythm, alliteration, and the evoking of sensory experience, especially that of the literal physical phenomena of winter affecting humankind, though with a floating of the signifiers in that they can be taken symbolically, especially in view of the preceding abstract nouns about the social and spiritual environment: the syntagm makes 'the wayes of fortune . . .' metaphoric, especially when the repeated genitives stress that *wayes* cannot be literal, and the series of abstract nouns strips away the physical denotation 'paths'; but then the participles throw stress back on the winter journey as vehicle of the whole metaphorical movement. The repeated 'till now' foregrounds the changed temporal aspect, placing addresser and addressee in the immediate present. Then the repetition and heavy stressing of the pivotal word 'now' at the beginning of the principal clause gives particular impact to the statement which summarizes the Christmas Day message, 'Now God comes to thee', with its loaded verbal choice contrasting with 'bring' to suggest the closer relationship with the bringer.

The remainder of the excerpt illustrates what that coming is, first negatively, and then positively, as the correlated syntax of 'Not as . . . but as' demonstrates. Looking back to the earlier part of the argument, Donne evokes 'dawn' (after night), and spring (after its lack, and after winter), only to deny their relevance to this coming, and instead he fills the paradigm he has set up with the sun (playing on the homophonic double signified 'Son') and the sheaves, adding to the impact of each by the temporal phrase which locates each at its peak, noon and harvest. Finally, the passage concludes with a rhetorical trick: at first it seems that the summarizing 'all occasions' is parallel to 'all penuries', in object position after 'to fill', but then the syntax is seen to pivot on it to make it the subject of the new principal clause's verb, 'invite', and then parallel to the following subject, 'all times'. This imparts a strong climactic effect to the final two clauses, in which Donne conflates what was separated in the opening sentence, while the paralleling of the objects of the verbs 'invite' and 'are' ('mercies' and 'seasons'), continues the dismantling of the opening oppositions, even while the present tense denies the flux of seasonal change.

Since the 'truth' of the content is not open to question, the effect of such elaborate rhetoric is to be powerfully emotive. By inviting the audience to perceive the variety of ways in which the normal conventions of language are played with (and against), the rhetoric functions to involve the audience in the gradual layering of meanings into a richly associative discourse.

While prose of such a kind was being developed, the

pressure for literary language to develop a base in everyday speech was being felt most heavily in the contemporary drama, to which we will now briefly turn.

## Textual shifts in Shakespeare's dramatic discourse

Apart from stage directions (in some periods), drama is couched in the direct speech of its protagonists, and this has two important ramifications for our study. First, there is the negative aspect of the absence of a narrator (and so the absence of the slanting of focalization which derives from a narrating voice). Because the discourse emanates from the protagonists within the drama, the point of view in any speech act is that of the speaker, not of a controlling narrator, and so its function is to attribute particular associated or disclosed characteristics to that speaker (and hence its function could be defined as hyperparadigmatic). Second, *implicature* is of crucial importance for the concept of the syntagm/paradigm axes (see Elam, 1980, 170–6). Participants in conversational exchanges normally share an assumption that their aim is to achieve effective and coherent communication. When the hypersyntagmatic relationship between speeches follows or breaches the conversational maxims which express implicature at the subtextual level, it expresses such important aspects of dramatic discourse as the degree of openness and equality of communication or the extent to which one or more speakers can dominate the process of exchange.

These superordinate aspects of dramatic discourse have major implications for syntagm/paradigm and signifier/signified interaction in terms of the density and intensity of semantic texture. This is clearly exemplified in Shakespeare's dramatic discourse, which changes from rhetorical to speech-based language in the period between *Romeo and Juliet* (c.1594?) and the mature tragedies of a decade later. This change is of particular stylistic interest if Greenblatt is correct in his observation that Shakespeare's plays 'are centrally and repeatedly concerned with the production and containment of subversion and disorder' (1985, 29). Much of *Romeo and Juliet*, particularly in scenes dealing with the emotional disorder of indiscriminate desire, is expressed through a style which draws attention to its own artifice:

*Benvolio* Alas! that love, so gentle in his view,
   Should be so tyrannous and rough in proof.
*Romeo* Alas! that love, whose view is muffled still,
   Should, without eyes, see pathways to his will.
   Where shall we dine? O me! What fray was here?
   Yet tell me not, for I have heard it all.
   Here's much to do with hate, but more with love:
   Why then, O brawling love! o loving hate!
   O any thing! of nothing first create.
   O heavy lightness! serious vanity!
   Mis-shapen chaos of well-seeming forms!
   Feather of lead, bright smoke, cold fire, sick health!
   Still-waking sleep, that is not what it is!
   This love feel I, that feel no love in this.

(I.i.168–80)

The semantic density of this extract is much less than that of
some of the Spenser examples considered, with only fourteen
adjectives to twenty-seven nouns (though in 'feather of lead' the
second noun has an adjectival function). The rank shift at the
beginning of Romeo's speech, whereby 'love' is modified by a
clause and then a phrase, thins the texture, and, while the later
part of the speech loads the syntagm in some of the ways
pointed to in Sidney's sonnet-writing, and the whole series of
seemingly incongruous oxymorons increases semantic density
and intensity (in that the relationship between adjective and
noun is one of contradiction), the speech lacks weight on the
plane of the signifieds. It is a rather conventional piece of
Petrarchan rhetoric, and in the last few lines, in particular,
syntagmatic flow is almost brought to a standstill by a
paradigmatic accumulation of familiar figures which, at their
final decoding, all share a single underlying signified; in other
words, the interplay of signifiers becomes predictable, and the
semantic texture is opened out accordingly. The imposing of a
recursive movement upon the syntagm culminates in the final
line of the extract, in which, apart from the key negative, the
second half of the line is a mirror inversion of the first:

1   2   3 4 4  3    2    1
This love feel I, that feel no love in this.

What purports to be a conversation between the two speakers
breaches the maxim of quantity, when Romeo's catalogue is so

much longer than Benvolio's, and the maxim of manner, in his overuse of oxymorons, especially when both speakers seem to be defining the concept signified by the signifier *love*, but as they do this, they do so perversely: love at this stage of the play is no more than a game played with language, as Romeo seeks to outdo Benvolio in extravagant rhetoric.

In the later tragedies semantic texture has become much denser, especially as created by adjective/noun combinations. *Macbeth* is almost contemporaneous with Bacon's *Aduancement of Learning*, and a comparison would suggest that genre is a factor in the very different types of persuasive language employed:

> *Macbeth*          Ere the bat hath flown
>    His cloister'd flight, ere, to black Hecate's summons
>    The shard-borne beetle with his drowsy hums
>    Hath rung night's yawning peal, there shall be done
>    A deed of dreadful note.
> *Lady Mac.*        What's to be done?
> *Macbeth* Be innocent of the knowledge, dearest chuck,
>    Till thou applaud the deed. Come, seeling night,
>    Scarf up the tender eye of pitiful day,
>    And with thy bloody and invisible hand
>    Cancel and tear to pieces that great bond
>    Which keeps me pale!
>
> (III.ii.40–50)

A wide range of registers is drawn on here: a formal register suggested by the complex sentence structures; the momentary intrusion of an intimate register of 'dearest chuck' in reply to Lady Macbeth's simple question; the technical register of falconry. Further, there is a greater semantic density than in the *Romeo and Juliet* extract (a ratio of seven adjectives to ten nouns), but, more significantly, intensity is increased by the different way the adjective/noun combinations function. Combinations are neither conventional, nor predictable, nor patterned. Instead the combinations are unexpected, and the adjectives carry a full semantic load in their own right. The auditor is much more conscious of the *process* of combination, and weighs each carefully, something that ceases to happen with Romeo's string of oxymorons.

Attention fixes on the interplay of signifieds rather than on the play of signifiers, and these signifieds become invested with complex associations. Thus 'cloister'd flight' carries more than a suggestion that bats frequent cloisters, since it also activates a range of connotations pertaining to cloisters. More complex still is the effect of the larger sequence running through 'shard-borne beetle', 'drowsy hums', and 'rung night's yawning peal', where the individual combinations are further affected by the paradigmatic congruences between 'drowsy' and 'yawning', on the one hand, and 'hums', 'rung', and 'peal' on the other: 'yawning', for example, evokes a human yawn, the mouth of a ringing bell, and, influenced by 'black Hecate' and the suggestion of decay in 'shard-borne', the common collocation of the yawning grave. Along the syntagmatic line, then, a number of overlaid paradigmatic associations are formed simultaneously; this process is largely set in train by the left-branching, hypotactic structure which insists on connectedness of the parts while deferring the information which explains what the connections are – and even when reached, the main clause still defers by using the dummy 'there' to push the grammatical subject back to final position. Lady Macbeth's question is hardly surprising, though she is only briefly the direct addressee, and is indirect addressee for most of both Macbeth's speeches. At this point in their exchange Macbeth breaches the maxim of relation, in his refusal to answer his wife's question while shifting register to address her with affectionate diminutives ('dearest chuck'), and the continuation of his speech thereby becomes a breach of both manner and quality, in that it is both irrelevant and an excess of information with respect to the second speaker's question, given that she is still formally ignorant of his meaning. It is one of many examples in the play where one of these characters exploits the dynamics of conversational exchange to achieve dominance over the other (Kennedy, 1983, 85–9).

Dense semantic texture is created in other ways also. There is some doubletting, but of verbs and adjectives rather than nouns, and of a kind which at least extends meaning ('cancel and tear to pieces'), or becomes virtually paradoxical, as in 'bloody and invisible', which is explicable in terms of the vehicle of the metaphor, 'seeling night' (the stitching hand is 'bloody'; the now blind hawk cannot see it), but becomes much more loosely evocative in relation to the tenor. It might be noted that in general the modifiers attached to the nouns within the extended metaphor impart a much more emotive impact to the metaphor than was the case with the epic simile from *The Faerie Queene*.

As a final illustration of the relationship between rhetorical and speech-based language in Shakespeare, we will take two passages from *The Tempest*:

*Miranda*                    Do you love me?
*Ferdinand* O heaven, O earth, bear witness to this sound
   And crown what I profess with kind event
   If I speak true! if hollowly, invert
   What best is boded me to mischief! I
   Beyond all limit of what else i' the world
   Do love, prize, honour you.
*Miranda*                    I am a fool
   To weep at what I am glad of.

                                        (III.i.67–74)


*Prospero* . . . as my gift and thine own acquisition
   Worthily purchased, take my daughter: but
   If thou dost break her virgin-knot before
   All sanctimonious ceremonies may
   With full and holy rites be minister'd,
   No sweet aspersion shall the heavens let fall
   To make this contract grow; but barren hate,
   Sour-eyed disdain and discord shall bestrew
   The union of your bed with weeds so loathly
   That you shall hate it both.

                                        (IV.i.12–21)

Ferdinand's protestation of love, in the first extract, is expressed in a syntagmatic style, although the sentence structure is rather formal. The clauses are carefully (and chiastically) balanced, so as to bring out the contrasts between 'kind event:mischief' and 'true:hollowly'; the texture is not semantically dense, with the only adjectives, 'kind' and 'best', functioning practically and intensively, and there is the same number of nouns as verbs (9). The second extract has a greater semantic density, but nevertheless still slightly lower than that of *Macbeth* (now 5.5 adjectives to 10 nouns), and the intensity is much less than in the *Macbeth* passage – most of the adjectives define and specify qualities of their nouns, but none is surprising, and some do verge on redundancy ('sanctimonious ceremonies'; 'holy rite'). The semantic intensity of these relatively straightforward signifiers is increased, however, by bringing in the added level of hypersignification suggested by Paul Brown's reading of the play as an exploration of colonialist discourse; this makes Prospero's island analogous to Virginia and Ireland (Brown, 1985). The defeat of the elements of disorder by the end of the play is condensed into the union between the two young lovers, which represents, incidentally, the antithesis of the unbridled desire underlying the *Romeo and Juliet* passage we began with. The figure Prospero selects here to assert his patriarchal control over premarital sexuality discloses its parallel with his colonization of the island, in that the agricultural vehicle reflects the political doctrine that the development of a virgin territory is subject to (ordained by?) higher powers. The strategy of personifying hate, disdain and discord rhetorically enforces the opposition between unbridled desire (resulting in desert) and chaste restraint (resulting in fertility).

## Changing semantic density and intensity in lyric poetry

DONNE (1572–1631)

It is illuminating to compare and contrast this development in drama with a similar development that takes place in lyric poetry, as exemplified in the work of John Donne (born in 1572, only some twenty years after Spenser and Sidney):

> I wonder by my troth, what thou, and I
> Did, till we lov'd? were we not wean'd till then?
> But suck'd on countrey pleasures, childishly?
> Or snorted we in the seaven sleepers den?
> T'was so; But this, all pleasures fancies be.
> If ever any beauty I did see,
> Which I desir'd, and got, t'was but a dreame of thee,
>
> ('The Good-Morrow', 1–7)

Donne is reacting against the enriching of semantic density which has been going on since the time of Wyatt. He puts in only two modifiers, 'countrey' and the numeral 'seven', and there are only 9 nouns to 12 verbs (a ratio of 7:10). Of those 12 verbs, two are 'was', and one is 'be', and they also include 'did' and 'got', though the others carry heavier semantic loading. The semantic texture is by count very thin. On the other hand, Donne almost flaunts his syntagmatic control within the stanza form, for there is very little by way of inversion and it is mostly normal prose-order, except for the 'all pleasures fancies be'; moreover, that syntagmatic control is emphasized by the way that the first line over-runs the line end, to be followed by a very early caesura, so that the very ordinary colloquial verb 'Did' is heavily foregrounded. When, in the last line, another colloquial verb, 'got', is prominently stressed, it might well seem that the semantic intensity is also slight, since such ordinary colloquial and indeterminate signifiers are carrying such weight. (This is especially so when 'got' follows on from 'desir'd', which is not only more elevated than, say, 'wanted', but also precedes 'got' within the line, pointing to a temporal progression in what is signified, from desiring to getting.)

Yet, as praise of one's mistress, the language makes a very powerful impact because paradigm and syntagm interact in such a way that the penumbra of associations clustering around quite simple words becomes important. For example, by being linked with 'pleasures', the one real adjective, 'countrey', becomes a floating signifier. There is an immediate activation of its bawdy, sexual connotations in colloquial language (more familiar from the 'country matters' of *Hamlet*, III.ii.123), and when it is counterpointed with the lexical set of 'baby' verbs, 'wean'd, suck'd,' and the associated adverb 'childishly' all sorts of connotations and associations are aroused. This floating is raised to a thematic level when the speaker contrasts his former lovers with the lady here addressed (as is made clear in 'till then'), and suggests that they are floating signifiers for the one true Platonic ideal signified, which is she. In effect, the dream at the end is being contrasted with the reality. Any intensity in this stanza does not depend on semantic density, but on spare and tightly controlled relationships which activate the penumbra of associations evoked by the signifiers.

Donne is the first of the so-called Metaphysical poets; his language depends very much on a syntagm/paradigm relation which is close to that of ordinary speech, even though it is more tightly patterned than in speech; there are rhetorical devices in it which activate a range of associations, but lexis on the whole is not very Latinate and elevated, and can become quite colloquial.

AN EXTENDED EXAMPLE: DONNE'S SONNET, 'OH MY BLACKE
SOULE . . .'

Earlier, we examined a prose extract at some length; here, we
seek to show the extent to which the syntagmatic/paradigmatic
interrelationship controls and yet allows play and flexibility of
interpretative activity when it interacts with a highly conventional
verse form. To do this, we have chosen one of Donne's Holy
Sonnets, 'Oh my blacke soule', and have set it out first in its
traditional sonnet form and then in a form which focuses
attention on its syntagmatic and paradigmatic patterning.
(Clauses, including non-finite clauses, have been numbered;
and items in some sort of paradigmatic relationship are in
vertical parallel.) Unless otherwise stated, numbers in the
subsequent discussion refer to the clause numbers.

> Oh my blacke Soule! now thou art summoned
> By sicknesse, deaths herald, and champion;
> Thou art like a pilgrim, which abroad hath done
> Treason, and durst not turne to whence hee is fled,
> Or like a thiefe, which till deaths doome be read,
> Wisheth himselfe delivered from prison;
> But damn'd and hal'd to execution,
> Wisheth that still he might be imprisoned.
> Yet grace, if thou repent, thou canst not lacke;
> But who shall give thee that grace to beginne?
> Oh make thy selfe with holy mourning blacke,
> And red with blushing, as thou art with sinne;
> Or wash thee in Christs blood, which hath this might
> That being red, it dyes red soules to white.

| | | | |
|---|---|---|---|
| 1 | Oh my | blacke Soule! | |
| 2 | | now thou art summoned/By | ‖sicknesse, deaths herald, and champion;/ |
| 3a | Thou art | | |
| | **like** a pilgrim, | | |
| 4 | | which abroad hath done/Treason, | |
| 5 | | and durst not turn to | |
| 6 | | whence hee is fled,/ | |
| 3b | or **like** a thief, | | |
| 7a | which | | |
| 8 | | till deaths doome be read,/ | |

```
7b                    Wisheth himself delivered from prison;/
9              But ‖ damn'd
               and ‖ hal'd     to execution,/
10            Wisheth
11                    that still he might be imprisoned./


12a   Yet grace,
13        if thou repent,
12b          thou canst not lacke;/
14      But who shall give thee
        that grace to beginne?/
15      Oh make thy selfe with holy mourning
                 blacke,/
        And  red            with blushing,
16                          as thou art with sinne;/
17      Or wash thee in Christs blood,
18                  which hath this might/
19a   That
20    being red
19b            it dyes
              red soules to
              white.
```

Approaching a Donne Holy Sonnet, a reader may anticipate particular theological presuppositions and a particular set of generic conventions which express them (cf. Flanigan, 1986, 55). More specifically, the sonnet form may inspire generic expectations about the octet/sestet division of the fourteen lines, and perhaps about the rhyme structuring of the quatrains. Primarily, though, *how* the sonnet means is shaped by the syntagmatic/paradigmatic structuring and its interrelationship with the sonnet form which makes up the framing parameter of the text – in other words, by the patterning of the language within a conventional, predictable framework.

The controlled release of information along the syntagmatic axis within a fixed form is very often underestimated, partly because of the power of the semantic thrust of the words selected to fill the paradigmatic slots, and partly because the terminal effect of line-end rhyme can function to mask the syntax and the syntagm. But their importance is shown immediately in the opening apostrophe to 'my blacke soule', for the colour term cannot, in collocation with 'soule', retain its physical, sensory denotation, so the reader must construe the signifier 'blacke' in such a way that its normal signified is displaced and replaced by a symbolic signified. This isn't a complex process, since 'soule' immediately signals a register pertaining to Christian discourse, within which the choice of 'blacke' conventionally evokes the concept of darkness and thence, by symbolic extension to yet a further signified, the suggestion of sin, a signifier not overtly included until clause 16. Other colour terms could have been chosen to fill the paradigmatic slot, so the contrast of the initial epithet with the final pair of epithets for the same paradigmatic slot, modifying 'soule(s)' in 19, retrospectively makes clear how important was the choice of 'blacke' for this opening apostrophe, with its connotative overtones deriving from the interaction of syntagm and paradigm as the speaker addresses the non-physical soul.

Another type of interaction occurs with the passive transform of the first finite verb, 'art summoned' (2). This immediately assigns the soul the non-active function it retains throughout the octet, but more importantly, it doubly foregrounds the agent of this passive verb by delaying its appearance until the end of the clause (syntactic end-focus) and until the beginning of the second verse-line (onset-focus). As with 'blacke', 'sicknesse' generates a double signification, now because the verb denotes a human action and hence marks the physical state 'sicknesse' as a personification. The whole of line 2 consists of a paradigmatic accumulation, and shows how such a cumulative technique can produce a layering of meanings and, to some extent, a floating of signification: the personification 'sicknesse' is amplified into a small allegory by the addition of two figurative concepts which form a lexical set with 'summon' and evoke the concept of trial by combat, in which the soul is defendant; and since sickness is given the status not only of death's forerunner, the herald, but also is fighting on death's behalf, the collapse of the usual distinction between herald and champion in a trial by combat stresses the power of sickness. Donne is thus playing with and against the norms of language in that he uses fairly ordinary and easily apprehended syntax to transfer the signifiers from their most common signifieds to less common, even if sometimes quite conventional, signifieds.

The rest of the octet is based on the parallel analogies of clause 3a/3b, 'like a pilgrim' and 'like a thief' respectively, with further qualifications within each simile. Within the first, the inversion after the relative pronoun 'which' foregrounds the adverb of place, 'abroad', significant because a treasonable pilgrim is subject to the death penalty not only at home but also if abroad; while in terms of the literal concept, the soul, having left God to come to the body, has sinned, and is afraid to return; but, being under the death sentence of sickness, is in a hopeless position in either location. The second syntagm changes the emphasis from the spatial to the temporal, tracing the chronological progress of the thief between his confinement in prison and his haling to execution; but the sequential time order is counterpointed with the thief's contradictory wishes concerning his spatial location.

Within the octet as a whole, the analogies for the soul's state reflect seventeenth-century cultural and societal hierarchies, as the descending social status and diminishing freedom of the soul are traced from the free man challenged to trial by combat, to the exiled pilgrim, and finally to the disreputable thief. Within the paradigmatic axis, the foregrounding of terms such as 'prison' (repeated in substantive and verbal form in 7 and 11, each time receiving both syntactic and verse-line end-focus) heavily emphasizes the isomorphic relationships amongst the individual, society, and the cosmos, as 'prison', literal for the thief of the simile, functions as a (once more, conventional) metaphor for the imprisoning of the soul by the body. In such ways, the hypersyntagm incorporates several concepts which to a twentieth-century reader unfamiliar with the Christian discourse on which Donne is calling might well seem too disparate to be brought together, though they were much more conventionally related for his contemporary audience.

The opening of the sestet foreshadows a contrast by its first word, the adversative 'Yet', and the next word 'grace' indicates the ground for the contrast. The embedded clause 13 that follows points to the conditional nature of the operation of grace, for it is 'if', not 'when', the soul repents that grace can be effective. But the most important aspect of 12 is the way in which the syntax works against the syntagm, when what seems initially a subject, 'grace', foregrounded by insertion of a different clause immediately following, becomes retrospectively the object of 'thou canst not lack'. Furthermore the choice of the negative form in the verb slot (substituted for, say, 'canst have') throws even more weight on the embedded conditional, for if the condition is fulfilled, the verb form stresses the consequent result (named first along the syntagmatic axis).

A key aspect of the sestet is a play with signifiers, with more than one signified denoted by the same signifier. For example, 'grace' in clause 12a is unequivocally 'the favour of God', but clause 14 requires some other sense for *grace* (now a precondition, not a conclusion, as 'that . . . to beginne' points up): perhaps 'attitude' or 'goodwill', or even 'a temporary immunity from a penalty'. Clause 15 repeats the poem's first epithet, 'blacke', but its placement *after* 'holy mourning' shifts the signified symbolism, and implicitly builds in life, the binary opposite of the opening agent, 'death', for the mourner is alive, after the death of another; and 'life' as the opposition to death is the focus of the sestet, building upon the death of Christ, the redemptive power of which brings eternal life to the repentant soul.

Play on 'blacke' gives way to play on 'red' in the rest of the sonnet, with the initial reference in 15 alluding to the shame which leads to repentance, the next reference to Christ's blood in 17, and then the intertextual allusion to Isaiah 1.18 in 19; the shift deliberately floats the movement of the signifed of 'red' in the final paradox which shows the gap between the term and its 'meaning'. Thus the third word of the sonnet, 'blacke', and the last word, 'white', control the movement of the sonnet from one symbolic extreme to its binary opposite, from the symbolized sin to repentance and forgiveness, from death to eternal life, from challenged passive defendant to one who has felt the might of Christ's blood; and the pun on 'dyes', the verb of 19, is yet another paradigmatic choice that foregrounds that opposition by carrying two signifieds behind the signifier.

An analysis of the text which concentrates mainly on the interrelationship of syntagm and paradigm proves, we think, very effective in bringing out how the poet both generates meanings within and controls a rather complex discourse.


## HERBERT (1593–1633)

The later Metaphysical poets do not flaunt their choices within language, and control of it, in quite the way that Donne does. The verse of George Herbert, for example, is less flamboyant, and, indeed, can be deceptively simple. In the brief poem 'Life' there are some grammatical 'poeticisms' which make the language a little less prosaic than Donne's – there are some minor inversions, such as the insertion of both the temporal phrase 'By noon' and the manner phrase 'most cunningly' between subject and verb in lines 4–5, and the redundant *do*-auxiliary appears three times ('did beckon', 'did steal', 'did . . . convey') – but a reader readily accepts such conventions as familiar aspects of a familiar mode:

> I made a posy, while the day ran by:
> 'Here will I smell my remnant out, and tie
>                     My life within this band.'
> But Time did beckon to the flowers, and they
> By noon most cunningly did steal away,                    5
>                     And withered in my hand.
>
> My hand was next to them, and then my heart;
> I took, without more thinking, in good part
>                     Time's gentle admonition;
> Who did so sweetly death's sad taste convey,             10
> Making my mind to smell my fatal day,
>                     Yet sugaring the suspicion.
>
> Farewell dear flowers, sweetly your time ye spent,
> Fit, while ye lived, for smell or ornament,
>                     And after death for cures.             15
> I follow straight without complaints or grief,
> Since, if my scent be good, I care not if
>                     It be as short as yours.

On the whole the syntagmatic axis is very straightforward, built up with mostly principal clauses, until in the last couple of lines there is a conditional clause embedded within a causal clause, with yet another conditional clause following. The syntax has become more complex as the poem pulls the strands of its thought together, but even here it is still not difficult to follow, especially because of the tight relationship between the two conditionals: the point of the title of the poem becomes more overt as the signifier 'it' of the last line is retrospectively shifted from its literal and grammatical referent, 'scent', and becomes symbolic of moral worth, and 'life'.

The semantic density is slight, as in Donne's verse; there are 8 adjectives (two of them, 'good' and 'short', predicative) to 27 nouns, though there are also 4 adverbs, so that modification is a little more in evidence than in Donne. It may seem that the semantic intensity is also slight, especially when there is a good deal of repetition: 'smell my remnant out' in the first stanza is echoed in 'smell my fatal day' in the second, and 'smell' occurs again in the third, though now as a noun, as is the semantically related 'scent' at the end; 'sweetly' is also repeated within a four-line stretch, with reference firstly to *taste* and then to *smell*. Both 'smell' and 'sweetly' are part of the poem's dominant lexical set dealing with scent and taste, and the primary function of the repetitions is to extend the signifieds from literal to figurative signification. Further, its recontextualization evokes a wide penumbra of associations for 'sweetly', which functions mainly to convey the point of view of the speaker. A crucial change of addressee between the first two stanzas and the last, in which the speaker directly addresses the flowers after having referred to them in the third person in the first two, makes still more overt the isomorphic analogy encompassing the temporal decay of both the human and plant worlds.

This contextual frame emphasizes both the sameness and the difference in the occurrences of 'sweetly'; a word with such a wide and loose denotative range is very dependent on the syntagmatic axis for its signification, but in line 10 this is set adrift between the behavioural signification suggested by its relation with the preceding 'gentle' and the sensory indicated by the following 'taste'. This broad penumbra of associations is extended further in the third stanza by a similar manipulation of the syntagmatic axis, in that 'sweetly' is now located between the attitudinal 'dear' and the sensory 'smell or ornament' (which adds sight to taste and smell).

Once again, then, as with Donne, a fine syntagmatic control opens out the significance of everyday signifiers. Herbert had already begun to do this in the very first line of the poem, in the choice of 'posy' for the flowers; it points to several signifieds – the group of flowers brought together into a new unity, the 'flowers' of rhetoric, a collection of poems,[7] and, by a further figurative extension, the characteristics and actions of a person which constitute a life. The poem's title creates an immediate context for the floating of the first major signifier of the poem, and from there the multiple levels of signification throughout the poem follow on without much difficulty, especially when the stress is on the function of the flowers, since it is what they do through their perfume and taste that is important in the lesson they pose for life. In choosing to focus on the sense of smell, Herbert draws attention to the way that sense operates, gathering information about the least tangible of the sensory phenomena. But the senses quickly become figurative, as the syntagmatic order plays its important role in activating the other levels of signification, for the progression in stanza 2 of 'hand → heart → minde' suggests the order, senses → emotion → intellect, by which death is apprehended.

# Milton (1608–74)

SYNTAGMATIC DEVIATION IN *PARADISE LOST*

Donne and Herbert used fairly simple syntagmatic and lexical choices to build up a good deal of semantic intensity, and the same might be said of other poets such as Marvell or Vaughan. In such a literary context, the writing, in both verse and prose, which stands out as remarkably deviant is Milton's. Perhaps the greatest impact of intertextuality on lexis in seventeenth-century poetry is also seen in Milton. As Nicholas R. Jones has observed, 'It is a clear understanding of the English Reformation that texts depend upon contexts for their utmost efficacy' (1982, 163). For Milton's greatest poem, *Paradise Lost*, the obvious intertext is the Genesis version of the Fall, and he could assume that his readers would compare and contrast that version with his epic reworking of it. With an already known 'story', variation and innovation will occur principally at the level of the discourse. In virtually any passage taken from the poem, syntagmatic deviation stands out:

1                    Thus the Orb he roam'd
     With narrow search; and with inspection deep
     Consider'd every Creature, which of all
     Most opportune might serve his Wiles, and found     85
     The Serpent suttlest Beast of all the Field.
2    Him after long debate, irresolute
     Of thoughts revolv'd, his final sentence chose
     Fit Vessel, fittest Imp of fraud, in whom
     To enter, and his dark suggestions hide     90
     From sharpest sight: for in the wilie Snake,
     Whatever sleights none would suspicious mark,
     As from his wit and native suttletie
     Proceeding, which in other Beasts observ'd
     Doubt might beget of Diabolic pow'r     95
     Active within beyond the sense of brute.

                                        (Book IX)

Of the two sentences which make up this extract, the first is somewhat removed from prose word-order, the second more drastically. In the first sentence, there are four clauses related quite simply, the second and fourth being co-ordinate principal clauses and the third a relative clause embedded within the second, but word-order within the clauses is deviant: the first has object/subject/verb order; in the second, the placement of the 'with' phrase ahead of its verb is only a minor transposition, but the parallel with the previous 'with' phrase draws attention to the inversion (and then within the 'with' phrase normal noun/adjective order is reversed in 'inspection deep'); in such a syntagmatic context, the normal word-order of the third clause becomes virtually a foregrounding device (this return to 'normality' is underlined rhythmically as well, since line 86 is also a regular iambic pentameter), emphasizing how the clause returns the reader most strongly to the pre-text, in that it is almost identical with the opening of Genesis 3:1. By thus drawing attention to his pre-text, Milton controls the range of connotation, in a way that points forward to the practice of the Augustan poets, who attempt to control the impact of the paradigmatic axis much more closely by the periphrases and formulae which are used to try to link signifier and signified more tightly.

The second sentence is more difficult, because of its sheer complexity, its numerous inversions, and its heavy use of ellipsis. This is all most clearly seen if the sentence is broken into its clauses (square brackets indicate ellipsis):

| | | |
|---|---|---|
| 1a | Him after long debate | |
| 2 | irresolute of thoughts revolv'd | |
| 1b | his final sentence chose ‖ | Fit    Vessel |
| | | fittest Imp of fraud |
| 3 | in whom to enter | |
| 4 | and [in whom] his dark suggestions hide from sharpest sight | |
| 5 | for in the wilie Snake whatever sleights [there were] | |
| 6 | none would [as] suspicious mark | |
| 7 | [but] as from his ‖ | wit |
| | and ‖ | native suttletie proceeding |
| 8a | which | |
| 9 | in other Beasts observ'd | |
| 8b | doubt might beget of ‖ | Diabolic pow'r active within |
| | | beyond the sense of brute |

Of these nine clauses, only 3 and 8 conform within themselves to normal word-order, and even then the sense of 8 is rather elliptical. The others have one or more irregularities. In 1, 4, and 6 the object/complement precedes the verb; there is some element of ellipsis in 4, 5, 6 and 7; in 5, 7 and 9 an adjunct precedes the verb on which it depends. At the level of clause relationships, the referent of clause 2 is indeterminate (either the adjunct of the preceding clause or the subject of the following); the referent of 'which' in clause 8a is 'sleights', way back in 5; and the repeated recourse to ellipsis makes the relationship between clauses 5, 6 and 7 almost impossible to determine. These deviations add up to a very contorted English – in his verse, as also in his prose, Milton writes with a word-order and clause relationships often reminiscent of Latin, even though English lacks both the inflections of Latin and its conventions of word-order. Syntagmatic structure could hardly be further away from the easy colloquial language used by Donne, for example, in both his verse and his prose.

Milton also differs from Donne in semantic density: to 25 nouns he has 18 adjectives, which is a high proportion and makes for a fairly dense semantic texture. But the intensity is not as rich as in Donne: some of the adjectives are predictable, almost clichéd, as in 'long debate' or 'wily snake', and the amount of information that the adjectives carry is not particularly intense. But then the rhythm and the syntax have a forward drive across the line-ends, and to have too dense a crowding of information in noun/adjective combinations when there are such contortions in the syntax could overweight one of the two axes at the expense of the other. The actual lexical choices in the passage are not very difficult, and not especially Latinate. Items derived from romance languages, such as *inspection*, *opportune*, *sentence*, *suspicious*, and the like, had been around since Middle English; *irresolute* and *brute* ('one of the lower animals') are early seventeenth-century; the occurrences of *orb* ('the earth') and *suggestions* ('incitement to evil') are the last recorded in these senses in the *OED*; and *imp* seems to be in transition between the original denotation 'a graft' (last recorded in 1706) and the superseding denotation 'an evil spirit' (first recorded in 1584). On the whole, then, lexis is straightforward and denotative; there is a more gradual, more cumulative build-up of meaning than in the short lyrics of the Metaphysicals; rather, the connection for this less intense semantic weighting is back more to Spenser and his long narrative. If one aspect of language changes, then it seems that it is usually compensated for in another aspect; the relative weighting of the features against each other seems to shift, and so when Milton is using the blank verse that interacts so strongly with the syntagmatic axis (with so many run-on lines, and such a strong forward progression), the paradigmatic axis is more muted in the part it plays. Milton is dealing with epic scenes, and has to elevate and distance them from the ordinary and everyday; to do so, he evolves a discourse which is removed from that of the everyday. With a weighty semantic texture combined with a basically denotative emphasis, he foregrounds the interaction of rhythm and syntagm in his lines rather than depending on the heavy connotative penumbra carried by words and phrases in the Metaphysical short poems. It is a major change in the way that the diction and syntax of English poetry are used.

## MILTON'S PROSE

As we have said, there is not a great deal of difference between the way Milton writes his verse and the way he writes his prose; the line division is the main difference. In both, the syntagmatic axis is more heavily weighted than the paradigmatic axis. We will conclude this chapter here with a brief illustration of this aspect of his prose, using part of one sentence from his *Doctrine and Discipline of Divorce* (1644). For the sake of analysis, the first few lines of the extract, which give the context, are set out as normal prose, but, after the colon, the remainder is set out in numbered clauses (or clause-equivalents) to bring out the complexity of the structuring, which may be masked by the syntagmatic ordering of the text; the principal clause is capitalized, and doublets are linked together vertically:

Love, if he be not twin born, yet hath a brother wondrous like him, called Anteros; whom while he seeks all about, his chance is to meet with many false and feigning desires, that wander singly up and down in his likeness:

1a  by them in their borrowed garb,
2    LOVE,
3a   though not wholly blind,
4          as poets wrong him,
3b   yet   having but one eye,

| 5 | | as being born an archer aiming, |
| 6 | | and that eye not the quickest |
| | | in this dark region here below, |
| 7 | | which is not Love's proper sphere, |
| 1b | partly out of the ‖ | simplicity |
| | ‖ | and credulity |
| 8 | | which is native to him, |
| 1c | often deceived, | |
| 2b | ‖ EMBRACES | |
| | ‖ AND CONSORTS HIM WITH THESE ‖ | OBVIOUS |
| | | ‖ AND SUBORNED STRIPLINGS, |
| 9 | | as if they were his mother's own sons; |

The Latin influence on the syntax here is particularly strong, and in an actual Latin sentence it would not be difficult with Latin's inflectional endings to put together the three parts that comprise clause 1, which explains why and how Love is deceived by the desires: because he is naturally simple and credulous, and because they deceive him by their borrowed garb. But for those who are only familiar with Present English, the syntax is highly convoluted, and very difficult to follow, especially when the subject of the principal clause, 'Love', is separated from its predicate by such a distance. Yet Milton has built in a number of cohesive pointers which signpost and link important elements in the sentence: for instance, the two correlated parts of 3 are linked by the 'though/yet' pair which explains negatively and then positively why Love's eyesight is poor; and then in the repetition in 3b and 6 of 'one eye/that eye', where the deictic of the second clause points back to the first. The choice of the deictic pointer 'these' instead of 'those' in the adjunct of the principal clause (when it finally arrives in 2b) makes a link back to the 'false and feigning desires' of the first part of the segment, and then to 'them' and 'their' of 1a, before leading on to 'they' in 9. And the reflexive 'him' of 2b also alerts us to the subject, 'Love', especially in view of the verbs chosen.

The importance of the syntagmatic axis lies in the weighting and ordering of the segment. A long left-branching structure precedes the main verbs ('embraces and consorts' in clause 2b), but only a brief and lightly-weighted right-branch follows them. An immediate effect is that the placement of 1a follows on from the earlier reference to 'false and feigning' before the focus turns back to love and the heavily-weighted explanation of his poor sight; then with the relative order of 1b and 1c the explanation for his deception occurs before the actual term, 'deceived', immediately preceding the pair of principal clause verbs which relate his affectionate actions towards the deceivers, while almost simultaneously the paired modifiers in 2b stress how the deceivers are unlike Love. Had the more normal order and weighting of Present English been followed, this telling juxtaposition of the contrasts between the protagonists would not have been foregrounded so strongly.[8]

## Notes and further reading

1 Scholars recently have become divided as to the social, cultural, and political significance of this theory of isomorphic structure. On the one hand, it can be adduced as the basis for finding that a text offers 'enlightening and entertaining illustrations of the dangers of deviating from one's place within the universal order' (Schuman, 1978); on the other, it is seen as 'fundamental to conservative political theory' (Delany, 1974; see also Aers, 1987), supporting social arrangements which suited the ruling class (which was largely the same as the literate class).

2 It is possible that *that* in line 3 is pleonastic, though it would still seem ungrammatical. For some comparable examples, see the discussion in Roscow (1981, 78–80).

3 For a discussion of *habitualization* as a problem in conventional coding, see Roger Fowler, *Linguistic Criticism* (Oxford and New York: Oxford University Press, 1986), pp. 31ff.

4 Hoby, in his translation of *The Courtier* (1561), writes of 'gorgeous and fine words' (Castiglione, 1974, 57).

5 The auxiliary *do*, like *gan* in Middle English, functions as a metrical filler and a device to facilitate rhyme by representing lexical verbs by their infinitives rather than by an inflected form. It occurs five times in this poem of twenty lines, with the inevitable consequence of thinning semantic texture.

6 *rankle* ('to fester') is literal in its application of 'poyson' to bones, though the transferred sense prevalent in Present English has begun to appear in the early sixteenth century.

7 'Posy', or a near-synonym such as 'garland', had often been used in the titles of poetry collections over the preceding half-century; one of Gascoigne's volumes, for example, was simply named *Posies*.

8   Further reading: for overviews of the period, see especially Gilbert (1979), for an account based on the classical tradition of the three styles; Partridge (1971), for an informative discussion of literary language from 1575 to 1675; Sherbo (1975), on 'poetic diction'. More specific studies, with a strong linguistic orientation, are Burnley (1983), Barber (1976) and Blake (1977 and 1983). See also: Elam (1980) for drama; Crombie (1984) and Harland (1986) for Donne's sermons; and Barrell (1988) for some cultural implications of Milton's style not evidenced in our examples.

## Exercises

1   Examine the interaction of syntagm, paradigm, and the signifier/signified relationships in lines 3948–84 of Chaucer's *Nun's Priest's Tale* ('Shortly I saye ... wol I telle his aventure'), taking particular note of where register shift occurs, which lexical sets are predominant, and how transitions between them are managed. What are the implications for the presentation of the narratorial point of view?

2   Consider the story/discourse relationship of stanzas 1–24 of Spenser's *The Faerie Queene*, Book III, Canto IX, taking up especially the semantic density and the intensity of signification in each. What are the implicit socio-cultural attitudes towards the male/female relationship?

3   Compare and contrast Bacon's Essay 'Of Marriage and Single Life' with Spenser's *The Faerie Queene*, Book III, Introduction and Canto I, stanzas 1–13, examining the impact of the chosen form upon the syntagmatic and paradigmatic structuring of the argument. How are the signifiers weighted as compared with the signified concepts?

4   Compare and contrast Shakespeare's *Twelfth Night* I.v.40–77 ('God bless thee, lady! ... Take away the fool, gentlemen') and *King Lear* I.iv.105–66 ('Let me hire him too ... This is not altogether fool, my lord'). How does the interrelationship of cohesion, congruence and coherence

point to the comic context of the one, and the tragic context of the other?

5   Compare and contrast Shakespeare's Sonnet 138 and Donne's 'Woman's Constancy' to bring out the subversion of the speaker's point of view and the deconstruction of courtly love conventions.

6   Compare and contrast Donne's poem 'The Sunne Rising' with the following extract from his *Sermon preached at Pauls upon Christmas Day in the Evening, 1624*, examining especially how the rhetorical patterning of the syntagm in the prose compares with the line patterning in the verse, and how each interacts with the paradigmatic choices and signifier/signified relationships. How does the difference in genre affect the extent to which the ideological presuppositions are conveyed?

> We begin with that which is elder than our beginning, and shall over-live our end, The mercy of God. *I will sing of thy mercy and judgement,* sayes *David*; when we fixe our selves upon the meditation and modulation of the mercy of God, even his judgements cannot put us out of tune, but we shall sing, and be chearefull, even in them. As God made grasse for beasts, before he made beasts, and beasts for man, before he made man: As in that first generation, the Creation, so in the regeneration, our re-creating, he begins with that which was necessary for that which followes, Mercy before Judgement. Nay, to say that mercy was first, is but to post-date mercy; to preferre mercy but so, is to diminish mercy; The names of first or last derogate from it, for first and last are but ragges of time, and his mercy hath no relation to time, no limitation in time, it is not first, nor last, but eternall, everlasting;. . .

7   Compare and contrast Milton's *Paradise Lost*, Book VI, 99–126 with the following extract from his *Areopagitica*, taking up the extent to which the syntagm, the syntactic units, and the rhythm overweight the paradigm and signifier/signified members of the triad. Then compare and contrast the two Milton passages with the two Donne passages of the preceding exercise, to bring out some of the

changes in how signification functions between the two periods of the seventeenth century. To what extent are such changes reflecting ideological differences between the two writers?

First, when a City shall be as it were besieged and blocked about, her navigable river infested, inroads and incursions round, defiance and battle oft rumoured to be marching up even to her walls and suburb trenches, that then the people, or the greater part, more than at other times, wholly taken up with the study of highest and most important matters to be reformed, should be disputing, reasoning, reading, inventing, discoursing, even to a rarity and admiration, things not before discoursed or written of, argues first a singular goodwill, contentedness and confidence in your prudent foresight and safe government, Lords and Commons; and from thence derives itself to a gallant bravery and well-grounded contempt of their enemies, as if there were no small number of as great spirits among us, as his was, who when Rome was nigh besieged by Hannibal, being in the city, bought that piece of ground at no cheap rate, whereon Hannibal himself encamped his own regiment.

# 3 Revolutions in literary English

Man, like the gen'rous vine, supported lives;
The strength he gains is from th'embrace he gives.
On their own Axis as the Planets run,
Yet make at once their circle round the Sun:
So two consistent motions act the Soul;
And one regards Itself, and one the Whole.
Thus God and Nature link'd the gen'ral frame,
And bade Self-love and Social be the same.

(Pope, *Essay on Man*, III.311–18)

## The rise of 'polite' discourse

Prose writing after Milton did not look back to his Latin-based prose as a model. In the following century, the so-called 'Age of Prose' (Gordon, 1966, Ch. 13), various forms of speech-based prose exerted a strong influence on writing practices, and deliberate, formal styles looked elsewhere for their models. Our object in the first half of this chapter is to pinpoint some of the main features which characterize the prose of the later seventeenth and eighteenth centuries, in order to suggest, first, why it has been so highly regarded, and, second, what happened to bring about its decline: for towards the end of the eighteenth century there occurred a radical change which affected the use of language in both prose and verse, a change the effects of which are still having an impact to this day. We have chosen to examine the prose before the verse, because verse form can initially mask some of the crucial features involved. The second half of the chapter will take up the nature of the transition from 'Augustan' to 'Romantic' verse.

We will begin by outlining some major characteristics of other influential kinds of seventeenth-century prose, but before doing so we will briefly draw attention to some general features important for our focused period. As the epigraph to this chapter reflects, on to the older scheme of the great chain of being, and its notions of order, hierarchy and harmony, post-Restoration thought was grafting a utilitarian ethic whereby self-interest and public welfare might be seen to coincide. Laura Brown (1985) has argued that the philosophy of the *Essay on Man* 'hangs between a capitalist ethic and traditional Christian morality . . . . and it defines man and his role in society in terms of both aggressive self-interest and Christian selflessness' (91). In the lines we have quoted the two are intertwined, first by the analogies, especially that between people in society and the planets revolving on their own axes while circling the sun, and then in the final couplet by the cohesive deletions (the subject of 'bade' and the noun 'love' modified by 'Social'), which in effect re-encode the idea of linking to suggest that it is reflected in the very syntax of the language. The concern with the relationship between self-interest and public welfare is subject to very complex (Brown would suggest ambivalent) analyses in the prose and verse of Swift and in the verse of Pope, and is responsible for much of the satiric impulse associated with the period. Inevitably, it also has profound implications for literary style, in both verse and prose. Apart from its more obvious semantic impact, it influences the way writers handle the relationship between cohesion, congruence and coherence, and hence influences the kind of emphases which characterize syntagm/paradigm and signifier/signified relationships. In particular, the changing attitude towards the dominant power of the syntagm, from one of exploiting its potential to one of growing revolt against it, has an important interconnection with the changing relationship between the actual reader and the narratee in the author/text/reader interaction. In general terms, then, as the seventeenth century moves towards the eighteenth, the changing attitude towards the reader in both discursive and fictive prose is one reflection of the gradual move away from a world view which perceives the relationship of people to the universe as being that of microcosm to macrocosm, towards one in which the primary relationship is that between people and society. (We have on principle used 'people' in this chapter, as a reminder that the 'Man' of Pope's title is rarely generic enough in his own terms of reference to include women, whose main function in his writings is as one satiric focus for his period's obsession with property.)

Milton's extreme Latinate syntax contorted the syntagm in

such a way as to issue a challenge to the reader's intellect, making no concessions that might render the structure of the argument easier to follow. Implicit in his style is an attitude towards readers and reading which suggests respect; the reader is addressed as if equal to the writer in learning, logic, and interpreting ability. This attitude contrasts with that implicit in the way Bacon or Donne, for example, carefully guides the reader/audience through the text, using repetition and patterning both to provide signposts and to construct an argument which persuades through rhetoric as much as or more than through logic. But this difference is only a matter of degree. None of the writers has attempted overtly to create a persona or 'voice' separable from himself, and hence a narratee separable from the reader (the two go hand-in-hand – once the speaker tends to become fictive his audience will tend to become fictive as well, though the developments need not be in any strict ratio or proportion, and when further embeddings of fictional narratives and relationships occur, the one-to-one relationship may well be disrupted).

## Some other seventeenth-century prose styles: Walton and Browne

In the less extreme Latinate style, as employed by Izaak Walton or Thomas Browne, for example, there is a slight shift in writer–reader relationships and the ways they are mediated, when both cohesive links along the syntagm and congruence within paradigmatic choices are relied on less heavily.

### WALTON (1593–1683)

Both Milton's prose and his verse suggest a Latinate style, but, since his lexical choices are not heavily Latinate, what creates the impression of Latinity is the syntax, with its inversions, its contortions, its splitting up of the clauses in the way that Latin does. Walton's prose includes some Latin-derived vocabulary, but his primary effects are also syntagmatic, though in a way very different from Milton's:

> From which place, before I shall invite the Reader to follow him into a Foreign Nation, though I must omit to mention divers Persons that were then in *Oxford*, of memorable note

for Learning, and Friends to Sir *Henry Wotton*; yet I must not omit the mention of a love that was there begun betwixt him and Dr. *Donne* (sometimes Dean of St. *Pauls*) a man of whose abilities I shall forbear to say any thing, because he who is of this *Nation*, and pretends to Learning or Ingenuity, and is ignorant of Dr. *Donne*, deserves not to know him.

(Walton, *The Life of Sir Henry Wotton*)

If this is compared back with the Bacon (*see* pp. 46–8), with which it has much in common, the chief differences centre on the less overt patterning of the Walton, and the more obviously evoked narratee. There is an overall balance in the sentence between left-branching and right-branching structure, as the sentence pivots at mid-point on its principal clause ('yet I must not omit . . .'), but there is also an element of looseness in the accretion of co-ordinate phrases and parenthetic explanations. Obvious elements of balance are played down by internal paradigmatic variation: the substantive 'the mention of' replacing the verbal 'to mention'; the English/verbal 'not to know' balancing the Latin/substantive 'is ignorant of', thus suppressing the obvious kind of doubletting which elsewhere in this example only appears in 'Learning or Ingenuity'. By such strategies, the careful structuring is masked, and the apparent increase in informality facilitates the involvement of the narratee in this emotive reminiscence. Walton uses the first person pronoun a number of times, and directly invites 'the Reader' to participate in the biography, and then implicitly to join with him, by way of his rhetorical *occupatio*, in scorn of the ignorant. But the 'I' that Walton advances is an aspect of himself in his self-conscious social function as biographer of another, and to that extent one aspect only of the whole man and hence, in effect, a narrator. The hypothesized 'Reader' is implicitly a member of the same social class as the narrator, a narratee, not the real individual reader, and so a gap is set up between the narratee within the biography and the real reader, whether in the seventeenth or twentieth century, who, while addressed, is only conventionally present in the discourse.

BROWNE (1605–82)

The situation in Browne's writing is rather different. His lexical choices are more heavily Latin-derived than Walton's, and there is more repetition of concepts at phrase-level, but he still achieves an intimate narrator–narratee communication:

> And therefore restlesse inquietude for the diuturnity of our memories unto present considerations, seems a vanity almost out of date, and superannuated peece of folly. We cannot hope to live so long in our names, as some have done in their persons, one face of *Janus* holds no proportion unto the other. 'Tis too late to be ambitious. The great mutations of the world are acted, or time may be too short for our designes. To extend our memories by Monuments, whose death we daily pray for, and whose duration we cannot hope, without injury to our expectations, in the advent of the last day, were a contradiction to our beliefs.
>
> (*Urne Buriall*)

Because the narrator has not adopted a stance superior to his narratee, the continual use of the first person plural pronoun implicitly conflates narrator and narratee in their shared experience of and attitudes towards inexorable temporality. The narrator's own quiescence is expressed by the consistent negation of the extended, pejorative lexical set referring to human hopes for the future – 'inquietude, cannot hope, ambitious, designes' – as opposed to the positive values of 'expectations' and 'beliefs' which are assumed to be shared by the narratee. An outstanding aspect of this style is the way Browne juxtaposes elevated and familiar terms (usually, though not always, in the form of Latinate as against native terms). This may be within a phrase, as in 'restlesse inquietude', or between balanced phrases, as when 'a vanity almost out of date' (elevated noun followed by a more commonplace qualifying phrase) is transformed into '[a] superannuated piece of folly' (with now the Latinate adjective followed by the colloquial noun-phrase). The sort of thing that differentiates Browne from Bacon (and from Johnson's Latinate prose of a century later) is the lack of continuous balancing and parallelism in the syntax, the wide variation in sentence length, and the embedding of co-ordinate clauses in a fashion similar to Walton. For instance, the very short sentence, ''Tis too late to be ambitious', succeeds two longer ones, and is followed by another short, though internally balanced, sentence before a longer, left-branching sentence which embeds a series of qualifications between its opening non-finite clause and the principal clause. Within this structure, the elements of repetition have an important function, for, while paradigmatic slots filled by elevated terms might have been filled by simpler terms, the mixing and multiplication of strange and familiar signifiers finally throw emphasis upon the signifieds lying behind them, and balance the appeal to the reader's intellect and emotions.

## An extended example: the Latin-based styles of Samuel Johnson and Ann Radcliffe

JOHNSON'S *RASSELAS* (1759)

It is instructive at this point to break strict diachronic progression and to leap forward some hundred years to a later great exponent of Latinate prose, Dr Samuel Johnson. His strongly cohesive and controlled style is most apparent in his argumentative discourse, but it also pervades his fiction. By his time, the novel, which is *par excellence* a mode of writing which presents people in relationship to society, is becoming established as a prose form with a variety of strategies of presentation, and so we will turn to *Rasselas* for an example of his argumentative prose. The following extract illustrates how aptly Johnson's style expresses his ideal of behaviour, which favours the long view over the fleeting moment and the intellectual over the physical (see Hansen, 1985):

[1]'I cannot forbear to flatter myself that prudence and benevolence will make marriage happy. [2] The general folly of mankind is the cause of general complaint. [3] What can be expected but disappointment and repentance from a choice made in the immaturity of youth, in the ardour of desire, without judgment, without foresight, without enquiry after conformity of opinions, similarity of manners, rectitude of judgment, or purity of sentiment.

[4] 'Such is the common process of marriage. [5] A youth and maiden meeting by chance, or brought together by artifice, exchange glances, reciprocate civilities, go home, and dream of one another. [6] Having little to divert attention, or diversify thought, they find themselves uneasy when they are apart, and therefore conclude that they shall be happy together. . . .'

(Ch. 29)

The syntagmatic structure of this writing has more in common with Walton and Browne than with Milton. Johnson does elsewhere employ sentences which branch leftwards more substantially than either of the last two sentences in this extract, but he generally uses right-branching sentences. What is more significant is the extent to which he balances and parallels words, phrases and clauses. There are a lot of doublets, but they are always extensive, as in 'prudence and benevolence' or 'disappointment and repentance', so that signifieds as well as signifiers are accumulated within paradigmatic slots. The repetition of 'general' in [2] underlines the balancing of cause and effect in the relationship of 'folly' and 'complaint'. Phrases are carefully and cumulatively balanced along an intricately linked chain in [3], as the '[made] in the' pair expands into the 'without' trio, which in turn enfolds the four 'x of y' phrases depending on 'inquiry after'. Finally, balance is skilfully effected on a larger syntagmatic level in the co-ordinated principal clauses of [6], where inter-reflecting paradigmatic choices ('find themselves:conclude', 'uneasy:happy', 'apart:together') assert connections which override the differences in the syntactic structure of subordination within the co-ordinated clauses. It is an *exquisite example* of the intersection of syntagm and paradigm. We have pointed to balance and parallelism in earlier writers, but the individuality here lies in the nature and *proportion* of the balancing, and in the subtle interaction of syntagm and paradigm.

Johnson's lexical choices are also in themselves important, with regard to the type of signifiers chosen – whether abstract or concrete, whether denotative or connotative. Johnson judiciously mixes Latinate and native terms. Bacon and Donne also use many native terms, especially Donne, whose non-native terms tend to stand out because of their unusualness; the difference is evident in the choices Johnson has made in filling the paradigmatic slots. In a language like English which has so many near-synonyms and so much flexibility in sentence construction, choice for a particular paradigmatic slot often lies between a more native and a more Latinate term for roughly the same signified, and between a more or a less elevated grammatical construction. This type of choice is to be seen operating in [5] in the contrasting clauses 'exchange glances, reciprocate civilities, go home, and dream of one another': with the elevated language (instead of, say, *'look at and speak to each other') peaking in the second clause, and the rest of the sentence entirely native English, the speaker's ironical (not to say comically undercutting) view of the gap between social behaviour and inner emotion is very economically presented. The other area of paradigmatic choice is the range of grammatical options. A writer often has the choice of framing an idea adjectivally (either contiguous or predicative), verbally, or substantively. For example, at the end of [3], instead of *'proper judgment, or pure sentiment' Johnson has opted for the more abstract nouns, 'rectitude' and 'purity', which suggest that distancing which is part of the effect of Latinate language.

That the passage purports to be the speech of Rasselas is another pointer to the distance Johnson has travelled from, say, Shakespeare, for there is very little that is speech-like in the sentences, and, even if we compare them with Romeo's rhetorical description of love, Rasselas' intellectually argued and humorously satiric generalization about what makes marriage work within a social framework is far less emotive than Romeo's oxymorons.

In sum, Johnson's Latinism, in contrast to Milton's, lies predominantly in lexis, in his greater use of Latinate terms where native terms are available, and in smaller-scale grammatical choices which either foreground or stem from his lexical choices. So while both Milton and Johnson can be described as Latinate writers, they differ totally in the ways they relate the syntagmatic/paradigmatic axes. Johnson's syntax is foregrounded by its balance and parallelism, but the whole impression of formality, elevation and distance (especially when his speaker is discussing such a potentially emotive topic as the causes of marriage) is very differently achieved from Milton's attempted naturalization of Latin syntax in English. As contrasted with Milton, Johnson signposts his strongly cohesive structure within and between sentences much more clearly: his sentences are predominantly right-branching, and he is not inclined to embed clauses one within another; repetition of subordinators and recurrence of semantically related terms clearly mark relationships within sentences; and the basic cohesion of the discourse is very strong when there are so many logical markers to guide the reader's intellect through it.

RADCLIFFE'S *THE MYSTERIES OF UDOLPHO* (1794)

We here move forward a further fifty years to a different type of fiction writing, and to a very different type of effect produced by the interaction of syntagm and paradigm, in which is foreshadowed the radical change in the literary use of language brought about within 'romantic-style' writing. Ann Radcliffe's Gothic novel marks a transition between Latin-based and so-called 'Romantic' prose (Gordon, 1966, 157–9):

[1] They had to cross two courts towards the east wing of the castle, which, adjoining the chapel, was, like it, in ruins: but the silence and gloom of these courts had now little power over Emily's mind, occupied as it was with more mournful ideas; and she scarcely heard the low and dismal hooting of the night-birds, that roosted among the ivyed battlements of the ruin, or perceived the still flittings of the bat, which frequently crossed her way. [2] But when, having entered the chapel and passed between the mouldering pillars of the aisles, the bearers stopped at a flight of steps, that led down to a low arched door, and, their comrade having descended to unlock it, she saw imperfectly the gloomy abyss beyond; – saw the corpse of her aunt carried down these steps, and the ruffian-like figure, that stood with a torch at the bottom to receive it – all her fortitude was lost in emotions of inexpressible grief and terror.

(cit. in Wright, 1956, 157)

There are syntagmatic features in these two sentences which, in their length, turgidity and convolutions, are reminiscent of the Latinate syntax of Milton. For example, a subordinate clause may be represented by an absolute participial construction (that is, a non-finite clause which, though it can stand alone, has only a participle instead of a finite verb). This construction – very common in Latin, but rather less so in English – appears here in 'their comrade having descended to unlock it'; it seems to be used to attempt to suggest contemporaneity in defiance of the constraints of a linear syntagmatic line. The use of participial clauses in place of clearly defined subordinate clauses with their own individual markers blurs the relationships between the information being given by the various syntactic units, and so loosens the tightness of that type of linkage which subordinators build in by specifying the type of relationship between the clauses which they introduce. Subordinate clauses as opposed to participial ones also function to bring out the hierarchy of importance in the information incorporated within the syntagm; if that information is placed in a subordinate clause rather than a principal clause, it is marked as being less important, though it will also indicate the type of relationship it has to the principal clause by way of its subordinator, as in the Johnson passage. Thus Radcliffe attempts to suggest that the information in the participial clause is not lower in the hierarchy than that in the surrounding clauses.

Another quasi-Latinate element in Radcliffe's prose is the attempt at a complex, left-branching structure in Sentence [2]: the main sentence frame is temporal clause plus principal clause ('But when . . . the bearers stopped . . . and . . . she saw . . ., all her fortitude was lost'), but the overtly marked break at 'saw' functions to transform this parenthetic extension of the subordinate clause's verb into what is virtually an emotive exclamation, foregrounding point of view both visually and attitudinally.

Yet in spite of its absolute participial clause and its left-branching sentence, the passage could not be considered comparable to Milton as an example of Latinate style – indeed, the syntagm may seem to be less important than, and overweighted by, the paradigmatic choices. It is, nevertheless, important to see how the syntagm functions and the way that it differs from the earlier passages, especially when it is so central to the build-up of the atmospheric and strongly emotive impact.

What is particularly significant about the syntagm is the loosening of coherence within the sentences. This is evident in the participial clauses embedded almost immediately at the opening of [2] – at first 'having entered . . . and passed' seems to be, and indeed is, attached to 'the bearers', but there are so many other loosely embedded units that a reader will probably attempt to attach this pair to 'she' once it becomes clear that 'she' is the principal subject of the sentence. Perhaps, in the end, it doesn't matter, because any clear syntagmatic line is being dissolved in order that the text might function on an emotive level, presenting emotional responses and factual information more or less simultaneously in an attempt to overcome the inherent constraints of the linear syntagmatic line. What is beginning to emerge here in this passage is the sort of syntax that is losing its tight coherence, and leads on to the open-endedness and lack of coherence (and especially of cohesion) which is characteristic of some late nineteenth-century and some twentieth-century writing.

In its syntagmatic structure, then, this extract differs markedly from the *Rasselas* passage, and its treatment of the paradigmatic axis is just as different. The type of paradigmatic choices and their repetitive focus tends to overweight the Latinate-type syntax, rendering it less noticeable than in Johnson and Milton. On the one hand there is a major lexical set presenting such conventional Gothic paraphernalia as corpses, graves, hooting birds and bats, and the ruins of castles, battlements and chapels. These involve concrete nouns, and in the way they build up atmosphere they complement the second main lexical set, that consisting of abstract terms of emotion, with 'emotions' overtly referred to at the end. This second set includes the repeated 'gloom[y]', with 'mournful' and 'dismal', and in case the emotion signified goes unrecognized it is spelled out in 'grief and terror'. So while 'emotions' itself may be vague, the lexical set of terms that specify the emotion signified is somewhat restricted. Further, this sort of Gothic style makes extensive use of connotative modifiers, which both activate a penumbra of associations and carry a fairly heavy semantic load, as in the 'mouldering pillars' in the chapel, where there is a sensory as well as emotive element functioning to create the impact on the reader. Such language betrays a clear attempt to manipulate the emotions of the reader, and helps to account for uncooperative reader responses to such texts: if the reader focuses on the signifiers rather than on the signifieds, the over-foregrounded reaction of the narrator and of Emily easily becomes comic. This is particularly the case when the emotions are said to be 'inexpressible'; so much is said to be striking the character subliminally ('she scarcely heard . . . or perceived'; 'she saw imperfectly'), and yet the narrator insists on being explicit with the narratee, going out of her way to express the 'inexpressible'.

The role of the narratee within this passage is thus very important, and represents another major difference from the extracts discussed above, especially when the conflict between reason and sensibility in a Radcliffe novel reflects the beginning of a major socio-cultural shift towards an emphasis upon the relationship between the individual Self and Nature. The whole scene is presented through a third person narrator, though one who very clearly presents Emily's point of view and gives *her* emotive reactions, as in 'ruffian-like figure'. But the Gothic paraphernalia of 'the low and dismal hootings of the night-birds' and the somewhat contradictory 'still flittings of the bat' point to things of which, it is said, Emily is scarcely aware; Radcliffe's narrator is really concerned to use these to influence the narratee by creating atmosphere. The choice of deictics, as in '*these* courts', implies that narrator and narratee are present to experience with their senses this horrifying spectacle where Nature is important in its own right, but is also reflective of the emotions of the protagonist (as in 'dismal') and the narrator. As readers, we can either share the narratee's experience and empathize, or else conclude that the narratee is being too obviously manipulated by the narrator, and dissociate ourselves from the narratee, finding the attempt to evoke a response comically overdone. We could also argue, of course, that it is bad writing.

The comparison between Johnson and Radcliffe shows how the use of certain elements of the Latinate style (whether syntagmatic, paradigmatic, or both) can function very differently, and how their interaction with other kinds and uses of language can be weighted in different directions because of other aspects of the text, especially the shift in cultural and linguistic presuppositions which was taking place in the later part of the eighteenth century.

## Dryden (1631–1700)

Prose between Milton and Johnson was predominantly speech-based. We will now return to examine developments within this prose, beginning with Dryden, who evidences a substantial departure from any kind of Latinate style in the period after Milton. His writings also illustrate why high praise has been accorded the prose of the period:

[1] For this last half year I have been troubled with the disease (as I may call it) of translation; the cold prose fits of it (which are always the most tedious with me), were spent in the *History of the League*; the hot (which succeeded them), in this volume of verse miscellanies. [2] The truth is, I fancied to myself a kind of ease in the change of the paroxysm; never suspecting but that the humour would have wasted itself in two or three pastorals of Theocritus, and as many odes of Horace. [3] But finding, or at least thinking I found,

something that was more pleasing in them than my ordinary productions, I encouraged myself to renew my old acquaintance with Lucretius and Virgil; and immediately fixed upon some parts of them which had most affected me in the reading. [4] These were my natural impulses for the undertaking.

*(Preface to Sylvae, 1685)*

This creates the impression of almost unselfconscious talk, having more similarity with the colloquial, undisciplined style of Hakluyt than with any other piece of prose we have so far considered. There are no doublets; the only Latin-derived terms are thoroughly acclimatized ones, and the lexicon is generally native; and the speech-like idioms and syntax create a strong effect of colloquialism. Short sentences are interspersed with longer ones, as with [4], and in place of the long, hypotactic sentences of the earlier period, Dryden's compound sentences consist of short clause units linked together, in the main, by co-ordination and parataxis. There is some clause-embedding, but, as it usually consists of ironical self-commentary, it enhances the effect of colloquialism and spontaneity. This is especially so with qualifications such as 'But finding, or at least thinking I found', which give the impression that the speaker has not entirely thought out in advance what he is going to say. Linkage within sentences is often effected by semantic relations, as when, for example, the three principal clauses of [1] are linked by the meronymy of 'disease', 'cold . . . fits', 'hot [fits]'. Such lexical congruence also functions as a cohesive device between sentences – the 'disease' of [1] is carried on to the 'paroxysm' and 'humour' of [2]. The ellipsis of 'fits' and of 'were spent' from the third clause of [1] is a cohesive device typical of speech, which further enhances the impression of colloquialism and renders the balance between the second and third clauses less obviously artful. Another colloquial aspect of cohesion is the ellipsis of subordinators that are not needed, as in 'The truth is, [that] I fancied'. This is the sort of conjunction commonly left out in speech when there is no problem about following the progress of the thought; and it helps Dryden to give the impression that the discourse is that of well-bred speech in a social setting, where intellectual play is pre-eminent. The clauses of the left-branching sentence [3], however, are held together by explicit grammatical subordinators ('But, or, and, which'), as seems more necessary to the more complex sentence structure. So the cohesive links that we suggested were starting to break down in Radcliffe's prose are still very much in evidence here.

Another new element within this discourse lies in the treatment of the narrator, as compared with, say, Walton. Dryden is much more consciously playing a role than is Walton; there is a more perceptible gap between the writer and the speaker, and the writer is gently laughing at the speaker's cultural role-playing; this comes through in the way that the first parenthesis draws attention to the self-reflexive function of the disease metaphor for translation, and the next pair of parentheses continues to foreground the metaphor, 'the cold prose fits', 'the hot', while maintaining the self-reflexivity. There follows the play between the emphatic opening, 'The truth is', and the following uncertainty in 'I fancied to myself', with the 'ease/paroxysm' contrast carrying on the play with the signifiers for disease. The speaker is in fact advancing an explanation and defence of his work, and it needs considerable tact to talk about one's work without either aggrandizing or deprecating one's achievements. One means by which Dryden's speaker steers the middle course is by focusing attention on the signifiers as much as or more than on the signifieds, so that the play on something like the disease metaphor is *shown* to be play; another is the interpolation of modifiers within the continuous verb form, as in 'was more pleasing' and 'had most affected me'. These modifications not only make the prose more like speech, but they also function to qualify the speaker's claims which might otherwise seem presumptuous. The repeated use of 'I' presupposes a 'you' throughout, to whom the 'I' is speaking, and the narratee here is being treated as an intimate, especially in view of Dryden's gentle poking of fun at his speaker. The friendly relationship of narrator and narratee here helps to make that outer relationship between writer and reader equally relaxed and close, as they play intellectually with signifiers (a key concept in a passage about translation and the signification of meaning in different languages).

## Richardson's *Pamela* (1740)

The more loosely connected syntagm of speech-based language, as contrasted with the various types of Latinate style, can be multi-functional in eighteenth-century prose, especially fiction. In this respect, the first-person narration of the letter-novel is an interesting successor to the kind of discourse seen in the Dryden passage, as the following extract from Richardson's *Pamela* shows:

> The wretch (I think I will always call her the *wretch* henceforth) abuses me more and more. I was but talking to one of the maids just now, indeed a little to tamper with her by degrees, and she popt upon us, and said, 'Nay, Madam, don't offer to tempt poor innocent country maids from doing their duty. You wanted her to take a walk with you. But I charge you, Nan, never stir with her, nor obey her, without letting me know it, in the smallest trifles. – I say walk with you! and where would you go, I tro'?' – 'Why, barbarous Mrs Jewkes,' said I, 'only to look a little up the elm-walk, since you would not let me go to church.' . . . .
>
> Now I will give you a picture of this wretch. She is a broad, squat, pursy, *fat thing*, quite ugly, if any thing human can be so called; about forty years old. She has a huge hand, and an arm as thick as my waist, I believe. Her nose is flat and crooked, and her brows grow down over her eyes; a dead, spiteful, grey, goggling eye, to be sure she has; and her face flat and broad: and as to colour, looks as if it had been pickled a month in saltpetre: I dare say she drinks. . . .
>
> (1962 edn, 97)

The speech-based style is evident here in the short clauses strung together by parataxis or co-ordination, and in the parentheses, omission of linking words, contractions such as 'don't', plain lexicon, and colloquialisms such as 'popt upon us'. In the first paragraph the narrator's discourse does not differ in these respects from the represented direct speech. In the second paragraph, however, the relationship between the pieces of information that Pamela gives is left fairly open. This is in keeping with the speech-based prose of the letter, since links in speech are often implied rather than spelt out, but it also evidences within smaller syntagmatic movements the hypersyntagmatic tendency for *Pamela*'s discourse to appear to the reader as 'episodes that do not contribute to a clear objective' (McKee, 1985, 624). Such discontinuity functions at both levels to focus attention on point of view and attitudes conveyed. In this particular example, the reader is made aware of the manipulation of Pamela's point of view – and that of her narratee/audience – by the process of description itself, since it is intertextual in the way that it inverts the mode of describing a beautiful woman.

The description begins with a cumulative series of apparently factual (though negatively loaded) adjectives before 'thing', which is followed by the generalized evaluative summary, 'quite ugly', and then the odd, parenthetic qualification, 'if any thing human can be so called'. The intertextual effect of the qualification is to evoke the convention of describing the lady's supra-human beauty as 'divine'; intratextually, it acts as both a logical and syntactic break within the syntagm, and its function seems to float. On the one hand, it suggests that the whole preceding description is of someone barely human; on the other, it is a reminder of Pamela's prissy sanctimoniousness. In other words, the narrative strategy points to the gap between the protagonist Pamela within the 'story', the narrator Pamela who is making the judgement within the discourse, and the writer who encodes the whole.[1] Since there is no logical link between 'quite ugly' and the following clause, the break suggests Pamela's lack of logic in her revulsion against Mrs Jewkes, and functions to build up her attitude and characterization. Then the truncated clause 'about forty years old' is chained on paratactically, suggesting that there is still a link between this final remark in the sentence and what precedes it, while leaving that link totally indeterminate. The carry-over of 'thing' from the principal clause to the parenthesis impedes the linking of the final clause back to its proper antecedent ('fat thing'), and so floats the meaning. Thus it might suggest that being over 40 is inconsistent with being human, or merely that Pamela is stringing together random thoughts as they occur to her. Again, the logic breaks down, but her display of emotion is reinforced by that breakdown; where the narratee within the discourse (here the implied recipient of the letter) is being invited to respond to the emotion, and empathize with Pamela's predicament in being imprisoned by such a wretch, the real reader may well judge Pamela's illogical emotion as exaggerated and over-done, and conclude that it reveals as much or more about her as narrator (and possibly about the social status of maids of the period) than about Mrs Jewkes herself. This romantic-style prose appears well before the Romantic period, and its effect, in keeping with the major stress of the Augustan period, is to reflect the society of the time, and to appeal rather to the reader's intellect and judgement than to his/her emotions.

From that general response to Mrs Jewkes, Pamela makes mention of her hand and arm, with the somewhat irrelevant 'I believe' at the end of the comparison of her arm and Pamela's own waist; it is unnecessary, and perhaps suggests hesitancy about the validity of the comparison, but also inverts a conventional hyperbole whereby waists are as slender as arms. The odd order in which Mrs Jewkes' facial features are described – nose, eyebrows, eye, facial proportions, and lastly colour – helps to foreground the distance between her appearance and conventional beauty. The treatment of the eye is particularly interesting. First there is the problem of why it is singular instead of plural as in the preceding clause. The probable answer is, again, the intertextual one – a coquette conventionally allures with her eyes, but in the period the singular is customary, as in the opening of Pope's 'Epistle to Miss Blount':

As some fond virgin, whom her mother's care
Drags from the town to wholesome country air,
Just when she learns to roll a melting eye,
And hear a spark . . . .

The four adjectives with which Pamela leads up to 'eye' are primarily connotative in effect, presenting emotive response more than factual data. The order is important, since the metaphorical 'dead' and judgemental 'spiteful' prevent 'grey' from being merely denotative. But if 'dead' suggests that the eye lacks vivacity, how at the same time can it show spitefulness? The choice of signifier at this stage reveals Pamela's attribution of that emotion to Mrs Jewkes, rather than proving that Mrs Jewkes is actually spiteful. And when the reader gets past the list of modifiers, it transpires that the syntax has been inverted into a left-branching clause, with 'she has' at the very end, and the object of 'she has' at the start of the clause; but the 'to be sure' before 'she has' is again breaking up the logic, and the over-emphasis (especially in view of the singular noun) is self-defeating, as far as Pamela is concerned. A description such as this makes very clear why the discourse given to a first person narrator so often functions to alert the reader that the narrator is unreliable and flawed. Everything is mediated through that narrator, and when syntax and diction combine to suggest that the point of view advanced by the narrator is strongly influenced by her emotions, the reader needs to judge the narrator as well as the character she describes. Thus the syntactic and logical gaps and the emotive language which we pointed to in the Romantic-style prose of Radcliffe, with its emphasis on the relation of Self to Nature, can also function in Augustan prose fiction to activate intellectual and judgemental involvement in the relation of people to society.

# Swift (1667–1745)

What begins to emerge from an examination of various prose styles, and from such aspects of them as the type of speaker/(in)direct addressee and/or narrator/narratee relationship(s), is an outline of various modes of discourse within which, and out of which, the discourse of fiction-writing develops. Another important mid-eighteenth-century phenomenon was the extension of fictive narrators to pamphlet writing, where they are used for ironical purposes. Jonathan Swift, in particular, not only exploits narrator unreliability with great skill but in doing so employs a whole range of narrator types familiar in fiction. This then leads on to a range of narratee types: the narrator of *A Modest Proposal*, for example, is essentially situated outside the level of 'story', as contrasted with Pamela, but his warped values readily distinguish him from Swift; a narratee/reader distinction exists at similar levels, as the narrator is taking for granted that his values are shared by the narratee, while the reader reacts emotionally against them. In *Directions to Servants in General* the narrator is situated within the 'story', taking part in it to the same degree as Richardson's Pamela partakes in her story. Finally, in the more obviously fictive *Gulliver's Travels*, Gulliver is both a narrator within the story, whose narratee is a member of eighteenth-century English society, and at times a speaker at one further level of embedding (that is, a protagonist whose speech to his direct/indirect addressee(s) is narrated by a narrator already situated within the story).

# Further precursors of Romantic-style prose

We have begun here to point to some of the differences in the treatment of the syntagmatic/paradigmatic axes between the Augustan and Romantic periods, and, before we show how they work in poetry as well as prose, we will make one last brief comparison between two prose writers of the late eighteenth century to show how devices which might be thought of as generally characterizing Romantic-style prose (in contradistinction to Latinate-style writing) can again function very differently.

Sterne's *Tristram Shandy* (1759–67) attracted the attention of Russian Formalists, such as Schlovsky, because it seemed to be a prime example of his concept of 'defamiliarization'. It certainly goes against virtually every convention expected in novels written before it, as Sterne apparently sets out to deconstruct the new genre of prose fiction. The following extract opens the first chapter of Book Three:

> — 'I wish, Dr. Slop,' quoth my uncle Toby, (repeating
> his wish for Dr. Slop a second time, and with a degree
> of more zeal and earnestness in his manner of wishing,
> than he had wished at first) — 'I wish, Dr. Slop,' quoth
> my uncle Toby, 'you had seen what prodigious armies    5
> we had in Flanders.'
> My uncle Toby's wish did Dr. Slop a disservice which
> his heart never intended any man, – Sir, it confounded
> him – and thereby putting his ideas first into confusion,
> and then to flight, he could not rally them again for the
> soul of him.                                           10
> In all disputes, – male or female, – whether for
> honour, for profit, or for love, – it makes no difference
> in the case; – nothing is more dangerous, Madam, than
> a wish coming sideways in this unexpected manner
> upon a man: the safest way in general to take off the   15
> force of the wish, is for the party wished at, instantly to
> get upon his legs – and wish the wisher something in
> return, of pretty near the same value, – so balancing the
> account upon the spot, you stand as you were – nay
> sometimes gain the advantage of the attack by it.       20
> This will be fully illustrated to the world in my chapter
> of wishes. –

The lack of hierarchical subordination in the passage is a key strategy, and by giving the very diverse bits of information virtually equal status, and by using the visual device of the dash as a major marker of both linkage and disruption, Sterne has set out to defy the constraints of the syntagm, in a way which differs very markedly from the practice of Radcliffe, though it has some affinities with the lateral associative thinking demonstrated by *Pamela*. Participial clauses, as in lines 1, 8 and 18, are associated with either principal clauses or mere isolated segments like those in 12–14, as the syntagm chains together unrelated fragments which challenge the reader to try to find some relationship at another level of the discourse. The choice of speech-like native terms, as in 'to get upon his legs', or 'of pretty near the same value', contrasts with more elevated terms like the intensive doublet 'zeal and earnestness', and 'confounded, confusion', in the first few lines; but the real breakdown of congruence comes at the semantic level, where the anaphoric use of 'wish' becomes the key strategy within the passage; 'wish', beginning as the cliché-type verb of the opening phrase, becomes a noun, then the verbal noun 'wishing', and in one form or another occurs no less than nine more times in the remainder of the passage. From being an abstract concept, the signifier 'wish' has its signified concept altered to something much more concrete, especially when it is associated with a lexical set of terms to do with military attack, and with phrases such as 'coming sideways' and 'the force of the wish'. When this last is followed by 'the party wished at', the perversion of normal idiom shifts the signified almost to the extent of becoming the reverse of its usual denotation.

Associated with the looseness of the syntagm and the floating of paradigmatic choices is the changing sex of Tristram's narratee, addressed as 'Sir' in line 8, and as 'Madam' in line 13. The self-reflexive nature of the discourse, signalled very obviously in the last paragraph, differs from that in Dryden, because of the lack of logical coherence at the hypersyntagmatic level, and the foregrounded narrator/narratee relationship differs from that in Richardson, because of the conscious playing with the discourse at the expense of the story. The devices that are used by romantic-style writers to break down the tyranny of the syntagm, by disrupting cohesion and congruence, and appeal to the reader's senses and emotions, are here used to activate the reader's intellect and sense of humour, to invite his/her participation in the game of laughing at him/herself for trying to find coherence in such comparative illogic.

A use of much the same devices with a contrasting effect occurs less than twenty years later, in Burke's speech in 1775, 'On Conciliation with the Colonies', from which this extract is taken:

> [1] The last cause of this disobedient spirit in the colonies is hardly less powerful than the rest, as it is not merely moral, but laid deep in the natural constitution of things. [2] Three thousand miles of ocean lie between you and them. [3] No contrivance can prevent the effect of this distance in weakening government. [4] Seas roll, and months pass, between the order and the execution; and the want of a speedy explanation of a single point is enough to defeat a whole system. [5] You have, indeed, winged ministers of vengeance, who carry your bolts in their pounces to the remotest verge of the sea. [6] But there a power steps in, that limits the arrogance of raging passions and furious elements, and says, 'So far shalt thou go, and no farther.' [7] Who are you, that should fret and rage, and bite the chains of nature? – [8] Nothing worse happens to you than does to all nations who have extensive empire; and it happens in all the forms into which empire can be thrown. [9] In large bodies, the circulation of power must be less vigorous at the extremities. [10] Nature has said it.

> (cit. in Selby, 1956, 22–3)

As with the Sterne, the predominating feature is the use of paratactic structures, such as the short sentences of [2] and [10], which are almost exclamatory in their effect. That there are ten sentences in twenty lines contrasts with most of the previous passages we have analysed, where there is more variation in sentence length, and here helps to make for a looser relationship, and a slackening of the cohesion of the passage. For instance, the precise relationship between [6], [7] and [8] is submerged, not made overt by subordinators, and there is no hierarchical privileging of one piece of information above the others. The emphatic statements which are presented as being self-evident allow the narratees (the House of Commons) no comeback, and the speaker's superiority to his audience is made apparent in, for example, [2], where he presents an incontrovertible fact, and by using the second person pronoun, 'you', instead of 'us', he emphasizes the distance between himself and them. The contrast with Sterne's humour as between equals and this didactic and hectoring stance of a superior to his inferiors demonstrates how the same type of syntactic structuring can be used for very different ends.

Burke's paradigmatic choices combine vague generalities and emotive semantic drift, as in the phrase at the end of [1], 'laid deep in the natural constitution of things', where the denotations of 'natural' and 'constitution', already somewhat imprecise, are overweighted by a penumbra of associations evoked because of the syntagmatic combination with the virtually non-signifying 'things'. The figurative language which is used throughout, either blatantly as in [5] or in a subdued fashion as in [2], brings in concrete detail, but Burke constantly switches perspective, from generalization to direct address to his narratees, from abstract to concrete, and in a phrase like 'the remotest verge of the sea', the unusual signifier 'verge' adds to the rhetorical colouring. Especially in his handling of abstract nouns, Burke, unlike some of the earlier Augustan writers, is inviting semantic drift, as in [6], where 'the arrogance of raging passions and furious elements' points to floating signifieds carrying a strong emotive charge, through the subdued figure of physical storms evoked by 'raging' and 'elements'; there is some indeterminacy as between the tenor and the vehicle here, especially with the definite deictic 'the', and its uncertain referent.

In contrast to Sterne's humorous incoherence, the coherence of Burke's prose is being rendered uncertain because of the interaction of the sensory and emotive appeal in the paradigmatic axis with the badgering implicit in the syntactic choices. The prose of the Romantic period is foreshadowed by Burke no less than by Ann Radcliffe; but before we move on to that period, we will look at Augustan verse and then at the transition to the Romantics.

## Syntagm/paradigm relations in Augustan verse

Syntagm/paradigm structures and relationships characteristic of prose writing inevitably re-appear in verse, since, regardless of mode, writers are likely to be influenced in broadly the same way by the dominant presuppositions and attitudes of their period. Thus the shift in attention from Man as a social being to the relationship between the Self and Nature is very apparent when, for example, Pope is compared with Wordsworth. The broad similarity between the verse and the prose certainly applies in some areas and attitudes, especially in the way in which the poet seeks to influence the reader; but on the other hand, the language of verse does conventionally incorporate syntagmatic structures not generally available to prose, and this element of deviancy may also encourage a greater range of individual differences between poets.

Then again, apart from the constraints which a period's poetic and linguistic presuppositions may place upon the range of a poet's paradigmatic choices (making certain registers fashionable, others unavailable, for example), some aspects of a strict verse form, particularly rhyme and metre, may add restrictions of another kind. Monosyllables and disyllables will tend to be preferred to polysyllables, and the latter, though quite easily accommodated, usually only appear one per line; it is not difficult to find examples where more than one appear, but they will tend be in blank-verse works such as Milton's *Paradise Lost* or Wordsworth's *Prelude*, and not in Pope's *Essay on Man*. Thus conclusions about a period style, and about contrasts between periods, while both possible and desirable, will always be hedged round with a certain tentativeness.

The way writers use the syntagmatic and paradigmatic axes is, of course, a central aspect of signification; differences in usage between various writers occur in the context of other kinds of differences, and in diachronic contrasts between periods these particularly involve differences of emphasis amongst the concepts being signified, as when there is a move from the greater emphasis on generality in the Augustan period to particularity in the Romantic period, from the impersonal to the personal, from the public to the private, from the self within Society to Self and Nature, from the intellectual to the emotional, and so on. Such oppositions are an oversimplification, but the tendencies they express are reflected in small and subtle changes in the interaction of the syntagmatic and paradigmatic axes, and especially in such relationships as that between signifier and signified, and between cohesion, congruence and coherence. Small changes can become cumulative, and lead on to much larger effects.

## Dryden and Augustan heroic couplets

Augustan verse is in many ways greatly influenced by the general attitudes within society and towards language current at the time. These are already present in Dryden's 'Mac Flecknoe' (1682):

All human things are subject to decay,
And when fate summons, monarchs must obey.
This Flecknoe found, who, like Augustus, young
Was called to empire, and had governed long;
In prose and verse, was owned, without dispute,                5
Through all the realms of Nonsense, absolute.
This aged prince, now flourishing in peace,
And blest with issue of a large increase,
Worn out with business, did at length debate
To settle the succession of the state;                         10
And, pondering which of all his sons was fit
To reign, and wage immortal war with wit,
Cried: ' 'Tis resolved; for nature pleads that he
Should only rule, who most resembles me.
Sh[adwell] alone my perfect image bears,                       15
Mature in dullness from his tender years:
Sh[adwell] alone, of all my sons, is he
Who stands confirmed in full stupidity . . .'

The last poet we considered was Milton, in some ways the most classical of English poets; Dryden, the forerunner of the Augustans, has already moved a long way from Milton. The decasyllabic (or 'heroic') rhymed couplet used by Dryden here is a characteristic form of the Augustan period as a whole. An important Augustan grouping of ideals concerns propriety associated with elegance and governed by reason, and hence order and discipline are highly prized. With that general societal emphasis on order and discipline, it seems in retrospect inevitable that the major verse form should be the highly formalized couplet, marked by its paired rhyming lines and use of the most common metrical form in English, the iambic pentameter with its immediately obvious pattern. The selection of such a form has major implications for what happens to the syntagmatic axis: where in Milton's blank verse the majority of the lines run on, each of Dryden's couplets has a definite pause at the end, with run-on lines being restricted to the odd lines (here five out of nine run on). The closed couplet places the syntagmatic axis under the constraint of having to produce a major clause break at every twentieth syllable, at the least.[2] Writers after Dryden tend to make lighter use of the run-on line, so that there tends to be a syntactic juncture every ten syllables. In fact, though, while Dryden has run on very heavily in these opening lines of 'Mac Flecknoe', he only does so six more times in the following 82 lines (at 33, 45, 57, 60, 81 and 94, and of these 45 and 60 are only lightly run on). Nevertheless, this still means that he runs on twice as much as Pope or Johnson. In the first 100 lines of Pope's 'Epistle to Dr. Arbuthnot' there are only six run-on lines (lines 3, 19, 21, 37, 51 and 95); in the first 100 lines of Johnson's 'Vanity of Human Wishes' there are five (lines 5, 7, 21, 65 and 87). The slightly more flexible interaction between Dryden's syntagm and couplet can add to the impact of the paradigmatic choices, as when 'he' in line 13 is given emphasis because of its final position and because it is the subject of the verb that is delayed to the next line; since 'he' rhymes with 'me', the link between Flecknoe and Shadwell is foregrounded before Shadwell's name is actually given. Pope uses the run-on line for similar effects, but in Johnson it does not override the individual line's internal balance. In

But scarce observed, the knowing and the bold
Fall in the general massacre of gold
('The Vanity of Human Wishes', 21–2)

'bold', as the second element of an extensive doublet, is pulled *back* into its line, and the stress-inversion at the beginning of line 22 further creates at least a mental hiatus between the two lines. The run-on effect is thus very slight. It seems, then, that the insistent rhyme within the couplet tends to lend itself to a syntagmatic break between the first and second lines.

Further, iambic pentameter imposes another constraint in that it inherently tends to have a break somewhere in the middle of the line (after syllable four, five or six); in Milton's blank verse, when the syntagm over-runs the line-end it tends to break within the next line at one of these mid-line places, as is still clearly the case in the Dryden at lines 4 and 14. The existence of these marked break-places promotes the development of point and balance within the couplet, so that, for example, it is feasible within satiric writing to balance the standard or norm in one unit, be it half-line or half-couplet, against the deviation in the other. An obvious example is lines 5–6 of the 'Mac Flecknoe' extract. This propensity for balance or point has another, perhaps less positive, implication, especially (but not only) for non-satiric verse. It has been argued (Amis, 1976) that the closed couplet form has significant implications not just for syntagmatic shape, but for the way the world is encoded, insofar as the couplet favours a poetic which deals in propositions rather than movements and 'suggests a view of subject or reality as existing rather than developing'. The form thus lends itself to the confident enunciation of 'universal truths', such as that in which the opening of 'Mac Flecknoe' grounds its satire.

The opening couplet of this poem also provides illustrations for most of the other remarks we have been making: after the generalizing and aphoristic first line, with clause-end and line-end coinciding, the second line develops a slightly more particular example of the general principle, and is heavily broken at its exact mid-point, first because the embedded temporal clause ends there, and second by the balanced semantic relationship of the two verbs, 'summons:obey'. We have previously noted how important such a semantic compo-nent is in the balanced prose style of Johnson at the other end of the Augustan period. It might also be remarked how quickly Dryden introduces into the paradigmatic axis notions of proper governance (in inverted form in the lexical set of 'monarch' terms which make up the structuring metaphor of Flecknoe as emperor of Nonsense), and in lines 12–13 two heavily-loaded terms representative of much that the Augustans admired: *wit* – 'the powers of the mind; imagination; quickness of fancy; judgment' (Johnson, 1773) – and *nature* – 'an imaginary being supposed to preside over the material and animal world; the native state or properties of things; the regular course of things' (Johnson, 1773). The first term, it may be noted, is a monosyllable, the second a dissyllable, whereas Johnson's attempt to gloss them has had to have recourse to polysyllables and abstractions.

## Constraints of verse form on paradigm and syntagm

There are, then, paradigmatic, syntagmatic and rhythmic constraints in Augustan couplets which would be inimical to such lines as:

The scenes which were a witness of that joy
Remained in their substantial lineaments
Depicted on the brain . . .

(The Prelude, I.599–601)

On the other hand, Dryden makes clever use of an isolated polysyllable in rhymed position in line 18 of 'Mac Flecknoe', where, after the late caesura and the tension between the run-on clause and the line-end have foregrounded the semantically weak 'he', the rhyme-word 'stupidity' concludes couplet and syntagm with a very heavy weight. The constraints which rhyme and rhythm place upon the lexicon, in combination with the constraints imposed by couplet form on the syntagm, inevitably have implications for the overall style of the verse, for they largely preclude the Latinate diction and syntagmatic elaboration which characterize the classical style of Augustan prose (that is, Johnson's style).

Thus the discriminations which can be made in prose texts amongst various degrees or mixtures of speech-based, Latinate and Romantic styles are not as applicable in verse. This partly explains why the language of poetry is often thought to be more 'concrete' than that of prose, for, when the more formal and elevated Latinate words are avoided, the abstractness and distance which such words bring with them are necessarily absent, and the lexicon will therefore contain a higher proportion of native or long-naturalized words, especially concrete nouns, which carry a different kind of semantic load. Further, where Augustan verse does employ abstract nouns, there is often a strong impulse towards personification, so that the degree of abstraction is reduced by the verbs and adjectives in the same syntagmatic context. A brief example from Johnson will illustrate the point without need for further comment:

Unnumbered suppliants crowd Preferment's gate,
Athirst for wealth, and burning to be great;
Delusive Fortune hears the incessant call,
They mount, they shine, evaporate, and fall.
On every stage the foes of peace attend,
Hate dogs their flight, and Insult mocks their end.

('The Vanity of Human Wishes', 73–8)

The constraints which strict verse-form places upon the syntagmatic axis will often produce distortions of word-order which would be solecistic in a prose text, but, since these have been a normal attribute of poetic style since at least the thirteenth century (and have only been consciously eschewed, to some extent, in the twentieth), poets employ them not just to satisfy the demands of rhyme and rhythm but also as deliberate foregrounding devices. Often, though, a reader is scarcely aware of their presence in verse, whereas in prose they would be heavily foregrounded because they go against the norm. In lines 3–4 of 'Mac Flecknoe', the O[bject]–S[ubject]–V[erb] order of 'This Flecknoe found' will seem, if noticed at all, elevated rather than solecistic, and the displacement of 'young' from the end of its clause to a position near the beginning, so that it occupies a rhyme position, acts as an emphatic device. The contortion and ellipses of lines 5–6 are minor compared with the witty, satiric effect of achieving end-focus within the couplet for 'Nonsense, absolute' ('normal' order would perhaps be *'[he] was, without dispute, owned [to be] absolute in prose and verse' . . . etc.). As a final example, the S–O–V order of line 15, by giving the final position, and thus emphasis, to the verb 'bears', and moving it a little further away from 'resembles' (which syntagmatically restricts the meaning of 'bears'), begins to drift the signifier to include 'carry a burden' as well as 'physically resemble', thus hinting at the onerousness of Shadwell's inheritance.

## Some stylistic vices, especially of the paradigmatic axis

There is nothing innately virtuous about syntagmatic deviation in verse, and when it coincides with excesses of conventionality and/or thinness in the paradigmatic axis, the result is verse of a rather uninteresting kind. The 'Pastorals' written by Pope in his teens are afflicted with these vices, and well illustrate the potential weaknesses of Augustan verse:

> So when the Nightingale to Rest removes,
> The Thrush may chant to the forsaken Groves,
> But, charm'd to Silence, listens while She sings,       15
> And all th'Aerial Audience clap their Wings.
>    Soon as the Flocks shook off the nightly Dews,
> Two Swains, whom Love kept wakeful, and the Muse,
> Pour'd o'er the whitening Vale their fleecy Care,
> Fresh as the Morn, and as the Season fair:       20

The Dawn now blushing on the Mountain's Side,
Thus Daphnis spoke, and Strephon thus reply'd.
   *Daphnis*
  Hear how the Birds, on ev'ry bloomy Spray,
With joyous Musick wake the dawning Day!
Why sit we mute, when early Linnets sing,            25
When warbling Philomel salutes the Spring?
Why sit we sad, when Phosphor shines so clear,
And lavish Nature paints the Purple Year?

                                      ('Spring')

Syntagmatic inversion here seems merely otiose. In the first line, the inversion of normal word order in 'to Rest removes' appears to have been made only for the sake of the rhyme and the rhythm, as does the placement of 'the Muse' at the end of the line in 18, instead of beside 'Love', which is the other subject of 'kept wakeful'. The use of the archaic interrogative V–S order in lines 25 and 27 is more functional, since it helps evoke the spatio-temporal 'other' in which pastoral exists. The passage encapsulates many aspects of Augustan poetry which led the Romantic poets of the late eighteenth and early nineteenth centuries to revolt against it; as an example of pastoral, it looks for its inspiration to previous texts rather than to personal observation and experience of the world. The Romantic objection to that sort of imitation is summed up in Keats's remark that 'if Poetry comes not as naturally as the leaves to a tree, it had better not come at all'; certainly there is no suggestion that the verse is natural in the sense of unpremeditated; the natural world is as stylized and formalized as the little pastoral drama which takes place within it, and neither setting nor action seems to offer any hint of the presence of the poet himself in or behind the poem. But of course Pope is not aiming to present a personal point of view; to expect one is an ideological stance inconsistent with the aims of the poem, though it should also be noted that Spenserian pastoral, perhaps the most obvious intertext apart from those in Greek or Latin, does offer access to the poet's point of view. Be that as it may, there are other features of this text which may make it less than satisfactory. Some of the adjective/noun combinations are clichéd or predictable, with the adjective contributing little or nothing in semantic intensity – an example is 'nightly Dews', since dew usually occurs at night; we have commented earlier (see p. 44) on this kind of textural thinness in parts of Spenserian narrative. The adjectives in the line 'Fresh as the Morn, and as the Season fair' are vague clichés, adding little information, while the inversion wrenches the syntax mainly for the purposes of the 'elegant' chiasmus and/or of the rhyme. 'Fresh' and 'fair' do suggest an attitude towards the signified concepts denoted by the nouns, but little more than that both are regarded as pleasant. This use of language contrasts with that of 'Mac Flecknoe', where the adjectives are functional, even where they might not seem to add a great deal to the signified evoked by the noun; in, for example, 'my perfect image' (15), the phrase characterizes Flecknoe as well as Shadwell, and enhances the satiric effect through its faint allusion to the Creation story of Genesis.

Further, the choices in the Pope extract of 'vale' for valley and 'morn' for morning are deliberately 'poetic', for the shortened forms are accepted in verse because of the need for monosyllables within the rhythm, but would be very obtrusive in prose. Adjectives created from nouns with a -y ending, as in 'bloomy' and 'fleecy', while they are useful for the rhythm of a line, are sometimes overdone in Augustan poetry, and tend to draw attention to themselves. There is a high level of redundancy in references to time of day and to bird song; and the Nightingale is twice mentioned, once by its ordinary name, once as Philomel, its name derived from Ovid. Other classicisms are 'Phosphor', a name for the morning star, and the use of *purple* to signify 'gleaming, bright, beautiful' (taken from Latin verse, in which the signified of *purpureus* 'purple-coloured' had been so extended; Vergil, for example, uses it with *ver* 'spring'). The choice of the signifier 'swain' for the shepherds is conventional in a pastoral poem, and even the names given them are conventional classical derivatives. Then, too, there are the periphrases, the round-about ways of saying something, which are also metonyms, a sub-set of figurative language, such as 'th'Aerial Audience' for the birds, or 'their fleecy Care', for the flock of sheep.

All of these features of the language choice tend to emphasize the signifiers, and the signifieds remain stylized and conventional, rather than pointing to a real scene such as the Romantics would have set out to evoke; even the personification of Nature 'painting' the year would have caused a Romantic reaction, for they would have seen Nature not as a painter but as a creator, and they themselves preferred to personify concrete things like hills, rocks and rivers rather than abstractions.

The lexicon of Pope's 'Pastoral' does contain many concrete, native words, but some of the items we have been pointing out clearly belong to that notorious feature of Augustan verse which used to be called, with pejorative intent, 'Augustan poetic diction'. The essence of this is the selection of over-elaborate signifiers for fairly ordinary signifieds, as in 'th'Aerial Audience' for birds, or 'their fleecy Care' for sheep, where the periphrastic phrases seem to over-elevate what is being signified, and so render the device of language itself questionable. The device consists of a formula which generally combines an adjective referring to some particular characteristic of the thing (that is, a metonym) and a more generalized noun. The function of periphrases is that they are an indirect expression of the signified, and have an ornamenting and/or elevating effect. But they are also a selecting and focusing device, pointing to certain aspects of the signified rather than to the simple signified itself, so the reader must move beyond the characteristic to the effect. Augustan poets themselves were just as aware of the potential for misuse of conventional diction and of devices like the periphrasis as are later critics. Pope's own later 'Essay on Criticism' (ll. 350ff.) is only one of the eighteenth-century attacks on the perversion of this poetic language.

## Two registers of Augustan verse

Augustan verse thus has two markedly different registers within its general lexicon: the conventional type of 'poetic diction' with its tendency towards empty adjectives and formulaic periphrases, which is usually part of the register for dealing with nature; and a register that deals primarily with mankind and society, and often uses very ordinary and everyday language. But such an over-simplified distinction cannot entirely bring out how the language of Augustan verse creates its impact, so to show this more clearly we will conclude this part of our discussion with an analysis of a mock-epic battle from *The Rape of the Lock* which exploits both registers:

> The Baron now his Diamonds pours apace;  75
> Th' embroidered King who shows but half his Face,

And his refulgent Queen, with Pow'rs combined
Of broken Troops an easy Conquest find.
Clubs, Diamonds, Hearts, in wild Disorder seen,
With Throngs promiscuous strew the level Green.          80
Thus when dispersed a routed army runs,
Of Asia's Troops, and Africk's Sable Sons,
With like Confusion different Nations fly,
Of various Habit, and of various Dye,
The pierc'd Battalions disunited fall                    85
In Heaps on Heaps; one fate o'erwhelms them all.

(Canto III)

Central to a reading of mock-epic is the recognition of
intertextuality, in this case the relationship between the trivial
card game and such epic battles as those described in the *Iliad*
and the *Aeneid*, or in Milton's *Paradise Lost*. In order to achieve
an epic elevation, Pope selects such 'poetic' terms as 'o'erwhelms', instead of *overwhelms*, and includes the Latinate
words 'refulgent' ('reflecting a brilliant light') and 'promiscuous'
('consisting of elements of different types massed together
without order'); there is the periphrasis of 'Africk's Sable Sons',
foregrounded by its contrast with 'Asia's Troops'; and there are
inversions such as that of adjective/noun in 'Throngs promiscuous', and in the A[djunct]–O[bject]–V[erb] order of line 78
(where V–O–A would be normal). In the pastoral such elements
of poetic diction – and the apparently empty adjective in 'wild
Disorder' might also be included – led to its stereotyped
weakness and artificiality; but here it is part of the satire of
poetic diction as well as of the card game; and by over-inflating
such a trivial social occasion, it mocks it. More ambiguous, and
more difficult to assess, are the semantic effects within the epic
simile of lines 81–6, since 'Asia's Troops, and Africk's Sable
Sons', located within a poetic device (epic simile) only available
at this time for parodic use, are apt to be infused with the
contemporary realities of British imperialism: the East India
Company in Asia was already becoming Britain's largest source
of revenue, and the slave trade between Africa and the West
Indies was increasingly lucrative. In such a context, the
analogies seem closer to contemporary realities than to classical
convention, and the commercial enterprises involved were, of
course, responsible for the exotic objects with which Belinda
adorns herself (see Laura Brown, 1985, 8–9).

Nevertheless, Pope maintains such a focus that while his description includes signifiers which normally belong to the register of warfare – broken troops, easy conquest, wild disorder, routed army, pierced battalions, and so on – it never *becomes* that of an actual battle, but always remains that of a card game, as the names of the suits make clear, and this masks, without removing, the essentially imperialist assumption behind the analogy. Crucial to the satiric effect is the way that the reader interprets the card game through the battle register; that is, the *signifieds* of the military terms are converted into *signifiers* now denoting things which are lesser both in size and significance. Thus, for example, through the process of double signification 'level green' (80) first denotes a battle field and then a card table. Another interesting game with signification is played out in the description of the King of Diamonds (76): it is, of course, entirely accurate, since this is the only King-card shown in profile; at the level of primary signification, though, it is totally redundant, a periphrasis over-determined by the preceding statement of its signified, but it also reflects a traditional iconography of deceit, and so suggests that, in a sense, Belinda's cards have been ambushed. This is taken further in the periphrasis of 'Africk's sable sons', which, occurring in the analogy to a rout, functions comically as a reminder that the black cards (in a game where Belinda has decreed that spades are trumps) are not at this moment winning the tricks.

## A contrast between Augustan and Romantic poetry: Thomson (1700–48) and Wordsworth (1770–1850)

The element of game in Augustan verse accords with the preponderance of satirical writing, a mode which strongly engages the reader's intellectual participation through the need for constant discrimination between positive standard and deviation. In non-satiric verse, however, the type of reader involvement is different; such verse usually has Nature as its primary focus, with humans now appearing as figures in a landscape, but the configuration has an effect different again from the nature verse of the Romantic poets. Indeed, strictly comparable passages from Augustan and Romantic nature poetry do not come readily to hand – a point which is

significant in itself. However, we will attempt to bring out some
of the differing characteristics of the verse of each period by
comparing an extract from Thomson and an extract from
Wordsworth; there are defining differences in paradigmatic and
syntagmatic choices, and in the manipulation of point of view,
especially in the way that emotions are both expressed within
the passage and invited from the reader. We will begin by
quoting both passages:

The full ethereal round,

Infinite worlds disclosing to the view,
Shines out intensely keen; and, all one cope                     740
Of starry glitter, glows from pole to pole.
From pole to pole the rigid influence falls,
Through the still night, incessant, heavy, strong,
And seizes Nature fast. It freezes on;
Til morn, late rising o'er the drooping world,                  745
Lifts her pale eye unjoyous. Then appears
The various labour of the silent night:
Prone from the dripping eave, and dumb cascade,
Whose idle torrents only seem to roar,
The pendent icicle; the frost-work fair,                        750
Where transient hues, and fancied figures, rise;
Wide-spouted o'er the hill, the frozen brook,
A livid tract, cold-gleaming on the morn;
The forest bent beneath the plumy wave;
And by the frost refined the whiter snow,                       755
Incrusted hard, and sounding to the tread
Of early shepherd, as he pensive seeks
His pining flock, or from the mountain top,
Pleased with the slippery surface, swift descends.

On blithesome frolic bent, the youthful swains,                 760
While every work of man is laid to rest,
Fond o'er the river crowd, in various sport
And revelry dissolved; where mixing glad,
Happiest of all the train! the raptured boy
Lashes the whirling top.                                        765

(The Seasons: 'Winter')

[Skating in winter]
So through the darkness and the cold we flew,
And not a voice was idle; with the din

Smitten, the precipices rang aloud;                                    440
The leafless trees and every icy crag
Tinkled like iron; while far distant hills
Into the tumult sent an alien sound
Of melancholy not unnoticed, while the stars
Eastward were sparkling clear, and in the west          445
The orange sky of evening died away.
Not seldom from the uproar I retired
Into a silent bay, or sportively
Glanced sideway, leaving the tumultuous throng,
To cut across the reflex of a star                              450
That fled, and, flying still before me, gleamed
Upon the grassy plain; and oftentimes,
When we had given our bodies to the wind,
And all the shadowy banks on either side
Came sweeping through the darkness, spinning still      455
The rapid line of motion, then at once
Have I, reclining back upon my heels,
Stopped short; yet still the solitary cliffs
Wheeled by me – even as if the earth had rolled
With visible motion her diurnal round!                        460
Behind me did they stretch in solemn train,
Feebler and feebler, and I stood and watched
Till all was tranquil as a dreamless sleep.

                                              (*The Prelude*, Book I)

There are some obvious differences. The Thomson passage has
as its topic the impact of a freeze on a rural landscape, and
proceeds by accumulating descriptive vignettes of typical
phenomena. The passage invites some interesting comparisons
with the passage from 'Spring' analysed at some length by
Barrell (1988, 108–18). It drops more immediately into the
layering of scenic details as, in lines 758–69, the effects of the
night's 'labour' are listed: after the first, the icicle, which
embraces both the domestically human ('the dripping eave')
and untamed nature (the 'cascade'), the order of presentation
proceeds from the foreground to take in hill, forest, pasture
land, and finally mountain top, in much the way Barrell has
identified as derived from the landscape strategies of Claude's
paintings. In all this, Nature is represented as operating
indifferently, its effects being rather matters for interpretation –
the impact of the 'dumb' waterfall, for example, has become

very like that of a life-like painting which might 'seem to roar', and the play of colours and shapes in the 'frost-work' allows the fancy scope for play. Unlike the 'Spring' passage, which situates the addressee as viewer ('your Eye excursive roams'), landscape in this passage is not formally viewed by a human subject, and the viewing 'eye' actually present is that of personified morning. But this is not the eye that imaginatively perceives the 'frost-work', and the implicit slipping between natural and human perceptions has the same effect as that Barrell observed in 'Spring': 'the perceiving self . . . is never obliged to construct its identity as something different from, and in opposition to, a constraining nature' (1988, 113).

In the Wordsworth, a number of subjects recur in order to focus attention on the abstract thematic elements of individual perception (auditory; visual; spatial). Thomson writes in the third person and present tense, and makes constant use of the definite deictic *the*, which all combine to make his scene general and typical; Wordsworth writes in the first person and past tense – he, too, makes heavy use of *the* (though intermingling some indefinite or zero deictics, as in 'a star' or 'far distant hills'), but here the different tense and person give the deictics a particularizing effect. Basically, Wordsworth presents a number of experiences repeated in the one location during a particular period of his life, but telescopes them so that it is *as if* he is describing a single experience. In Thomson, on the other hand, the whole time/space relationship is very different: even though time moves through night and morning into day, it is a typical frost-in-winter scene, and quite unlocated in a particular space (indeed, immediately following the extract cited, Thomson takes his reader on a tour of Northern Europe to Russia via Holland and Scandinavia). In other words, then, the paradigmatic choices in tense and deixis are having a marked effect on how the linearity of the syntagm is perceived – in Thomson's verse syntagmatic linearity seems to be emphasized, whereas in Wordsworth its effect seems to be minimized. Indeed, it can be argued that Wordsworth is deconstructing linearity, partly by the recursiveness of the experiences portrayed, but principally by the perceptual inversion of spatial relativity in the fleeing star and the sweeping banks, and then paradoxically in the wheeling cliffs but stationary skater. By encoding the figure of suspended motion in this way, Wordsworth is able to exploit the syntagmatic axis to encode the mind's passive receptivity to external natural forces (see Mudge, 1985).

## POINT OF VIEW AND REFERENTIALITY

Point of view is an important aspect of difference between the passages. Part of the generalizing effect of the Thomson is the assumption that the narratee stands and sees from the same place(s) as the narrator. Overt or implicit visualizing terms are used, with 'the view', and then 'appears', which introduces a long right-branching list of visualized phenomena, and includes many terms which reinforce the visual effect – the colour terms 'hues, livid, -gleaming, whiter', and the 'fancied figures' which, totally unspecified as they are, invite the reader to bring to bear his/her own memories or experiences. Most of the modifiers are quite denotative, giving precise factual information, such as 'Prone from the dripping eave', 'still', 'silent' and the series 'incessant, heavy, strong', though some of these may be used to express attitude, as also with 'fair' and 'pensive'. The latter collocates with 'shepherd' and 'swains', thereby evoking the pastoral, and as such is the point in this extract at which the aristocratic view of landscape most obviously impinges (compare Barrell, 1988, 115). That is, the figures in the landscape are seen as varieties of genre painting – pastoral cliché and rural sports – while it is nature which labours (757) and is naturally 'idle' (759). Real human work is referred to, but only as an absence (771). Here, as generally, attitude remains on the whole covert – an assumption that the narratee shares the speaker's perception of things.

Implicit in this attitude is a vast gap between eighteenth- and nineteenth-century theories of language: to put it crudely, the eighteenth century felt able to correlate appearance and reality, and so to assume that language functioned referentially, whereas, as Foucault (1970, Ch. 7) has argued, the next century had come to feel that appearances were rather external signs pointing to hidden meanings. Thus Wordsworth has to develop strategies which seek to compel language to be referential; hence his presentation of point of view is much more overt and emotive, mimicking the physical as well as the perceptual point of view of the speaker as Self as he records the impressions which strike his sensibility – the sense of touch ('through . . . the cold we flew'; 'our bodies [given] to the wind'), which is personalized rather than generalized as in Thomson, and the pervasive references to hearing and sight.

The elevated and Latinate language of Thomson's first three lines, especially the rather Miltonic periphrasis 'the full ethereal round', transforms the specifically visual into an evocation of general cosmic vastness. But Wordsworth's sky is more simply presented ('orange' is the only word not Anglo-Saxon), and its oppositional contrasts combining direction and light – 'Eastward' and 'sparkling clear' as against 'west' and 'orange . . . died away' – evoke a perception of process rather than of stasis. Thomson *refers* to processes, those of freezing, but describes them in terms of their immobile results; this can be seen clearly in the absence of finite verbs, except in embedded clauses, in the rest of the paragraph following 'appears'. All Wordsworth's other references to seeing coincide with an abundance of verbs expressing motion, a strategy nicely encapsulated by the happy ambiguity of 'glanced sideway', in which the eye, and then the skater's body, move towards the visual object. All this process is moving towards a stasis of a different kind, culminating again in the paradox of the closing lines, where Wordsworth now moves to the Latinate register that Thomson opens with –

> even as if the earth had rolled
> With visible motion her diurnal round!

– as a heightening device to prepare the reader to shift the next evocation of a physical scene on to the plane of transcendental contemplation where Self and Nature become one.

The way the syntagmatic axis interrelates details plays a very powerful part in such shifts. An earlier example presents a sequence of precisely described sounds – more properly, and significantly so, echoes – which culminates in 'an alien sound/Of melancholy not unnoticed'; this introduces strongly attitudinal and humanizing words ('alien', 'melancholy') interpreting the landscape, and uses the double negative to suggest a communion with living nature that takes place on the margins of liminality, and works both retrospectively and prospectively to suggest deeper significances in the descriptions of sounds and sky. By contrast, Thomson's *vignettes* are typical of the sort of pastoral scene which any sensitive Augustan observer might have perceived; he presents them in their own right, and without his overt intrusion or any sense of a religious dynamism inherent in the natural world. And the figures in Thomson's landscape are similarly perceived figures, interacting with and taking pleasure in the natural world, but separate from it.

## THE FUNCTIONS OF PERSONIFICATION

The kind of essential difference we have been pointing to between the two writers is also clear in the functions of personification in the two passages. Thomson's awakening morning is a product of fancy, depending largely on the convention of the sun as the eye of day, here in the periphrasis '[morning's] pale eye' to suggest winter sunlight, and on the literal fact that the sun is 'late rising' in winter. The personification thus decodes into a simple, literal scene, coloured slightly by the emotive 'unjoyous'. The personifications in Wordsworth are more covert: we have already pointed to the humanizing language used of the hills in 442–4, but would also add that 'melancholy' functions differently from Thomson's 'unjoyous', in that it overtly attributes human emotion to the inanimate landscape; the verbs which transfer motion from skater to landscape continually create a marginal personification, reinforcing the sense of marginal liminality throughout the second half of the passage; the earth is, more traditionally, an active female; and a human vocabulary is used to describe the cliffs, stretching 'in solemn train,/Feebler and feebler'.

In conclusion, Thomson seeks the mind's appraisal for the representative scenes of winter, and through that appraisal the resulting emotive response which the reader is invited to share; Wordsworth seeks to involve the reader in the experience much more directly, or else he overtly states the emotions to be recognized or shared. In their respective appeals to our sensory experience and emotions, Thomson makes us work harder, while Wordsworth does more of the work for us. This is not to suggest that the poets of the Augustan and the Romantic periods consciously work out how they are going to present their nature scenes, but the whole milieu of a period is reflected in the way that the poet chooses and organizes his language, and organizes the placement of his signifiers. In general, we would say that nature poetry is not the major strength of eighteenth-century poets; it is, rather, the poetry of 'Man' in general, especially the satire on deviant behaviour within society among representative men, that is characteristic of the greatest eighteenth-century poetry. By contrast, nature poetry *is* characteristic of the Romantic poets, a poetry that relates external nature to an individual conscious of selfhood. In eighteenth-century poetry, there is often a distancing of the speaker from the scene, and an appeal to the intellect, and through the intellect to the emotions; in Romantic poetry, there is often a strong sensory appeal, as the poet seeks to influence the reader's emotions more directly, reinforcing the emotive with the sensory.

## Syntagmatic and paradigmatic drift in Romantic poetry

The Thomson–Wordsworth comparison has suggested some general differences between Augustan and Romantic verse; some of the characteristics of Wordsworth's poetic discourse are further generalizable to other Romantic poets but, as always, there are synchronic as well as diachronic differences to be considered. Two aspects of the treatment of the syntagm are reflected, though in differing ways, in Romantic poetry at large: first, the meditative impulse encourages the looseness of syntagmatic relationships already observed in Radcliffe and in Burke, a syntagmatic drift whereby sentences accrete clauses by chaining them on from one another, rather than by relating separate subordinations back to the central line (this has a major impact on the developments in figurative language); second, whereas Augustan writers use syntagmatic relations to limit signs to denotative meanings, Romantics use the syntagm to create a drift within the sign, a drift of signification, so that connotative associations become more important than the central coherent core of denotation, even when congruence may seem initially to be breached. Let us for a moment go back to Pope:

Who shames a scribbler? break one cobweb through,
He spins the slight, self-pleasing thread anew:
Destroy his fib, or sophistry, in vain;
The creature's at his dirty work again,
Throned in the centre of his thin designs,
Proud of a vast extent of flimsy lines.
('Epistle to Dr. Arbuthnot', 89–94)

The extended comparison between 'scribbler' and spider enables a whole series of what might seem incongruously related words to carry duple denotation, but *no more* than duple. Thus the culmination of the argument, 'a vast extent of flimsy lines', refers precisely to the 'cobweb' of the vehicle and to the 'lines' of writing of the tenor; the attitudes to spiders and their webs ('creature', 'dirty work') and to scribblers ('fib or sophistry') are mutually enhancing, and develop a strong connotative effect even while the penumbra of associations round the double denotation is still tightly controlled. This is so because of the firm cohesion with which the clauses are linked. Lines 93–4 are parallel extensions of an idea apparently completed within the balanced couplet of 91–2 (and so retrospectively transform that couplet's signification into an open couplet),[3] but in the extensions, specifically to 'creature' and 'work', the text spins its own interlocked semantic web (extending by, respectively, 'Throned . . . Proud' and 'thin designs . . . flimsy lines'), so that the argument is strengthened without any risk of semantic or syntagmatic drift.

A Romantic poet formulates an exclamatory argument rather differently:

> And that simplest Lute,
> Placed length-ways in the clasping casement, hark!
> How by the desultory breeze caress'd,
> Like some coy maid half yielding to her lover,                   15
> It pours such sweet upbraiding, as must needs
> Tempt to repeat the wrong! And now, its strings
> Boldlier swept, the long sequacious notes
> Over delicious surges sink and rise,
> Such a soft floating witchery of sound                           20
> As twilight Elfins make, when they at eve
> Voyage on gentle gales from Fairy-Land,
> Where Melodies round honey-dropping flowers,
> Footless and wild, like birds of Paradise,
> Nor pause, nor perch, hovering on untam'd wing!                  25
>     (Coleridge, 'The Aeolian Harp' (first published 1796))

The movement of the mind is mimicked here by syntagmatic disorder, of which the anacoluthon in line 13 is only the most obvious example. More far-reaching in effect is the left-branching syntax thwarted both by the anacoluthon and by the tendency for tropes to collapse into their vehicles. The first sentence (12–17), then, begins with a grammatical subject 'that simplest Lute' which is immediately qualified but then left hanging until belatedly restated by 'It' in 16. This delay has a further consequence, as the clauses of lines 14 and 15 are free to generate connotation before the clause they qualify is reached. The second element of drift, after the anacoluthon at 'hark!', begins at 'caressed'; the denotation of 'caressed' would seem to be determined by 'desultory breeze', in that 'desultory' indicates that the caressing is an aimless touching, but because *caress* is normally marked as {+affectionate and +tactile} a figurative sense is also suggested, and hence the same kind of marginal personification we saw above in Wordsworth.

The response to this possibility, the 'coy maid' simile, is an example of the quintessential Romantic habit of embedding simile within metaphor, and, as is often the case, this has dire consequences. First, it contaminates the main line of thought by introducing a new and discordant penumbra of associations – the sound of the harp has become at its first mention a 'sweet upbraiding', and what is literal to the vehicle sits uncomfortably as the tenor; second, the final clause of the sentence, with its strongly attitudinal 'wrong', is a further extension of the sexual-seduction language of the vehicle and scarcely, if at all, develops the tenor. The kind of tight cohesive relationships within and between tenor and vehicle evidenced in the Pope example is far removed from this much looser and less coherent discourse.

A similar kind of syntagmatic chaining occurs in the second sentence, where a qualifying clause and an adjunct precede the main verbs, 'sink and rise'; and where a lexical set of *sea*-words ('surges sink and rise . . . floating . . . voyage') is not actualized as trope, giving way instead to the 'Elfins' simile, which in turn has embedded within it the extraordinary metaphor of the hovering Melodies, a metaphor created by the 'birds of Paradise' simile now embedded within *it*. Such syntagmatic chaos is calculated to widen the gap between signifier and signified, especially, too, as it collocates without controlling quite disparate lexical sets – 'delicious, soft, floating, twilight, gentle' as opposed to 'Footless and wild, untamed'. The interpenetration of these non-congruous sets promotes the free play of connotation at the expense of denotation. Such uses of language demonstrate why Romantic discourse is so easy to deconstruct (and suggest why deconstructionists chose to concentrate initially upon the period of discourse which best illustrated that theory's tenets).

DRIFT IN STANZAIC VERSE: SHELLEY (1792–1822)

The kinds of drift we have pointed to here are not confined to blank verse, but occur as readily in stanzaic verse where, as with couplets, the form might be expected to exercise some constraint over the syntagmatic axis. Shelley's 'When the Lamp is Shattered' (1824) opens with a heavy syntactic patterning which nevertheless does little to restrict drift:

> When the lamp is shattered
> The light in the dust lies dead—
> When the cloud is scattered
> The rainbow's glory is shed.
> When the lute is broken,                                      5
> Sweet tones are remembered not;
> When the lips have spoken,
> Loved accents are soon forgot.

The repetition of temporal-*plus*-principal clause structure, together with obvious semantic relationships linking clauses of the same type, creates the expectation that in some way meaning is also being repeated, but Shelley pushes against this expectation. Thus after the connectedness of lines 1 and 3 – they have identical grammatical form, and the rhyme-words 'shattered'/'scattered' clearly fall within the same semantic field – a similar relationship might well be expected between lines 2 and 4. But 'lamp' and 'cloud' belong to opposite fields of connotation, the former relating to notions of light, wisdom, intellectual illumination, and the latter to darkness, blindness, obscuration; such connotations are activated by the highly connotative linking of quite simple words in line 2, in which the phrase 'lies dead' imparts figurative senses to 'light' and 'dust'.

We enter here into a broader type of intertextuality than that generally found in Augustan verse, in that, while it would be possible to cite a few texts containing a phrase such as 'lies dead in the dust', such texts would hardly constitute specific pre-texts for Shelley's lines. A contrast is offered by Coleridge's 'its strings/Boldlier swept', which seems to owe something to Milton's 'Lycidas' (line 17), 'Begin, and somewhat loudly sweep the string': if the reminiscence does summon 'Lycidas' as an obligatory intertext, its function is to draw attention to the implicit siting of Coleridge's poem against the pastoral tradition.

But Shelley's lines are rather being located somewhat vaguely within the language of transience and mutability. And so the surprise movement of the fourth line to express illumination (note, too, the common collocables 'shed' and 'light') turns out to be in effect another expression of transience. Lines 3–4 nevertheless do remain deviant within the stanza, since the other temporal-*plus*-principal clause pairs assert in various ways that the breaking of the sign results in the destruction of signification.

In a sense, the stanza's own discourse becomes a paradox, since it expresses this destruction of signification by exploiting the capacity of the syntagm to float the signifiers placed within it. Another good example is the way the syntagm can impose new connotations on what might otherwise seem the simple denotation of 'have spoken'. The pairing of instruments, 'lute/lips', of their sounds, 'Sweet tones/Loved accents', and of their loss, 'remembered not/soon forgot', might seem to isolate the rhymed, grammatically similar non-pair, 'is broken/have spoken', but instead they are compelled to complete the pattern and behave as if they were totally isomorphic, with the result that the signification of each drifts towards that of the other. The play with signification in the opening stanza is thus very complex, and is a prelude to the further development of radical drift in both logic and figurative language as the poem progresses beyond stanza 1. We will comment further on this aspect of Romantic verse when we are discussing figurative language in chapter 6, but it can be noted here that the (often unconscious) self-deconstructive tendency we referred to in Coleridge reaches its apogee in the later Romantics, especially Shelley.

## BLAKE (1757–1827)

The syntagmatic destabilizing of signifiers takes a different form in Blake's verse. The following set of similes from *The Book of Thel* illustrates one way by which Blake pushes signifiers beyond their usual signifieds:

Ah, Thel is like a wat'ry bow, and like a parting cloud;
Like a reflection in a glass; like shadows in the water;
Like dreams of infants, like a smile upon an infant's face;
Like a dove's voice; like transient day; like music in the air.

(lines 12–15)

Thel (the speaker) symbolizes Innocence, and embodies it by being innocent of the knowledge that Experience provides. The series of similes builds up a tenor lying behind them all which represents the abstract concept *Innocence* semantically marked as

+ transient
+ delicate
+ beautiful

and hence a signified more complex than the simple signifier 'innocence' itself can point to. Individually, the similes may seem only to be related by slight connections along the syntagmatic axis, made by exophoric reference (rainbow and cloud belong to the sky;[4] 'a glass' and 'the water' both reflect, and it would not make a great difference to surface meaning if they were interchanged), and by grammatical isomorphism (the first two are structured 'like [adjective + noun]'; the second two, 'like [noun] in [noun]'), and by repetition ('infant'). The similes cannot themselves signify 'innocence', though the concept may be evoked by conventional associations of 'infant' and 'dove'; they do all point to something insubstantial and transient as tenor, and once this is identified as 'innocence' it becomes evident how particular signifiers are being pushed to allude to signifieds beyond their usual meaning, together building up a *symbol*.

Blake also extends meaning by yet another kind of intertextuality – an intertextuality in the sense that his poems interrelate with one another, and when the same or related signifiers appear in several poems they begin to develop new signifieds lying behind the usual signification. In the 'Songs of Experience', for example, around the signifiers within a lexical set denoting authority – 'Father/Priest/King'– there is built up a penumbra of association and connotation which marks these signifiers as {+repressive}; such connotation is often clear contextually, but is further enhanced by a second set signifying the tangible sign of that authority, 'rod/wand/sceptre/staff', and a third, 'fetters/briars/manacles/chains', which represents imprisonment, the result of repression. In 'Earth's Answer', the signifier 'Father' is associated with the modifiers 'cold, hoar, cruel, jealous, selfish' and with the actions of weeping, chaining and freezing. The intertextual method enables point of view to be expressed without the need for attitudinal modifiers, as in the second stanza of 'Infant Sorrow':

> Struggling in my father's hands,
> Striving against my swaddling-bands,
> Bound and weary, I thought best
> To sulk upon my mother's breast.

The connotations of 'father', as established within the body of 'Experience' poems, determine how the reader will interpret the struggling, striving, binding and weariness in this one; the infant's initial experience of life is thus seen to be already an experience of repression. An intertextual control of parameters of signification and especially of the penumbra of associations activated by the signifiers is different from the constraints built into texts of earlier periods, which depend upon cultural convention rather than upon the cumulative impact of an individual writer's own discourses, and has rarely been cultivated to the same extent since, though it certainly happens in the works of Yeats, Wallace Stevens, and Dylan Thomas, and to some extent in poem cycles such as Housman's *A Shropshire Lad*.

## Comic and satiric functions of drift: Byron (1788–1824)

A use of intertextuality which is both similar to and very different from Blake's is found in what seems a completely atypical Romantic poem, Byron's comic satire *Don Juan*. Defending Byron against the old charge that he lacks individuality and verbal complexity, and has done nothing to invest signifiers with meanings which overflow their normal capacity, Peter J. Manning (1979) has argued for Byron's individuality on the grounds of his extratextuality as well as his intertextuality, choosing his signifiers not only to allude to a vast number of pre-texts, but also to non-literary contexts. Wordsworth had recommended the use of the language of ordinary men, but neither he nor any of the other Romantic poets (indeed, nineteenth-century poets) ranges as widely as Byron (and before him, Pope) does through so many vocabularies and registers. And the continual movement from register to register functions, as Manning points out, to foreground 'the arbitrary agreements on which the making and maintaining of meaning rest' (1979, 229). However he does not emphasize how in this (as in much else) Byron looks back to the late Augustan writers, and adapts techniques like those of Sterne, whose endemic inter- and extratextuality also functions comically to foreground the process whereby literary art creates its illusions through language, and so becomes self-referential, and, as Manning remarks, creates those 'myriad slippages and maladjustments of that social network [that] create the gaps in which his irony and satire operate' (ibid.).

Central to this essentially metafictional strategy is, as with Sterne, and before him, with Fielding, Byron's narrator, whose intrusive and disruptive voice constantly mimics and mocks contemporary Romantic discourse, though it is Byron's actual practice that constitutes the most penetrating criticisms of his contemporaries. The narrator's cavalier treatment of the syntagm repeatedly exposes the tendency towards syntagmatic drift we have pointed to in the prose of the late Augustan age, as well as in the poetry of Coleridge and Shelley, while the lack of congruity in his paradigmatic choices is associated with a destabilizing of signification which becomes a crucial strategy for his comic satire. The following stanzas from Canto I of *Don Juan* may be taken as typical:

He pored upon the leaves, and on the flowers,           745
    And heard a voice in all the winds; and then
He thought of wood-nymphs and immortal bowers,
    And how the goddesses came down to men:
He missed the pathway, he forgot the hours,
    And when he looked upon his watch again,           750
He found how much old Time had been a winner—
He also found that he had lost his dinner.

Sometimes he turned to gaze upon his book,
    Boscan, or Garcilasso; — by the wind
Even as the page is rustled while we look,           755
    So by the poesy of his own mind
Over the mystic leaf his soul was shook,
    As if 'twere one whereon magicians bind
Their spells, and give them to the passing gale,
According to some good old woman's tale.           760

Juan's pubescent stirrings are here transformed into an allegory of misreading, though it might equally well be said that Romantic readings of Nature's immanent mysteries are being slyly reduced to emotional self-indulgence. The first stanza initially poses Juan as a mock-Wordsworth in his apperception of the humanized landscape, but breaks this mode at the late caesura in 746, which allows the connective 'then' to occupy the final, rhyme-stressed position, thus asserting that Juan's next thoughts follow appropriately, as well as chronologically. They do not, of course. Byron has simply exploited syntagmatic cohesive ties to override conceptual disparateness. By switching intertextual field to the inimical Augustan-type pastoral tradition, he ironically opposes poetic artifice to the notion of transcendent presence implied by the figure of the wind's voice. The next move is to relate fiction to 'life', as the rhetorical heightening of the parallel clauses of 'He missed . . . he forgot' gives way to the overtly humorous bathos of the final couplet, in which the incongruous colloquialisms – 'old Time . . . a winner . . . lost his dinner' – bring fancy down to earth.

The second stanza follows a structure similar to the first. It begins with the citation of specific intertexts, then heightens the style by the analogy between the wind rustling the pages of a book and the movement within Juan's soul, and by the syntactic inversion with which it begins; this displacement of the agent 'by the wind' to the beginning of its clause makes the sense difficult to grasp and increases the complexity of the syntactic relationships within the analogy. But, to say the obvious, it is all too much, and the lexical choices of 'poesy' and 'mystic' only comically exacerbate it. The intricate syntagmatic structure exists for the sake of the syntagmatic drift which sets in immediately following line 757, when another analogy is appended, expanded by a co-ordinate clause, and then undone by the disruptive narrator's concluding sceptical qualification to the narratee.

This stanza also invites, in the repetition of 'wind' (746, 754 and in 759 as the synonym 'gale') and 'leaf' (745, 757), a comparison with Sterne's repeated shifting of the signification of the signifier 'wish' until it becomes not only comically anasemic but also one of the metafictional strategies which permeate *Tristram Shandy*. On the one hand, 'wind' is stripped of the significance with which it is invested in line 746, becoming merely an unmarked agent. On the other hand, 'leaf' reappears in an entirely new sense, 'page', and gains potency from its modifier, 'mystic'; the two occurrences are connected isomorphically, since Juan pores over both, and metafictionally, in that by explicitly showing that meaning in the 'mystic leaf' is not innate but attributed, Byron dismantles the implicit assertion of immanence in the original use (745).

Byron is usually contrasted synchronically with the other Romantic poets, to his disadvantage, but when he is thus compared diachronically with Sterne it can be appreciated how skilfully each enacts the deferral of meaning consequent upon misreading, and exploits the presence of a disruptive narrator and his comic interaction with the narratee, which invites close reader participation in the enjoyment of the games that language can be seen to play.

## Keats (1795–1821)

As both comparison and contrast, we can place against the Byron extract the central stanzas from Keats's 'Ode to a Nightingale':

> Away! away! for I will fly to thee,
>   Not charioted by Bacchus and his pards,
> But on the viewless wings of Poesy,
>   Though the dull brain perplexes and retards:
> Already with thee! tender is the night,                35
>   And haply the Queen-Moon is on her throne,
>     Cluster'd around by all her starry Fays;
>       But here there is no light,
> Save what from heaven is with the breezes blown
>     Through verdurous glooms and winding mossy
>       ways.                                            40
>
> I cannot see what flowers are at my feet,
>   Nor what soft incense hangs upon the boughs,
> But, in embalmed darkness, guess each sweet
>   Wherewith the seasonable month endows
> The grass, the thicket, and the fruit-tree wild;       45
>   White hawthorn, and the pastoral eglantine;
>     Fast-fading violets cover'd up in leaves;
>       And mid-May's eldest child,
> The coming musk-rose, full of dewy wine,
>     The murmurous haunt of flies on summer eves.       50

The speaker's self-dramatization here is obviously different from the role created by and for Byron's narrator – in place of his disruptive and distancing strategies, Keats constructs a fiction of the presence of the self. That is, the experience is rendered as if actually occurring (initially by the narrative shift between lines 31 and 35, and then sustained by the use of present tense and

of the proximal deictic 'here'). But because the experience is
not actually referential, but takes place in the imagination, Keats
simultaneously evokes self-presence through precise sensory
details and deconstructs it through tropes and a grammar of
negation that deprives the speaker of the primary sense of sight.

How this double movement operates is succinctly shown in
lines 31–2 in the very complex reference to 'Bacchus': the lines
assert the immateriality of the poetic imagination in the contrast
'not . . . but on', and the rejection is both of artificial stimulants
and of mythopoeic intertextuality; yet the vehicle of the
metaphor 'fly on the wings of Poesy' suggests a materiality
associated with the bird being addressed, and the modifier
which would at the same time deny it, 'viewless', is an unusual
poeticism whose meaning is partly to be recognized from its
earlier uses by Shakespeare and Milton (*Measure for Measure*,
III.i.124; 'The Passion', 50).

Within a few lines, a personification of the type rejected
appears in 'Queen-Moon' (36). In fact, Keats has recourse to
various artifices of language to move his poem out of the
ordinary. The more obvious ones are: the archaisms 'pard',
'haply', and the second person singular pronoun 'thou/thee/thy'
(a common Romantic convention); other poeticisms, such as the
aphetic 'eves'; unusual combinations such as 'verdurous
glooms', where 'verdurous' becomes subject to drift, and
develops a new denotation (now 'characteristic of *verdure*'
rather than 'rich in *verdure*'), and 'embalmed darkness', where
the noun brings out the adjective's associations with death.
More complex are effects gained by synaesthesia, which can
evoke multiple sense impressions and make the text strange at
the same time; thus 'light' is *blown* by breezes, and the series
'soft incense hangs' combines touch, smell and, to some extent,
sight (though the speaker visualizes without seeing). The list in
45–50 combines sensory precision with a temporal slipping that
draws the mind away from the object. The invisibility of the
violets is reiterated – 'covered up, etc.' – and yet they are 'fast-
fading', emblematic of the transience of inspiration. The last
three lines of the extract achieve this temporal slipping through
typically Romantic syntagmatic drift – there is a sequence of
four paratactic phrases, each chained on to the phrase before it;
one shift is from the figurative, the personification in 'mid-May's
eldest child', into an elaboration of its literal aspect, a move which
reverses the classical process whereby the literal is rendered as

virtually transparent. Within this is placed the highly connotative metaphor 'dewy wine', which compacts together a large number of associations – rich scents, freshness, taste, for example. The power of the larger syntagmatic movement is very evident here, since an actual wine would hardly be praised for being 'dewy', so the reader brings the separate associations of each word to the text and attaches them to the implied tenor, 'nectar'.

The second element of drift is in the time references, which slide from mid-May to summer, from the rose in bud to the rose in full flower. Such drift pushes the reader away from the merely literal, drawing attention to the text's implicit self-reflexivity, its comment on the creative process which gives expression to the felt inspiration of the Self. Perhaps somewhat surprisingly, Keats and Byron thus come together, despite their more overt differences in lexical choices and the roles of the speakers. For Keats, too, builds an effective deconstructive strategy on a lexical range, on intertextuality, and on syntagmatic drift. There is similarity, as well as diversity, between these poets, and between these and the other Romantics. From here, we must turn to the even more complex situation of Romantic period fiction, and then follow this through into the still more diverse writing of the Victorian age.[5]

## Notes and further reading

1   In her typology of narratees, Shlomith Rimmon-Kenan (1983, 94–6) observes that the narratee is always 'situated at the same narrative level as the narrator' (p. 104); this presupposes a one-to-one relationship between narrator and narratee (which in Rimmon-Kenan seem to be terms applied also to speaker and addressee within the story) which does not always apply in embedded narration, as for example when the direct and indirect addressees of Mrs Jewkes's speech in the first paragraph of the extract (Pamela and Nan) exchange roles, as Mrs Jewkes turns from one to the other, while the narratee of the letter is a further indirect recipient of the direct speech of the protagonists within the story.

2   Dryden occasionally extends a couplet to a triplet, but of the five examples in the 217 lines of 'Mac Flecknoe' three have a discrete co-ordinate clause as the third line. The device is employed much less frequently by the time of Pope, though it can have a marked impact, as in 'Epistle to Arbuthnot',

323–5, where in the see-saw comparison for Sporus the triplet extends his antithetical attributes over three lines, as the third summarizes the preceding pair.

3   For figures and discussion of Pope's 'open couplets' – couplets which 'postpone the completion of meaning' – see Jones (1969), pp. 209ff.

4   The rainbow/cloud pair, of course, inevitably slip into the intertextual space such as that surrounding lines 3–4 of Shelley's 'When the Lamp is Shattered'.

5   Further reading: Gilbert (1979), Gordon (1966), and Barrell (1988), for eighteenth-century 'mixed genre' poems (not discussed here); Leech and Short (1981) and McCrea (1980), for the basic elements of Johnson's style and the uses to which he puts them; Marks (1984) for eighteenth-century poetic styles; Morris (1983) for illuminating comments on art, signification, and referentiality; on selfhood and intersubjectivity in *Pamela*, see McKee (1985); and for an extended discussion of Keats's syntax, Patterson (1979).

## Exercises

1   How significant for a study of textuality is the growing range and importance of types of prose writings in the seventeenth–eighteenth–early nineteenth centuries? Do writers show major textual differences in their handling of the categories they choose for prose non-fiction and fiction? Find examples of some of the categories (e.g., sermon, essay, biography, epistolary novel), and analyse the methods employed in building up the signification of meaning (and the narrator/narratee relationship).

2   Examine some pieces of Augustan writing (both verse and prose) which are marked by irony/satire/humour and explore how the effects are produced by examining the triads of syntagm/paradigm/signifier-signified and of cohesion/congruence/coherence. To what extent do the same triads help to show differences between earlier and later eighteenth- and early nineteenth-century writings?

3   Compare and contrast Pope's *Rape of the Lock*, I: 121–48 with Keats's *Eve of St Agnes*, stanzas 24–6, to show how major ideological presuppositions have affected the hand-

ling of elements of textuality, especially the extent and type of reader participation in the (re)construction of signification.

4   Compare and contrast the two following passages of discursive prose, the first from Samuel Johnson's *Plan of a Dictionary*, the second from Shelley's introduction to *Prometheus Unbound*, to bring out how the use of language in each reveals major differences between their respective periods:

(i) When first I undertook to write an English Dictionary, I had no expectation of any higher patronage than that of the proprietors of the copy, nor prospect of any other advantage than the price of my labour; I knew that the work in which I engaged is generally considered as drudgery for the blind, as the proper toil of artless industry, a task that requires neither the light of learning, nor the activity of genius, but may be successfully performed without any higher quality than that of bearing burthens with dull patience, and beating the track of the alphabet with sluggish resolution.

  Whether this opinion, so long transmitted and so widely propagated, had its beginning from truth and nature, or from accident and prejudice, whether it be decreed by the authority of reason, or the tyranny of ignorance, that of all the candidates for literary praise, the unhappy lexicographer holds the lowest place, neither vanity nor interest incited me to enquire. It appeared that the province allotted me was of all the regions of learning generally confessed to be the least delightful, that it was believed to produce neither fruits nor flowers, and that after a long and laborious cultivation not even the barren laurel had been found upon it.

(ii) The moral interest of the fable, which is so powerfully sustained by the sufferings and endurance of Prometheus, would be annihilated if we could conceive of him as unsaying his high language and quailing before his successful and perfidious adversary. The only imaginary being resembling in any degree Prometheus, is Satan; and Prometheus is, in my judgement, a more poetical character than Satan, because, in addition to courage, and majesty, and firm and patient opposition to omnipotent force, he is susceptible of being described as exempt from the taints of ambition, envy, revenge, and a desire for personal aggrandisement, which, in the Hero of *Paradise Lost*, interfere with the interest. The character of Satan engenders in the mind a pernicious casuistry which leads us to weigh his faults with his wrongs, and to excuse the former because the latter exceed all measure. In the minds of those who consider that magnificent fiction with a religious feeling it engenders something worse. But Prometheus is, as it were, the type of the highest perfection of moral and intellectual nature, impelled by the purest and truest motives to the best and noblest ends.

This Poem was chiefly written upon the mountainous ruins of the Baths of Caracalla, among the flowery glades, and thickets of odoriferous blossoming trees, which are extended in ever winding labyrinths upon its immense platforms and dizzy arches suspended in the air. The bright blue sky of Rome, and the effect of the vigorous awakening spring in that divinest climate, and the new life with which it drenches the spirits even to intoxication, were the inspiration of this drama.

5  Compare and contrast Pope's 'Temple of Fame', 11–20, with Keats's *Fall of Hyperion*, 19–31, showing how the particular point of view in each leads on to broader aspects of perception of the relationship between the speaker and nature. Then compare both with Blake's 'The Garden of Love' from *Songs of Experience* to show how his very different perceptions are encoded.

6  Compare and contrast Wordsworth's sonnet 'Upon Westminster Bridge' with Blake's 'London' from *Songs of Experience* and with Byron's *Don Juan*, Canto X, stanzas 82–3. To what extent do the very different views of London reflect differences in the writers' attitudes to the (lack of) referentiality in language? How does each strive to compel the language to be referential?

7  Compare and contrast Coleridge's narrative techniques in (selected sections from) *The Rime of the Ancient Mariner* with those of Keats in 'La Belle Dame Sans Merci' and with those of Radcliffe in (selected sections from) *The Mysteries of Udolpho*. Do similarities outweigh differences?

**A shifting focus:
the nineteenth century**

Ah, what a dusty answer gets the soul
When hot for certainties in this our life! –
In tragic hints here see what evermore
Moves dark as yonder midnight ocean's force,
Thundering like ramping hosts of warrior horse,
To throw that faint thin line upon the shore!
(George Meredith, *Modern Love*, 50)

## Movements in early nineteenth-century prose

From Dryden's time onwards, speech-based prose had steadily
gone on to establish itself as the basis of English prose style,
especially for fiction-writing. Although the eighteenth century
attempted to oppose it with other styles – a reintroduced Latin-
based style on the one hand, and the affective style of the
Gothic novelists on the other – by the early nineteenth century
prose writing had begun to use a speech-based style modified
to varying degrees through periodical recourse to the Latinate
and Romantic modes. The purposes of writing had also
changed, and with them had changed the relationship between
writers and readers. At this point of our overview, notions of 'a
period style' become even more elusive for attempted typologies of prose writings than for typologies of verse. The sources
upon which early nineteenth-century prose drew had become
so varied that 'a typical sample' is an imaginary critical
construct. Nevertheless certain trends and tendencies can be
identified as characteristic of prominent styles, and relationships
can be drawn between these and the intellectual milieu within
which they function.

A consequence of the Romantic stress on the imagination and
emotions was a diminished emphasis on intellectual responses
shared by educated society in favour of the individual's
emotional ones. The Gothic novel, for example, represents an

attempt to resolve the conflict between referential uses of language – the language which creates novelistic realism – and poetic uses of language which express inner experience (Haggerty, 1984). This effort is most apparent in scenes in which stimuli are observed acting upon the fertile imagination of a focalizing character, and which seek an empathetic response from the reader. The evocation of scene or landscape displays most clearly a shift in the function of figurative language, now placed primarily in the service of emotive response rather than as a support for rational argument. The emotive use of landscape as it interrelates with the evocation of selfhood permeated fiction in general, and seems to have remained a permanent feature of fiction ever since. The slackening of cohesive ties and the tendency to allow, or even cultivate, syntagmatic drift, which we earlier noted in Radcliffe and in the Romantic poets, also comes to be an important element in nineteenth- (and twentieth-)century fiction, and is one of its most significant developments.

## Scott (1771–1832): treatment of scene

Walter Scott's novels are notorious for their romantic treatment of a scene in relation to the characters who move through it, but they also reveal something of the range of possibilities for which this can be exploited, as is shown by the following extracts from *The Heart of Midlothian* (1818). In this first extract, we will break up the complex third sentence into its component clauses:

[A] The windows commanded an enchanting view of the little vale over which the mansion seemed to preside, the windings of the stream, and the firth, with its associated lakes and romantic islands. [B] The hills of Dumbartonshire, once possessed by the fierce clan of MacFarlanes, formed a crescent behind the valley, and far to the right were seen the dusky and more gigantic mountains of Argyleshire, with a seaward view of the shattered and thunder-splitten peaks of Arran.

> [C]
> 1a *But to Jeanie,*
>     2a whose taste for the picturesque,

3 if she had any by nature,
2b had never been awakened or cultivated,
1b *the sight of the faithful old May Hettly,*
4 as she opened the door to receive them in her clean toy, Sunday's russet gown, and blue apron,
5 nicely smoothed down before her,
1c *was worth the whole varied landscape.*

(Ch. 45)

The scene is quite overtly visualised, as indicated by 'view' (twice) and 'were seen', but sentence [C] makes it obvious that the scene is presented as if the narrator were seeing it, not Jeanie (who at this point has never entered the house to see the view from the windows). Indeed, the narratee is invited both to savour the scene and to share some superiority of perception with the narrator. The language of the first two sentences contains both attitudinal and evocative terms ('enchanting, windings, romantic, dusky, shattered, thunder-splitten'), and the narrator's reference to the 'fierce clan' of the past goes beyond mere local colour to impart an increased romantic ruggedness to the scene. Both sentences are right-branching and loosely paratactic, with tendencies towards drift; both conclude with a correlative 'and . . ' further extended by a 'with . . ' addendum. By contrast, sentence [C] is carefully left-branching, the principal clause being split into three parts with four other clauses embedded within it. Adding 'sight' to the set of 'view' and 'seen', and virtually framed by 'picturesque' and 'landscape', the sentence consciously opposes what Jeanie does see, human and domestic values, against the rugged, romantic landscape, and readjusts the narratee's feelings of superiority towards the plain and simple Jeanie by redefining the preceding scene-description as 'cultivated taste for the picturesque'. Scott's contrasting of two kinds of syntax (and of lexis) thus evokes contrary value systems, but, because Jeanie is herself as much observed as the landscape (she is 'our heroine' a couple of sentences later), the reader has little difficulty in reconciling the two.

The following extract, from Chapter 51, is more atmospheric in its reading of natural phenomena as a system of signs:

> the dead and heavy closeness of the air, the huge piles of cloud which assembled in the western horizon, and glowed like a furnace under the influence of the setting sun – that

awful stillness in which nature seems to expect the thunder-burst, as a condemned soldier waits for the platoon-fire which is to stretch him on the earth, all betokened a speedy storm.

This is in form left-branching, but a problem with suspension of this kind in landscape description is that the principal clause can come as an anti-climax. As it is, the very free parataxis and the succession of disconnected tropes throw emphasis on the individual details, and then on signifiers rather than signifieds, so that by the end of the long 'condemned soldier' analogy the looseness of coherence has brought the sentence to the verge of anacoluthon and necessitates the summative subject 'all'. This, in contrast to the previous example, makes heavy use of figurative language for its emotive effects, even at the risk of such an incongruence as '*piles* of cloud *assembled*', in which the Romantic habit of perceiving natural objects as animate seems to jar against the material 'piles'. The first passage, illustrating one strand of Romantic style, uses the specific details of 'stream, firth, lakes, islands, hills, etc.', interwoven with emotive terms, to provide the scene with a concrete particularity that creates the illusion that narrator and narratee visualize the same landscape. The second passage discloses, as it were, a Gothic heritage in its heavy combination of atmosphere, emotion and symbolism, which subordinate the objective scene to the response evoked. The effect on the characters within the text is to inspire them to a (very stilted) debate over the relationship between man and nature, and then the scene turns out to be the prelude to the murder of one of the speakers by his own illegitimate son.

## Jane Austen (1775–1817): syntagmatic control of represented emotion

Published two years earlier than *The Heart of Midlothian*, Jane Austen's *Emma* does not seem to be overtly influenced by Romantic prose in its depiction of emotional states or in the presentation of conflict amongst imagination, perception and reason, even at such moments of crisis as Harriet's revelation that it is Knightley she aspires to:

Harriet, who had been standing in no unhappy reverie, was yet very glad to be called from it, by the now encouraging manner of such a judge, and such a friend as Miss

Woodhouse, and only wanted invitation, to give the history of her hopes with great, though trembling delight. Emma's tremblings, as she asked, and as she listened, were better concealed than Harriet's, but they were not less. Her voice was not unsteady; but her mind was in all the perturbation that such a development of self, such a burst of threatening evil, such a confusion of sudden and perplexing emotions, must create. She listened with much inward suffering, but with great outward patience, to Harriet's detail. Methodical, or well arranged, or very well delivered, it could not be expected to be; but it contained, when separated from all the feebleness and tautology of the narration, a substance to sink her spirit; especially with the corroborating circumstances which her own memory brought in favour of Mr. Knightley's most improved opinion of Harriet.

(Ch. 47)

There are several lexical items here dealing with emotions, and they have their nodal points as 'delight' with respect to Harriet and 'suffering' with respect to Emma. Beyond this, however, the emotion of neither woman is very far defined, apart from the parallel set of 'development/ burst/ confusion' describing Emma's state. Even that set, which begins to take on the appearance of an exclamatory paradigmatic expansion typical of Romantic style, is syntagmatically controlled. The '[x] of [y]' structure which makes up each phrase is manipulated in two ways to build up the emotive impact – each is made longer than the one before by the addition of a modifier to the [y] element; and the [x]-nouns are arranged in a pejorating sequence:

such a development of self
such a burst of threatening evil
such a confusion of sudden and perplexing emotions.

Together they are the compound subject of the verb 'must create' which comes, when it finally does, curiously and anticlimactically modified by the modal 'must', not as the factual 'creates'. The distance and quality of generalization imparted by the syntagmatic control and the final modal both stress the presence of the narrating voice and draw attention to the ideological conflict underlying Emma's reactions: she responds as she does not only because Harriet's announcement has prompted Emma's realization that she wants to marry Knightley herself, and so her self-interest is threatened, but also because Harriet's ambition is inappropriate to her class and status. A similar kind of control is exercised over the repetition of 'trembling[s]' earlier in the passage, where the same signifier is used to indicate opposite emotions; on the first occasion, the conjunction with 'delight' determines meaning, but on the second the shift of word-class (adjective to noun) helps the reader determine a different signified by making the appropriate hypersyntagmatic links with the surrounding pattern of ironical opposites. Thus the negative expression of Harriet's 'no unhappy reverie' paradigmatically evokes Emma's depression; Harriet's innocent perception of Emma as 'such a judge, and such a friend' precisely evokes how poor a judge and friend Emma has been. The signified of 'trembling[s]' changes, but without any suggestion of drift.

But perhaps the major controlling strategy for the episode is the sustained contrast between 'inside' and 'outside'. We noticed earlier a tendency in Romantic poetry for texts to reflect on the linguistic processes of communication as a part of their own attempt to communicate, and it is most interesting to see this phenomenon appearing also in Austen. Thus Emma's voice is 'not unsteady' while her mind is in 'perturbation'; 'outward patience' masks 'inward suffering'; and Harriet's conversation is marked by a large gap between 'narration' (the surface, or discourse) and 'substance' (or story). Austen here exploits the novelist's capacity to slip between third person narration and indirect representation of a character's thoughts, in that by the end of the final sentence the reader is aware that Emma's point of view is being presented in this sentence – the markers are the emotive 'feebleness and tautology' and the access to Emma's 'own memory'.

The paragraph began by focusing through Harriet's point of view for the opening sentence (the naïve acceptance of 'judge and . . . friend', coupled with the formal 'Miss Woodhouse', are sufficient indicators), and then moved to narrator point of view for the whole middle section before shifting again in the final sentence. Emma's predicament at this moment is a product of her consistent failure to perceive the proper relationship between signs and things, intentions and actions, words and world. Ironically, of course, she is doing it again here, since Knightley has no marital interest in Harriet. Emma's misuse of reason and judgement have still to be set right, but at this point the novel epitomizes, in her arrogant (mis-)reading of Harriet's 'text', how it is that Emma goes so wrong. In Austen's overall control and the presence of much hypotaxis and balance within the syntagmatic axis, she appears to continue the speech-based prose of the eighteenth century, and a generalization to that effect would be unexceptionable, but in lexis and theme she proves not entirely immune to Romantic influence. Such uses of language tend to confirm Edward Neill's recent argument (1987) that the conflict in the novel between Emma's Romantic imaginings and her 'English ideology' (of which Knightley, the embodiment of both gentility and reason, is the pinnacle) is symptomatic of a larger fissuring in society and the literature it produces.

## Emily Brontë (1818–48): manipulating reader response

We will compare the *Emma* extract with an episode from *Wuthering Heights* (1847) which also represents emotional perturbation in an inward/outward frame, but in a much more Romantic (even Gothic) mode:

This time, I remembered I was lying in the oak closet, and I heard distinctly the gusty wind, and the driving of the snow; I heard, also, the fir-bough repeat its teasing sound, and ascribed it to the right cause: but it annoyed me so much, that I resolved to silence it, if possible; and, I thought, I rose and endeavoured to unhasp the casement. The hook was soldered into the staple: a circumstance observed by me when awake, but forgotten. 'I must stop it, nevertheless!' I muttered, knocking my knuckles through the glass, and stretching an arm out to seize the importunate branch; instead of which, my fingers closed on the fingers of a little, ice-cold hand! The intense horror of nightmare came over me: I tried to draw back my arm, but the hand clung to it, and a most melancholy voice sobbed, 'Let me in – let me in!' 'Who are you?' I asked, struggling, meanwhile, to disengage myself. 'Catherine Linton,' it replied shiveringly (why did I think of *Linton*? I had read *Earnshaw* twenty times for Linton). 'I'm come home: I'd lost my way on the moor!' As it spoke, I discerned, obscurely, a child's face looking through the window. Terror made me cruel; and, finding it useless to attempt shaking the creature off, I pulled its wrist on to the broken pane, and rubbed it to and fro till the blood ran down and soaked the bed-clothes; still it wailed, 'Let me in!' and maintained its tenacious gripe, almost maddening me with fear.

(Ch. 2)

Brontë here quite deliberately runs the risk, by pressing hard on the reader's emotions, of a reaction against the tenor of the text. This is particularly so in the final sentence, where the narrator, Lockwood, details the cruel action towards the child which potentially, at least, invites a revulsion from him. But this does not detract from the emotive impact, because of the way Brontë has skilfully manipulated the language to diminish the reader's perception of the narrator's responsibility. There are constant reminders that the incident related is a nightmare, not waking reality ('I thought . . . when awake . . . nightmare' etc.), which distances actor from event, but there are also crucial grammatical manipulations. The first clause of the sentence, 'Terror made me cruel', names both cause and effect of the following action, so the narrator himself recognizes that he is cruel, rather than it being left to the reader to name his action as cruelty. Further, 'Terror' is the grammatical subject and Lockwood the object, in a mild personification which passes the blame for the cruelty to the abstract emotion.

A similar device occurs a little earlier, when, in his remark that 'the intense horror of nightmare came over me', Lockwood once again makes himself the grammatical object of the clause, and thence the passive object of something seemingly external to himself; thus the emotion evoked by the nightmare receives primary stress. In contrast to this, the girl-child is to some extent depersonalized by the use of 'it' throughout, and she is referred to as 'the creature', which distances her further still. The subjective experience of nightmare thus takes on the appearance of objective reality.

Another manipulation of reader response lies in the slight ellipsis of the causal link between the narration of the action and its result, which throws the onus on the reader to draw the inference that rubbing the child's wrist on the broken glass cuts it and so causes it to bleed. The gap probably passes unnoticed, but it is there, and the reader, by filling in that gap, becomes an imaginative participant in the action, thus making it more difficult to maintain distance and to form judgements. Lockwood has overtly admitted that he is a flawed narrator, and that further influences reader responses to him.

Lockwood's narratorial function is also a reflection of how the incident models the complex way that the novel's events are mediated through narrators occupying positions peripheral to those events. Romantic-style writing – from Radcliffe to Mary Shelley, and thence to Dickens, Hardy, Lawrence and so on – develops a tradition whereby external phenomena are focalized through the subjective perception of characters situated within the story, and hence function as a direct mirror of inner states. Such writing frequently hovers on the borders of melodrama, so that if it fails to restrict the reader's responses to the emotional, and allows the intellectual to enter in, the effect evoked may be contrary to that apparently intended – laughter, rather than empathy, as can occur with Ann Radcliffe or Mary Shelley. Brontë's slightly removed narrators, though, offer a slant mirror, through their fallibility, prejudice and ignorance, and this affords one kind of control over reader response.

Reader responses are also subject to the control of the syntagmatic axis. Syntactic structure here consists mainly of short principal clauses linked by co-ordination. In the first sentence, for example, a series of perceptions and actions is presented through a bunch of clauses beginning with 'and' or 'but', the only subordination being the simple causal 'so much, that' and the parenthetic and elliptic conditional 'if possible'. There is a tendency for ellipsis in subordinate clauses – the second sentence is very compressed, in that it is a whole series of subordinate clauses so elliptical that they almost conceal how much temporal information they provide about what Lockwood has seen earlier and has now forgotten. But set against the compression of that second sentence is the expansion of the third, where the series of co-ordinate clauses emphasizes temporal sequence without imposing a hierarchical order, so that the climax is achieved partly by simple end-focus, partly by the semantic intensity of the pair of adjectives modifying 'hand', and partly by the orthographic signalling of exclamation. This whole structure is characteristic of Romantic-style syntax. There is, however, a tight semantic congruence between the sentence's two last clauses:

| stretching an | arm out to | seize | the importunate | branch |
| my | fingers | closed on | the | fingers |
| | | | of a little, ice-cold | hand |

An obvious effect of this linking is to foreground the contrast between the personified branch and the human hand, laying the ground for the depersonalizing effected through the presentation of hand, face and voice as if disembodied. Although there are in this passage some lexical items which are emotively loaded, such as 'intense horror', 'shiveringly', and 'terror made me cruel', the bulk of the narration is seemingly so objective that a response is covertly evinced from the reader, and this response will be emotive rather than intellectual. So, while fully exploiting the resources of Romantic prose, Brontë has also refined it to create a subtler, less hectoring, relationship of writer to reader.

Austen, Mary Shelley, the Brontës: not a new, but an increasingly significant, aspect of nineteenth-century fiction is the number of books now written by women. Until further evidence is assembled, it seems that little that is conclusive can be said to suggest that early nineteenth-century women novelists display a significantly different lexis or select different syntagmatic forms or different tropes. Women writing towards the end of the century occasionally expressed a sense that not only were some aspects of human experience conventionally unavailable to women writers, but the language in which these might be expressed was similarly unavailable;[1] we have not seen any evidence for the development of a feminized lexicon in women's writing of the Victorian period.

## Darwinism and the otherness of the physical world

As the nineteenth century progressed, it became increasingly heterogeneous in intellectual life and literary output. The years surrounding 1860 rate special mention, since they saw the publication of such challenging works as Darwin's *On the Origin of Species* . . . (1859), Mill's *On Liberty* (1859) and *Utilitarianism* (1861), Huxley's *Man's Place in Nature* (1863), Spencer's *First Principles* (1862), Muller's *Lectures on the Science of Language* (1861–4), and Arnold's *Culture and Anarchy* (1869). Fiction published in 1859–62 included novels by Braddon, Wilkie Collins, Dickens, George Eliot, Kingsley, Lytton, Meredith, 'Ouida', Payn, Thackeray, Trollope and Wood, to name, perhaps, just the major figures. Merely to list these illustrates the diversity of Victorian writing, and gives some indication of the complexity of the intellectual climate in which both the development of certain Romantic assumptions and a reaction against them occur.

Although it would not be surprising to learn that Darwin, for example, exerted a significant influence over later Victorian literature, not merely on content, or 'story', but also on discourse, it might be surprising to be told that Darwin's own discourse is indebted to his reading of Dickens's fiction. Gillian Beer (1983, 62) has suggested that the way Dickens's style 'insists upon the recalcitrance of objects – their way of mimicking the human order without yielding their own *haecceitas* [thisness]' possibly offered Darwin a means to express the relation of man to the rest of the natural order. It is pertinent to note at this point that the mode of inductive realism, especially its assumption that the essence of a fictional character can be created by the accumulation of externals, is an important characteristic of nineteenth-century fiction; it is also quite fundamental to poetry, and can be seen, for example, in Browning's practice and in Hopkins's notion of inscape and instress. Beer identifies a number of tendencies in nineteenth-century literature which Darwin's work at least reinforced, and these include some which have an important bearing on the study of literary language.

The detailing of 'facts' in describing the material world may proceed without there being any sense of some greater end or precedent design, but they still have as principal end the perception of the wonder or strangeness of phenomena in themselves, and a gradually growing sense of their otherness from self. A result was, in Beer's words, that 'the grotesque, the beautiful and the wonderful in the everyday was a major Victorian imaginative theme. The study of "fact" was . . . an exploration of the fantastic' (1983, 81). An organicist approach to the world, and to literary representations of the world, reduces the discreteness of mental categories and so perhaps also facilitates such linguistic phenomena as the incongruence of extreme register-shift. Any identifiable historical period has its own methods of organizing signification; Darwin, it must be stressed, was a symptom, not a cause, of contemporary shifts in language use and style – they are already as clearly apparent in Browning's early poetry as in Hopkins's late poems, and always remained unacceptable to some readers and writers.[2]

Another important straw in the wind is represented by Ruskin's pre-Darwinian reformulation of the concept of sympathy, or of accord between inner and outer world, as the 'pathetic *fallacy*' – 'The highest creativity is that to which the primrose is for ever nothing else than itself – a little flower apprehended in the very plain and leafy fact of it, whatsoever and how many soever the associations and passions may be, that crowd around it' (*Modern Painters*, 3:209, cited in Beer, 1983, 50). Victorian writers *are* much more likely to seek to evoke a sensory experience for its own sake, without moving from the senses to the emotions or to the intellect, as earlier writers had done.

The eighteenth-century Enlightenment, with its conception of an ordered universe in which everything was in its place, had not deeply questioned the usual western religious view that the world was anthropocentric. Nineteenth-century theories of evolution implicitly called this in question, though they did not immediately affect conceptions of language. As Beer comments, the language of the period generally remained 'anthropomorphic by its nature and anthropocentric in its assumptions' (50), though the assumption of an underlying and precedent design had already been somewhat undermined by the Romantics' emphasis upon the congruity of the inner and the outer worlds. Even where this congruity was no longer assumed, the loosening of grammatical cohesion, with its corollaries of semantic drift and the generation of associative penumbras, which had been employed by Romantic writers as an important linguistic strategy for undermining dogma and reason and for liberating the imagination, remains characteristic of post-Romantic writing, though there were some attempts to revive more classical qualities in reaction against Romantic looseness and emotionalism (Sinfield, 1971, 37). The 'vagueness' often perceived in Tennyson, for example, seems to us to be a consequence of developments in the Romantic style.

## Implications for representation: narrator–narratee relationships

Beer also suggests (1983, 44–6) that the challenge to teleological order and to omniscience has an important impact on narrator–narratee relationships; divested of authority, 'Victorian novelists increasingly seek a role for themselves within the language of the text as observer or experimenter, rather than as designer or god' (45), and so the speaking voice of the narrator increases in significance. Once again this is a matter of degree, since Sterne had long since employed a narrator who was idiosyncratic, individual, and very fallible, and Dickens had experimented with decentred narration, notably in *Bleak House* (1852–3). The following extract from Esther's narrative will illustrate how the narrator's voice is individualized and how her relationship with the narratee is rendered ambiguous:

Richard had been gone away for some time, when a visitor came to pass a few days with us. It was an elderly lady. It was Mrs Woodcourt, who, having come from Wales to stay with Mrs Bayham Badger and having written to my guardian, 'by her son Allan's desire,' to report that she had heard from him and that he was well, 'and sent his kind remembrances to all of us,' had been invited by my guardian to make a visit to Bleak House. She stayed with us nearly three weeks. She took very kindly to me, and was extremely confidential: so much so that sometimes she almost made me uncomfortable. I had no right, I knew very well, to be uncomfortable because she confided in me, and I felt it was unreasonable; still, with all I could do, I could not quite help it.

She was such a sharp little lady, and used to sit with her hands folded in each other, looking so very watchful while she talked to me, that perhaps I found that rather irksome. Or perhaps it was her being so upright and trim; though I don't think it was that, because I thought that quaintly pleasant. Nor can it have been the general expression of her face, which was very sparkling and pretty for an old lady. I don't know what it was. Or at least, if I do, now, I thought I did not then. Or at least – but it don't matter.

Of a night when I was going upstairs to bed, she would invite me into her room, where she sat before the fire in a great chair; and, dear me, she would tell me about Morgan ap Kerrig until I was quite low-spirited! Sometimes she recited a few verses from Crumlinwallinwer and the Mewlinnwillinwodd (if those are the right names, which I dare say they are not), and would become quite fiery with the sentiments they expressed. Though I never knew what they were (being in Welsh), further than that they were highly eulogistic of the lineage of Morgan ap Kerrig.

'So, Miss Summerson,' she would say to me with stately triumph, 'this, you see, is the fortune inherited by my son. Wherever my son goes, he can claim kindred with Ap Kerrig. He may not have money, but he always has what is much better – family, my dear.'

(Ch. 30)

The narrator's voice is individualized mainly by her habits of modification ('very; extremely; sometimes . . . almost; I knew very well; dear me; I dare say'; etc.), and by her trailing, co-ordinate syntax. The passage is really about the significance of the relationship between Esther and Mrs Woodcourt, but like so much else in *Bleak House* signs obscure as much as they reveal. There is a self-reflexivity here that teases the reader. Near the beginning of the passage information is presented in a sequence of terms for Mrs Woodcourt which both explain and particularize: 'a visitor', 'an elderly lady', 'Mrs Woodcourt'. In the second paragraph, in a sequence dealing with her feelings about Mrs Woodcourt, Esther is evasive and withholds something she knows – the cause of her hostility and depression – from her narratee ('the unknown friend to whom I write' of Chapter 67). Then the third paragraph, which moves from the narrator–narratee realm of discourse into story events, resituates Esther as Mrs Woodcourt's narratee, where she in turn experiences the same opacity of signification (Mrs Woodcourt's 'evidence' being in Welsh). Now Esther knows, and the reader knows, that her discomfort is because Mrs Woodcourt is obliquely warning her off Allan Woodcourt, who is, after all, the ostensible cause of his mother's (over-extended) visit to Bleak House. This has to be deduced in a general way, decoding discourse to reveal the hidden text, just as Esther puts aside the discourse of the Welsh verses to reach their 'story' (but implicitly finding that the story has been resignified and reapplied). Thus Esther's presentation of external 'facts' serves to disclose an order and a meaning which lies hidden under the surface.

The simultaneous process of concealment and disclosure depends for its existence and effectiveness on the implicit relationship between fallible narrator and her narratee, and this in turn has a significant impact on the text/reader interrelationship, for individual readers can interpret the Esther/narratee relationship in two different ways: one is to adopt the position assigned to the narratee, and take the remarks confided in the narratee as showing Esther's human frailty, and inviting empathy for her situation and her interpretation of it; the other is to react against the narratee, and to see the revelation of another side of Esther which brings out her hypocrisy in not aligning her public and her private behaviour.

Rather than pursuing expository clearness, Dickens has created an obscuring surface which, when penetrated, discloses a complex of attitudes and emotions. We have been arguing that in some pre-Romantic prose writers, and in the Romantics themselves, emotive appeal was associated both with a loosening of syntagmatic and grammatical cohesion and with a loosening of congruence amongst paradigmatic choices. It is at least partly true to claim that, in a reaction against the Age of Reason, the Romantics saw emotive appeal as located in opposition to intellectual comprehension; Victorian reactions against what they perceived as Romantic excesses, however, occur in a context partly conditioned by the Romantics and in an intellectual climate no longer informed by the certitudes of the previous century. The convenient binary opposition of emotion and intellect will no longer serve, especially when the appeal of the sensory comes to the fore without its earlier link to either intellect or emotion. The implication for the paradigmatic/syntagmatic axes of text is the generation of further diversity and experimentation with variety, but in the context of the loosened cohesion evolved by the Romantics.

# New developments in the paradigm/syntagm relationship: Tennyson (1809–92)

The consequences of the Romantic developments of the syntagm can be seen in the poetry of Tennyson. Tennyson, as Sinfield has argued (1971, 38), combines Romantic and Neoclassical qualities, deriving values from personal experience in the Romantic manner, but striving to express these in an art which recaptures 'the harmony and beauty which the Enlightenment had observed in the functioning of the whole universe'. The result is a new kind of paradigm/syntagm complex, in which a classicizing tendency appears in the paradigmatic choices, but in which the syntagm remains essentially Romantic. Section 54 of *In Memoriam* shows how syntagmatic indeterminacy creates semantic drift and destabilizes signification:

> Oh yet we trust that somehow good
>   Will be the final goal of ill,
>   To pangs of nature, sins of will,
> Defects of doubt, and taints of blood;                4
>
> That nothing walks with aimless feet;
>   That not one life shall be destroy'd,
>   Or cast as rubbish to the void,
> When God hath made the pile complete;                8
>
> That not a worm is cloven in vain;
>   That not a moth with vain desire
>   Is shrivell'd in a fruitless fire,
> Or but subserves another's gain.                12
>
> Behold, we know not anything;
>   I can but trust that good shall fall
>   At last − far off − at last, to all,
> And every winter change to spring.                16
>
> So runs my dream: but what am I?
>   An infant crying in the night:
>   An infant crying for the light:
> And with no language but a cry.                20

This is a poem about doubt, coming from the middle section of *In Memoriam* where the problem of doubt is explored, and raises the question of the extent to which any poem can deal with doubt as its subject without generating a self-deconstructing discourse. The speaker's doubt is continually foregrounded, as in the opening line, where 'yet' and 'somehow' problematize 'trust'; the 'trust' of line 14 echoes the opening line, and is again a qualified affirmation, now by 'but'; and the choice of 'dream' in line 17 self-consciously throws doubt on the whole preceding attempt at affirmation, suggesting that it is all illusory. The answer to the last stanza's question, 'but what am I?'

foregrounds through repetition both 'infant' and 'cry', and these two terms also undercut any suggestion of certainty.

## THE SYNTAGMATIC AXIS

The poem is organized around binary oppositions – good/ill, faith/knowledge, light/darkness – and contrasts an elaborate grammatical structure in lines 1–12 with the more fragmented utterance of the rest of the poem. The first three stanzas consist of a single right-branching sentence which is built up on a series of 'That' clauses dependent on 'We trust' in the first half-line. Overtly evidenced here is Tennyson's well-known habit of accumulating closely related or analogous concepts within a frame. Yet the apparent orderliness breaks down in the elaboration within the first of these clauses; it is difficult to determine the precise grammatical context of the series of *head noun + possessive noun* phrases following 'goal of ill', because the change of particle from *of*, in 'goal *of* ill', to *to* seems to indicate that the phrases are not simply particularizations of 'ill' nor simply adjuncts of 'goal'. This loosening of grammatical cohesion leads to uncertainty not only as to how the phrases relate to what has preceded, but also as to how they relate to one another.

The problem is in origin grammatical, because grammar cannot determine the relationship between the units of such a structure. Thus *of* might signify 'caused by', 'inherent in', or 'endemic to', and might shift from phrase to phrase. The difficulty is further compounded by the disruption of congruence amongst the terms selected for those phrases. All of the nouns in the stanza are generally abstract, and, whereas 'good' and 'ill' help to define one another by binary opposition and end-line focus, the nouns of lines 3–4 are less constrained. The four possessive nouns form sets chiastically ('nature . . . blood', 'will . . . doubt'), but the head nouns don't pattern in this way; the attempt to link 'sins' and 'defects', indeed, rather draws attention to the contrast between the terms, in that the second is judgementally weaker, and there is a similar attitudinal contrast between 'pangs' and 'taints' which tends to mask how the outer chiastic pair refer to inherent faults and the inner pair to acts of choice. So amongst this group of phrases there is a constant shifting of the point of view in moral terms, which is partially masked by the common grammatical structure; but in the long run the meaning is left fairly indeterminate.

The tactic, in each of the four 'that'-clauses which follow, of affirming precedent purpose by negating examples of its opposite, succeeds in foregrounding emblems of doubt. So when the parallel principal clauses run from 'O, yet we trust', to 'Behold, we know not anything', to 'I can but trust', the signified of 'trust' has been drifted considerably through the negative examples provided. Even the positive 'that' clauses of the fourth stanza are syntagmatically undermined: the adverbial sequence in line 15, 'At last – far off – at last', postpones 'good' to some place remote in space and time, and its placement between the verb 'shall *fall*' and its adjunct 'to all' contributes towards destabilizing the verb's meaning, so that there is a lingering suggestion that *fall* signifies destruction.

## THE PARADIGMATIC AXIS

The syntagmatic axis can, in the ways we have described, destabilize the signification of meaning; but of course it interacts with the choice of which particular signifiers are placed in the paradigmatic slots. Two aspects of lexis, in particular, require further comment: first, the use of the concrete nouns 'worm' and 'moth', and second the uses of 'pile', 'subserve' and 'infant'. The concrete nouns 'worm' and 'moth' only incidentally point to particular signifieds within the natural world, since a broad intertextuality imbues them with more general and symbolic reference, asserting them as emblems of purposive prescience. Sinfield (1971, 192) has remarked on 'pile' as 'a very material word to use of human souls' which helps undermine the purposive role attributed to God here. Further, though, the building metaphor implicit in 'cast as rubbish . . . made the pile' shifts the meaning of *pile* to include the less common signified 'a large building' as well as 'a heap of things', and thus imparts some degree of elevation to the subject.

A similar effect is achieved by use of the rather rare word, 'subserves'. An effect more arcane to a modern reader is found in 'infant', where Tennyson exploits his period's interest in etymological allusion to pun on the root meaning from Latin *infans* 'unable to speak'.[3] This reinforces, at the end of the poem, the contrast between articulate 'language' and the inarticulate 'cry', and hence the poem's final self-deconstruction: the language of the poem is itself a cry, and hardly communicating clearly. Despite its apparent syntactic cohesion and clearly marked relationships within and across the stanzas, the poem can be said to lack coherence, in view of the grouping of the abstract nouns and the querying of language at the end. Earlier in *In Memoriam*, section 5 directly addresses the inadequacy of language as an expressive medium, finding that

> words, like Nature, half reveal
> And half conceal the Soul within

and that words convey significance 'in outline and no more.'

The unobtrusiveness of register-mixing in Tennyson's verse is effected by pervasive minor deviations from language norms which serve to separate his poetic discourse from common speech discourse. Section 54 has less deviation than most of the sections of *In Memoriam*, but nevertheless diverges significantly from the norm. The patterned anaphora of 'nothing/not one/not a/not a' is unusually rhetorical; 'hath' is an archaic poeticism; although the positioning of adjuncts in English is flexible, that of 'with vain desire' (line 10) ahead of its verb is less common than that of 'in vain' in line 9 – the two adjuncts are not grammatically parallel, but the repetition of 'vain' effectively points up the shifted position of the second phrase; 'or but' is a non-standard copula; 'know not anything' is either archaic, if a version of 'do not know anything', or strikingly emphatic, if a version of 'know nothing' – there is no way to decide which; and 'So runs my dream' inverts subject and verb. In this context of frequent grammatical deviations along the syntagmatic axis, register-deviations within the paradigmatic axis are not heavily foregrounded. A comparison with Browning's very different practice will be instructive here.

## Cultivated incongruity: Robert Browning (1812–89)

In earlier periods, incongruity was usually associated with comedy or satire; from the Romantic and Victorian periods on, this link is broken, and incongruity appears in non-satiric and non-comic contexts. Browning cultivates it extensively, though not always happily, and a later flaunting of incongruity carries over into twentieth-century literature. Browning employs a vast and diverse range of registers within a single poem, and, unlike Tennyson, makes no attempt to mask the transitions. This mixing of registers may help to account for the difficulty many readers feel in determining the tone of the speaker in particular poems. The loosening of congruence in Browning's monologues can be jarring, as when he combines elements from an archaic register to suggest that the speaker lives in time past, and a conversational register to suggest contemporaneity:

My sons, ye would not be my death? Go dig
The white-grape vineyard where the oil-press stood,
Drop water gently till the surface sinks,
And if ye find . . . Ah, God I know not, I! . . .
Bedded in store of rotten fig leaves soft,                    40
And corded up in a tight olive-frail,
Some lump, ah God, of *lapis lazuli*,
Big as a Jew's head cut off at the nape,
Blue as a vein o'er the Madonna's breast . . .
Sons, all have I bequeathed you, villas, all,                 45
That brave Frascati villa with its bath,
So, let the blue lump poise between my knees,
Like God the Father's globe on both his hands
Ye worship in the Jesu Church so gay,
For Gandolf shall not choose but see and burst!              50
Swift as a weaver's shuttle fleet our years:
Man goeth to the grave, and where is he?
Did I say basalt for my slab, sons? Black —
'Twas ever antique-black I meant! How else
Shall ye contrast my frieze to come beneath?                 55
The bas-relief in bronze ye promised me,
Those Pans and Nymphs ye wot of, and perchance
Some tripod, thyrsus, with a vase or so,
The Saviour at his sermon on the mount,
Saint Praxed in a glory, and one Pan                         60
Ready to twitch the Nymph's last garment off,
And Moses with the tables . . .

('The Bishop Orders His Tomb . . .')

The Bishop is speaking, and a number of speech-like features are included to convey the impression of a speaking voice: the exclamatory interruption of the line of thought in 39; the prominent use of questions and exclamations; colloquialisms such as 'a vase or so' (58), and 'twitch the last garment off' (61), which is both lexically and grammatically colloquial. On the other hand, intermingled with these, in places even overlapping them, are some archaic forms: the use of 'ye' throughout; the quasi-Biblical language of 51–2, but only marked as such by the archaic form 'goeth'; while the use of exclamation in 39 is speech-like, the syntax of 'I know not, I' is archaic; some lexical items – 'ye wot of', 'perchance' – are likewise obsolete well before the nineteenth century. Also contrasting with the colloquialism is the embedding of clauses in 40–1 following the interruption, so that there is quite a distance between the verb 'find' and its object 'some lump', and the use of the very specialized register of terms for the stones that the Bishop wants for his tomb.

The poem has a satiric effect, but this does not derive from the incongruities within the language, but rather from the double point of view, that of the Bishop himself, and that of the poet which invites judgement of the speaker. The distinction is made primarily by disparities in *content* which bring out the gap between the Bishop's religious position and actual worldliness. This is obvious in the materialistic and sexual rivalry with Gandolf, in the sons he should not have, and in his last desperate clutching at worldly possession. It is presented in more complex fashion in, for example, the jumbled components of the frieze the Bishop envisages, which juxtapose the sacred and the profane in such a way as to suggest that, for the speaker, all representations are empty signs – the female figures of 'Saint Praxed in a glory' and the about-to-be-denuded Nymph can coexist because of the Bishop's carnal incomprehension of anything beyond the material.

There is an equally revealing juxtaposition in the analogies found for the lapis lazuli, and within them a mark of the Bishop's complete inability to penetrate the surface of signs in 'Blue as a vein o'er the Madonna's breast'. Here his focus is on the beauty of an art-work, a feature which recalls traditions about the Madonna's beauty, but his reading of it is physical and sexual, apparently unaware that the Madonna's breasts are an intercessory symbol.[4] One of the most popular themes of Renaissance painting, the Madonna and Child is a revealing diachronic index to the nature and quality of religious thought. Browning's bishop fails miserably. But whereas the disparity between his status as a Bishop of the Christian Church and his un-Christian behaviour is functional, is indeed the basis of the poem, the incongruities of language do not seem to be contributing to it. In later poets like Hopkins and Dickinson, however, incongruities of language (especially disruptions in the syntax) seem to be more functional thematically, and are already so in contemporary novelists such as Thackeray.

## Thackeray: irony and paradigmatic choice in *Vanity Fair* (1847–8)

*Vanity Fair*, which began appearing two years after 'The Bishop Orders His Tomb', is also satire, of course, and so a reader might expect incongruity to be exploited, as it is in the following passage:

> Faithful to his plan of economy, the Captain dressed himself in his oldest and shabbiest uniform and epaulets, leaving the newest behind under his wife's (or it might be his widow's) guardianship. And this famous dandy of 5
> Windsor and Hyde Park went off on his campaign with a kit as modest as that of a sergeant, and with something like a prayer on his lips for the woman he was leaving. He took her up from the ground, and held her in his arms for a minute, tight pressed against his strong 10
> beating heart. His face was purple and his eyes dim, as he put her down and left her. He rode by his General's side, and smoked his cigar in silence as they hastened after the troops of the General's brigade, which preceded them; and it was not until they were some 15
> miles on their way that he left off twirling his mustachio and broke silence.
>
> And Rebecca, as we have said, wisely determined not to give way to unavailing sentimentality on her husband's departure. She waved him an adieu from the 20
> window, and stood there for a moment looking out after he was gone. The cathedral towers and the full gables of the quaint old houses were just beginning to blush in the sunrise. There had been no rest for her that night. She was still in her pretty ball dress, her fair hair hanging 30
> somewhat out of curl on her neck, and the circles round her eyes dark with watching. 'What a fright I seem,' she said, examining herself in the glass, 'and how pale this pink makes one look!' So she divested herself of this pink raiment; in doing which a note fell out from her 35
> corsage, which she picked up with a smile, and locked

into her dressing box. And then she put her bouquet of
the ball into a glass of water, and went to bed, and slept
very comfortably.

The town was quite quiet when she woke up at ten   40
o'clock, and partook of coffee, very requisite and
comforting after the exhaustion and grief of the morning's occurrences.

(Ch. XXX)

The narrative strategy is quite different from Browning's, in that
Thackeray uses a rather obtrusive narrator to present the
characters and to give point to the primary ironic gap, that
between the behaviour of each of the characters in his or her
particular situation and notions of a more usual or more apt
behaviour. Becky is subject to a harsher judgement than
Rawdon; he may be ridiculous, but she is callous, and simple
text-order determines that her behaviour will seem all the worse
after the description of his.

Further, the verbal irony which evinces these judgements,
while the same in kind in each paragraph, differs in degree.
That is, the irony mainly consists of inappropriate paradigmatic
choices, but with differing degrees of disparity. The two places
where the narrator most directly intervenes illustrate the
difference. In the second sentence (line 5 ff.), the proximate
deictic 'this' signals the narrator's overt entrance into the
discourse. The contrast between past and present, consumption
and economy, game and earnest – all encapsulated within the
semantic balance of 'famous dandy of Windsor . . . kit as
modest' – creates a favourable impression; the term 'dandy',
true of Rawdon but inappropriate to his present circumstances,
has been carefully distanced. And when the narrator moves to
the non-visual with the phrase, 'something like a prayer . . .',
the qualification suggests an ironic comment on Rawdon's
general unfamiliarity with prayer, but doesn't prevent his real
emotional state from being indicated.

At the narrator's second overt entrance, at the beginning of
the second paragraph, the crucial determinant of tone is the
phrase 'unavailing sentimentality'; it has already been signalled
that Rawdon could be going to his death, and this choice of
signifiers strongly evokes an awareness of those *not* chosen,
such as 'helpless grief', made all the more evident when 'grief'
does appear at the end of the episode, but by then rendered

virtually anasemic. These ironic choices retrospectively cause 'wisely' to undergo marked semantic drift; what kind of wisdom is this, and from whose point of view? The reminder of the narrator's presence is also a reminder of the need to pass judgement, heavy-handed though the whole process might be.

Inappropriate paradigmatic choices also occur in the first paragraph, notably in the quasi-romantic touches: in 'pressed against his strong beating heart', the hesitation as to whether 'strong' modifies 'beating' or 'heart' is enough to foreground the innate absurdity of the phrase; and in 'His face was *purple* and his *eyes dim*', where perhaps paradigmatic choices such as 'flushed' and 'misted' would convey the emotion less obtrusively (and with less similarity to the effects of alcoholic excess), there is perhaps an arch reference to the 'purple' quality of the prose at this point. Rawdon is clumsy, and perhaps a little melodramatic, but nevertheless what seems an external description still invites narratee (and reader) to perceive the genuine love and sacrifice that he demonstrates beneath his physical distress. As with the Browning, but through different methods, two views of the character emerge; but whereas Browning directly elicits a judgement on the Bishop, Thackeray's text sets Rawdon and Becky up for comparative judgement.

In the second paragraph Becky's physical point of view is twice presented, when she looks out the window and in the mirror. She sees herself, and thinks only of herself, but in the third sentence (line 22 ff.) the narratee, who looks with her, seeing perhaps with different eyes, sees the symbolic level whereby it ought to be Becky, not the towers and gables, that blushes. Thackeray's use of incongruity to produce such effects is more functional than Browning's less carefully directed incongruities, though it is sometimes heavy-handed. A comparison back to the irony of Jane Austen would bring this out quite clearly.

The grammatical and syntactic structures out of which Thackeray's syntagmatic axis is constructed are predominantly simple co-ordinations. A conversational style is further promoted by ellipsis of non-essential function words: a verb in the first clause; a relative in 'the woman [ ] he was leaving'; a verb from each of the clauses loosely attached to 'She was still in her pretty ball dress'. A high frequency of (non-finite) participial clauses attached to principal clauses overlaps with this tendency. The prose is most formal in the use of syllepsis in 'went off . . .

with a kit . . ., and with something like a prayer', but the linking
of these two items imparts a comic function to the device.

## The syntagmatic axis and the mental processes of fictional characters

Thackeray's handling of the syntagmatic axis is symptomatic of
the way Victorian fiction accretes information, and is, at least
partly, a legacy of mid-nineteenth-century realism. It characterizes much of George Eliot's writing, even after she had
abandoned the mode of simple inductive realism,[5] and is the
staple of most of the period's 'popular' novelists. As illustration,
we will consider first a small extract from *Middlemarch*, and
then one from Rhoda Broughton's *Belinda* (1883).

GEORGE ELIOT'S *MIDDLEMARCH* (1871–2)

When she entered the Yew-Tree Walk she [Dorothea]
could not see her husband; but the walk had bends, and
she went, expecting to catch sight of his figure wrapped
in a blue cloak, which, with a warm velvet cap, was his
outer garment on chill days for the garden. It occurred      5
to her that he might be resting in the summer-house,
towards which the path diverged a little. Turning the
angle, she could see him seated on the bench, close to a
stone table. His arms were resting on the table, and his
brow was bowed down on them, the blue cloak being      10
dragged forward and screening his face on each side.
'He exhausted himself last night,' Dorothea said to
herself, thinking at first that he was asleep, and that the
summer-house was too damp a place to rest in. But then
she remembered that of late she had seen him take that      15
attitude when she was reading to him, as if he found it
easier than any other; and that he would sometimes
speak, as well as listen, with his face down in that way.
She went into the summer-house and said, 'I am come,
Edward; I am ready.'      20
He took no notice, and she thought that he must be
fast asleep. She laid her hand on his shoulder, and
repeated, 'I am ready!' Still he was motionless; and with
a sudden confused fear, she leaned down to him, took

off his velvet cap, and leaned her cheek close to his   25
head, crying in a distressed tone,

   'Wake, dear, wake! Listen to me. I am come to
answer.'

   But Dorothea never gave her answer.

(Book V, Ch. 48)

The segment is presented from a restricted perspective, in that until line 24 everything is mediated through Dorothea's seeing and thinking; this is perhaps most obvious in line 23, where 'He took no notice . . .' represents Dorothea's limited perception and withholds from narratee and reader the information that Casaubon is dead, but is also more widely emphasized by the strings of appropriate terms:

| *Sight* | *Conception* |
|---|---|
| could not see (2) | it occurred to her (5–6) |
| expecting to catch sight (3) | said to herself, thinking (12–13) |
| she could see (8) | (she remembered (15)) |
| screening his face (11) | she thought (21) |
| (had seen (16–17)) | |

Events and perceptions occurring within the garden and summer house are set out in chronological order, interrupted only by the descriptions of Casaubon's habitual dress and recent postural habit. The grammar and syntax reinforce this presentation. Clauses are linked mainly by co-ordination, with most subordinations being of the simplest kind, that is, temporals and relatives. Non-finite, present participial clauses express simultaneous action ('Turning . . . she could see' (7–8); 'leaned her cheek . . . crying' (25–6)) or details seen simultaneously ('the blue cloak being dragged forward and screening . . .' (10–11)). The most complicated syntax is in lines 15–18, where 'she remembered' is followed by two dependent noun-clauses, each of which enfolds additional clauses – the first an infinitive clause, then a temporal, then a comparison; the second an embedded co-ordinate clause. But the information contained in all these clauses is still presented in the order of chronological perception – the first noun-clause recalls the pose, its recent origin, then the manner, and the second recalls an associated, occasional action.

   Different effects to be gained from linking clauses by co-ordination and/or parataxis, and building through suspense towards a climax, can be seen in a comparison of lines 23–9 with lines 37–9 of the Thackeray: 'And then she put her bouquet of the ball into a glass of water, and went to bed, and slept very comfortably.' This lists a banal and commonplace sequence of actions, but the larger ironic context, especially the strong presence of the narrator's voice, imbues the sentence, and especially the intensifier + modifier 'very comfortably', with a satiric effect. The Eliot also concentrates the tenor of the larger context into the smaller sequence, but transforms it into a surprise. The sudden shift in presentation of the scene from Dorothea's visual/conceptual stance to the external-narrator-stance contributes to this effect, and also to the way in which all that has preceded the revelation must now be retroactively reinterpreted. Paradigmatic choices also play a major part in creating these effects. The extract doesn't make very heavy use of modifiers, except for three small but vital sets which have as their nodes associations with *comfort*, *discomfort* (with over-tones of death), and *emotional upset*:

| 1 Comfort | 2 Discomfort | 3 Emotional upset |
|---|---|---|
| blue (4) | chill (5) | sudden confused (24) |
| warm (4) | stone (9) | distressed (26) |
| velvet (4) | damp (14) | |
| blue (10) | motionless (23) | |
| velvet (25) | | |

Our inclusion of 'motionless' in Set 2 may seem surprising, since it is the odd term in the set, but the retroactive effect reconstitutes the terms into this grouping.

The members of Set 1 and the first three of Set 2 perform two main functions. First, they impart verisimilitude to the scene; they are details which Dorothea can be assumed to know, and are thus concrete details included for the reader's benefit. As such, they reflect the Victorian habit of presenting physical detail for its own sake, whether for sensory effect or to represent 'reality'.

Secondly, though, they function as devices of suspense: initially, the signing function of the 'figure wrapped in a blue cloak' is to disclose to Dorothea Casaubon's whereabouts, but even as it does this it conceals his state; the velvet cap is 'warm' and protects against 'chill', and its removal discloses the coldness of death; the threats to Casaubon's well-being – 'chill, stone, damp' – become transformed into emblems of death. So what Eliot has done is to use some of the methods of inductive realism but to exploit at the same time the limitation inherent in it if a tight relationship between signifier and signified is too complacently assumed.

## BROUGHTON'S *BELINDA* (1883)

Eliot's writing is much subtler than Broughton's, which as well as demonstrating some general tendencies exemplifies some major defects in Victorian female writing. R. C. Terry has remarked that the effective antecedents of the 'sensation' novels which began appearing in the 1860s are the Gothic novel and the novels of the Brontës (1983, 8). The influences are apparent even in such relatively restrained texts as *Belinda*. In the following extract, which is laying the ground for the sentimental and melodramatic ending germane to Broughton's chosen genre, syntagmatic and paradigmatic selections are made not only to create a sense of excitement but to blend together the perceptions of the narrator, narratee, and character. Broughton avoids the kind of distancing achieved by Eliot's clearer distinction between character's and narrator's perceptions. As Showalter has remarked, mid-Victorian women novelists 'made a powerful appeal to the female audience by subverting the traditions of feminine fiction to suit their own imaginative impulses, by expressing a wide range of suppressed female emotions, and by tapping and satisfying fantasies of protest and escape' (1982, 159). To achieve these ends, needless to say, attention to discourse is essential.

The context of the extract is that Belinda has just secretly left her husband and is travelling to meet David Rivers, the man with whom she is planning to live:

> The morning is lovely, with morning's fresh look of newness, as if the ancient hills had but just been turned out of their Maker's workshop. Lapis-blue is the lake, as a summer lake should be; and with its little islands laughing in summer forest-green upon its radiant lap.      5
> Over one mountain shoulder, indeed, a few slight cloud-shadows, thrown light as gauzy scarves, still lie. But on his brother's granite knees there is strong resolute sunshine, and in their ravines shadows cut hard and black.      10

Oh, cruel world! Again you are jeering her with your
beauty! Her eyes roll wildly round, and thought after
thought courses with mad rapidity through her head.
Little irrelevant incidents out of far-away childhood,
fragments of forgotten books, texts of scripture. 'I will     15
look unto the hills from whence cometh my help!' That
is what teases her most. And yet what applicability is
there in it to her? Does any help come from the hills to
her? Beneath the trees that lip the lake, and through
whose leafage come ever glimpses of its dazzling gaiety,     20
the sweet road winds.

(*Belinda*, Period 4, Ch. 6)

The choice of third-person present singular in which to narrate
this novel allows Broughton to slip continually between narrator
commentary and the character's free indirect thought. In
contrast to Eliot's method, there is no clear indication of who
sees what in the first paragraph – or at least of who formulates
the language in which the scene is described. The moral
pressures which weigh upon Belinda are in this way presented
more subtly than are the more direct attempts at representing
emotion, where such phrases as 'roll wildly' (12) and 'mad
rapidity' (13) are the clichés of mental breakdown. Broughton
generally depends heavily on modifiers when portraying
passion, but the habit too often results in what Terry has
described as 'throbbing prose' (1983, 111). Between the
phrases just cited, though, comes the 'thought after thought'
which signals the slipping in point of view; as the fragments of
memory become more specific in focus they appear more as a
rendering of indirect thought, culminating in the questions
(18–19).

This method of opening access to a character's mind is
another kind of departure from inductive realism; it is typical of
Broughton's style, and strongly invites reader empathy. The
passion expressed in the extract is conveyed as much by
syntagmatic ordering and by tropes as by lexis: the short
exclamatory sentences (a legacy of Romantic style), the
co-ordinate or paratactic structure of the longer ones, the
frequent ellipsis of verbs, and the use of minor inversions like
'Lapis-blue is the lake' (a common trick of Broughton's style),
combine to convey excitement and strained emotion.

Like Eliot, Broughton also demands retroactive rereading: the half-quotation from Psalm 121 (15–16) instils a new meaning into the previously observed scene. There is a suggestion of femininity in the observing consciousness, as lake, islands, and mountains are figured as a family group, the 'little' islands being children in their mother's 'lap', with the masculine mountains behind. But the peaceful domesticity implied by this metaphor, denied to Belinda in her life with her dessicated old husband, and not possible in the life of a 'fallen woman' which she envisages as her future, exists only as a deconstructed possibility. There is an ominous shift between the first mountain, which is not at first obviously masculine (the 'gauzy scarves' suggest otherwise), to the threatening masculinity of 'his brother', described in epithets denoting hardness and strength. The 'Maker's workshop' cliché, reinforced by 'thrown' (7), has shifted its tenor by the end of the paragraph, and further still by the end of the extract, to imply the presence of a patriarchal control which creates beauty in the world and refuses to allow it to blossom in the life of a woman.

The drift here from the received Christian view of the universe to a more sceptical, post-Darwinian, more feminist view is projected hypersyntagmatically in the moral ambiguity of the novel's ending. Having surrendered to the pull of morality and turned back, Belinda is rewarded by finding that her husband had conveniently died that morning without discovering the farewell letter she had left for him to find.

As with the Gothic style which is its antecedent, this kind of writing requires a passive reader, and the more resisting reader might well find unintentional humour in such features as the syntagmatic ordering of detail in lines 7–10, rather than a deliberated progression. More importantly, such extreme alternation between covert narration with focalization through a character's perceptions (as in the presentation of scene in lines 1–10) and overt narration (as in line 11 ff.) can prompt the reader to focus upon the *narrator's* attitudes and emotions. We have already pointed to such an effect with Thackeray's ironic narrator and his sense of collusion with a mentally alert reader. In the present example, though, the shift in modes of narration may rather lead to an amused reaction against the narrator's hyperbolic and over-emotive use of the conventional Romantic strategy of placing a figure in an anthropomorphic landscape. A useful comparison could be drawn here with an obvious intertext, the famous stolen boat episode in Wordsworth's *The*

*Prelude*, I.357–400. In Broughton, the relationship between figure and landscape is located in the narrator's mind, and Belinda's own thoughts and perceptions, when overtly present in the second paragraph, are focused on memories and texts rather than on her awareness of and response to the world's beauty. This focus becomes more problematic still if a reader chooses to interpret the psalm reference as misquotation of one of the period's best-known 'texts of scripture', in which case attention to Belinda's state of mind may become more judgemental than empathetic.

To a non-passive reader, then, problems of textuality may obstruct reception of the narratorial attitude being conveyed towards the protagonist and the narrator's overt sympathy with her. The discourse may not overtly prompt uncooperative reader response to perceive its discrepant aspects, just as Ann Radcliffe's text does not, but it does not prevent such a response from one who, as happens in Richardson's *Pamela*, refuses to empathize with and be manipulated by the narrator.

## The loosening of cohesion in poetry

The basis of all we have said so far about nineteenth-century literature rests in the diachronic development of the simpler but looser syntagmatic line. This continues throughout the Victorian period, to become the staple of much twentieth-century fiction, especially fiction remaining within the traditions of realism. But it is also subject to resistance and extension – resistance in the elaborated prose of Henry James, and extension in writers like Emily Dickinson and Hopkins, who make the loosening of cohesion the basis of their poetry. There are already precedents in Browning for disruption of the hypersyntagmatic axis, as Gerhard Joseph implicitly recognizes in his comments on 'frame-within-a-frame recessiveness' in the dramatic monologues (1985, 404–5), but these other poets largely discard the narrative element of Victorian poetry and disrupt smaller syntagmatic units.

DICKINSON (1830–86)

The unusual capitalization and punctuation practices employed by Dickinson destabilize the syntagmatic axis, problematizing the relationships of word to word and of line to line. The reader proceeds by decoding grammatical puzzles and pondering the significance, in the paradigmatic axis, of abstractions which, unusually freed of constraints from the syntagmatic axis, may evoke a wide penumbra of associations. A convenient example is poem 435, which, while it displays the tendencies we are concerned with, is not particularly difficult, and does not complicate signifier–signified relationships with details of figurative language. The overall effect of the poem is figurative, however, and when read alongside other Dickinson poems dealing with restraint and confinement – especially, for example, poems such as 'They shut me up in Prose' (613) – 'Much madness . . .' emerges more clearly as an analysis of society's repressive response to the unconventional woman poet (McNeil, 1986, 16; Mossberg, 1982, ch. 6):

> Much Madness is divinest Sense –
> To a discerning Eye –
> Much Sense – the starkest Madness –
> 'Tis the Majority    4
> In this, as All, prevail –
> Assent – and you are sane –
> Demur – you're straightway dangerous –
> And handled with a Chain –    8

Recognizing, before Freud, that sanity is a relative, not an absolute, condition, and is defined by the degree of conformity to social norms, Dickinson sets out here to break down the conventional opposition of madness and sanity and the hegemony of the social majority in determining such differences. Her opening proposition – 'Much Madness is divinest Sense' – begins to do this in three ways. First, by opposing the term 'Madness' to 'Sense', rather than to 'Sanity', it becomes subject to semantic drift within the sets:

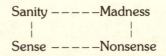

and so a stable signification is denied. Later, the second quatrain adds new pairs to interact with the original sets:

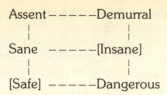

The opposition of 'sane' and 'dangerous' works in the same way as the opposition in line 1, but by now the arbitrary cultural convention which imposes a link between signifier and signified has become very clear: these new pairs only act as glosses on the original pairs as a form of social control.

Secondly, the opening proposition attacks the principle of opposition by asserting the identity of the opposed terms: madness *is* sense. Thirdly, the modifiers set against each other a relative, 'much', and a superlative conjuring the greatest wisdom imaginable, 'divinest', thus simultaneously asserting the wisdom of madness and rendering the assertion itself relative, not absolute. That the role of the modifiers is crucial becomes even more apparent when the third line seems to repeat the process, but reverses the order of the nouns, elides the verb, and substitutes another superlative (the second phrase being now a variant of the cliché 'stark madness'). The unbalancing modifiers prevent the propositions from becoming the playful paradox, 'Madness is Sense, Sense Madness', on the 'Beauty is Truth, Truth Beauty' model (taken up in Poem 449). In Dickinson, *some* of each is an extreme of the other, but then the problem immediately arises that the usual way of identifying which is which is social consensus.

Because the verse-line acts here as a syntagmatic unit, the process of unbalancing continues as the rhyme scheme indicates a quatrain structure (though the off-rhyme 'Eye/Majority' in itself also defies tidy structure), but the only run-on line is line 4, as lines 4–5 comprise a syntactic unit. Further, grammatical relationships within this unit do not completely control signification, since the antecedent of 'All' could be 'this' (thus assuming the ellipsis 'as [in] All') or (perhaps less likely) 'Majority', that is, the Majority acting as the Whole. This is only a small indeterminacy, but is symptomatic of a pervasive freeing of context which is then apt to generate semantic drift. A different kind of syntagmatic disruption is the poem's final disclosure; that is, the poem discloses the punishment for rebellion, but refuses poetic closure. The syntagmatic axis, and the conflict, extend forwards.

Such a strategy was to become familiar in twentieth-century poetry, as were many of the grammatical disruptions to which Dickinson has recourse: unconventional uses of pronouns; verbs unmarked for number or tense; changes of word-class (adjective as adverb, for example, or noun as adjective).[6] As with more recent poets, the disruption of normal structures is a challenge to, even subversion of, conventional wisdom and hierarchies; expectations are overthrown 'in order to set up and illustrate the new, less restrictive equilibrium of meaning that is the point of the poem' (C. Miller, 1983, 145).

## HOPKINS (1844–89) AND HARDY (1840–1928)

Other poets sharing an impulse to disrupt and subvert language, though very different from one another, are Hopkins and Hardy. Like Dickinson, Hopkins was little published in his lifetime, so his influence has been diachronically displaced. Hardy's impact was principally on the lexicon of poetry; late Victorians such as Arnold seem to have been moving towards a restricted poetic lexicon, which these two poets broaden again, creating possibilities to be picked up in modern poetry after the rather enervating impact of the Pre-Raphaelites. Hopkins's contortions of word-order, on the other hand, while inherently an obvious reaction against contemporary Victorian writing, must (like those of Dylan Thomas) in a diachronic perspective be regarded as idiosyncratic. The lexicon of both poets is extended by dialectal words, lexical archaisms, back formations, word-class shift, and new compounds. The differences between them are just as important, and can be seen in the following extracts. First, the octet of Hopkins's 'As Kingfishers catch fire':

As kingfishers catch fire, dragonflies draw flame;
   As tumbled over rim in roundy wells
   Stones ring; like each tucked string tells, each hung bell's
Bow swung finds tongue to fling out broad its name;    4
Each mortal thing does one thing and the same:
   Deals out that being indoors each one dwells;
   Selves – goes itself; myself it speaks and spells,
Crying *What I do is me: for that I came.*    8

Secondly, the first two stanzas of Hardy's 'Neutral Tones':

We stood by a pond that winter day,
And the sun was white, as though chidden of God,
And a few leaves lay on the starving sod;
   – They had fallen from an ash, and were gray.     4

Your eyes on me were as eyes that rove
Over tedious riddles of years ago;
And some words played between us to and fro
   On which lost the more by our love.     8

Both poems are typically Victorian in the way they handle the syntagmatic axis. Despite obvious grammatical differences stemming from compression and inversion, Hopkins's syntagm is not very dissimilar to Tennyson's, in as much as intensity is achieved by accumulating variations around an initial concept – though not even Tennyson says the same thing ten times in ten different ways as Hopkins does here. A glance through almost any of Hopkins's poems will confirm that this is a general characteristic. Hardy's syntagm is propelled by the narrative, though lines 3–4 obviously accumulate related bits of data. The language of both poems also portrays the natural world as anthropomorphic. Hopkins's notion of immanence is a facet of pre-Darwinian theology; Hardy's analogy between decay in Nature and the end of a love relationship, even though it does reflect Hardy's post-Darwinian evolutionary pessimism in the way the realms of Nature and humans follow the same pattern, still implicitly personifies – the 'chidden' sun is white, presumably, with fear, and the continuant 'starving' denotes more than 'barren'. Ruskin's *caveat* has not yet sunk home.[7]

The two extracts can be considered in the light of our earlier remark that Tennyson assimilated potentially deviant elements with little strain because he had separated his discourse from speech norms by means of continual minor deviations. Hopkins increases the width of the separation; Hardy decreases it. Hardy's co-ordinated clauses have a structure and word-order that scarcely depart from speech norms, so that the sudden deviation of 'On which lost the more by our love' is heavily foregrounded. When examined, though, the contortion seems both excessive for the line's function and curiously difficult to unravel, since either 'on' or 'by' must be redundant (presuming the sense is '[words] on/by which our love lost the more' – the problem apparently arises from the attempt to use the idiom 'the more by' intransitively). It is a simple point, but readers readily accept almost any level of deviation once it is perceived as the normal idiom sustained for a poem, or by a poet. Gross breaches of this idiom prove discordant. So, while Hardy is moving towards the closer fit of poetic and speech word-order characteristic of much twentieth-century poetry, departures from it will seem solecistic.

Thus Hopkins surprises less, because on the one hand the reader expects to find all kinds of deviant language in Hopkins, and on the other hand it appears as constantly as in Tennyson. A line such as 6, which is compacted by ellipsis — of the pronominal subject of the principal clause ('[it] deals') and of the relative heading the subordinate clause ('[which] . . . dwells') — which inverts the order of verb and complement ('dwells indoors each one'), and which boldly creates a metaphor by substituting an adverb, 'indoors', for the preposition 'within', is nevertheless normal for a discourse which continually omits minor parts of speech, which invents new forms by affixing ('roundy') and new verbs by back-formation ('selves'), which employs dialectisms (*tuck* 'to touch; to strike a drum'), and which violates deep structure by paradigmatic substitution of a signifier abnormal in the context ('broad', instead of 'wide').

All of these innovatory techniques are also to be found in Hardy's verse, though not all at once. In the extract from 'Neutral Tones' the only variations that are made within the paradigmatic axis are the poetic/archaic 'chidden of' and the extension of 'starving' to include also the archaic/dialect signified 'suffering cold'. But Hardy's deviations, whether syntagmatic or paradigmatic, scarcely detract from the overall ordinariness of the language which makes him an important transition figure into the twentieth century.

## The otherness of the other

As a final comment on the transition from the nineteenth century to the twentieth, we will consider a poem published in 1923, Wallace Stevens's 'The Snow Man'. The separation of adjective and noun in the title, as distinct from the usual compound forms 'snowman, snow-man', emphasizes the playing off of animate against inanimate, and of self against other, which is the poem's theme:

*The Snow Man*

One must have a mind of winter
To regard the frost and boughs
Of the pine-trees crusted with snow;

And have been cold a long time
To behold the junipers shagged with ice,                          5
The spruces rough in the distant glitter

Of the January sun; and not to think
Of any misery in the sound of the wind,
In the sound of a few leaves,

Which is the sound of the land                                    10
Full of the same wind
That is blowing in the same bare place

For the listener, who listens in the snow,
And, nothing himself, beholds
Nothing that is not there and the nothing that is.                15

The poem consists of one highly cohesive sentence, but,
despite the complexity this might entail, the coextensiveness of
speech and verse discourse is now complete. The first six and a
half lines consist of two co-ordinate sentences, linked by
parallelism, ellipsis, and congruent lexical sets (regard/behold;
frost/snow/ice; pine-trees/junipers/spruces:

| One must have | a mind . . . to regard . . . | frost . . . | pine-trees |
| | | snow | |
| [one must] have been cold . . . to behold . . . | ice . . . | junipers |
| | | | spruces |

Undermining this pattern and order, however, is the uncertain
meaning of the unusual phrase 'a mind of winter'; it is formed
on the analogy of such phrases as 'heart of gold', 'mind of
steel', but violates the pattern by substituting the temporal for a
concrete object. Signification thus remains suspended until the
negative of line 7; in the meantime, the poem seems to be
within the tradition of realistic nature poetry, with its precise
presentations of scenic detail. That someone, carefully unspecified by the indefinite 'one', is *seeing* these details ('regard/
behold') is a further allusion to the tradition. The pivotal
negative governs the result of seeing: 'not to think of any

misery' introduces a brief moment of Romantic anthropomorphism, analogous to that we saw in 'Neutral Tones', except that Stevens focuses on the mental process whereby the sound of the wind and the leaves comes to signify misery. In lines 10–12 he plays this arbitrary attachment of sign to referent against the cohesive devices of repetition and hypotaxis, in order to shift the signifieds of 'sound' and 'wind' in preparation for placing the mindless listener in opposition to the mindful beholder. The result of this dialectic is to disanthropomorphize the landscape, seeing it as neither Hardy's analogy with human feeling – 'beholds/Nothing that is not there' – nor Hopkins's significant immanence – 'beholds . . .the nothing that is'. Victorian thought and poetics have here been transformed into a discourse powerful and new.[8]

## Notes and further reading

1   For a brief account of the situation see Showalter (1982), Chapter 1, and especially pp. 24–9.
2   Browning, of the poets, perhaps comes most readily to mind here. See Nichols (1983); Gibson (1981) examines the importance of 'the world's materials' and 'fact' in Browning's poetic. Hopkins is a later exponent of the grotesque. It is an obvious feature of Dickens's fiction.
3   For a discussion of this example within the context of Victorian attitudes to language, see Scott (1980, 376), and, more generally, Ruthven (1969, 9–37).
4   See Barbara G. Lane, *The Altar and the Altarpiece* (New York: Harper & Row, 1984), 5–8: Figure 5 (p. 7) reproduces a fifteenth-century Italian miniature in which on either side of God the Father kneel Christ and Mary, he touching the wound in his side, she touching her naked right breast. Both, of course, are intercessory symbols.
5   Eliot's 'realism' has been much discussed. See especially Knoepflmacher (1968), Gallagher (1980) and McGowan (1980).
6   For detailed discussion of Dickinson's disruptive devices, see Porter (1966), Ch. 7; a more recent study, mainly from a feminist perspective, is C. Miller (1983).
7   According to Langbaum (1970, 101–26), poetry which functions by opposing the pathetic fallacy is not found before Wallace Stevens and Marianne Moore.

8 Further reading: Beer (1983), Langbaum (1970) and Showalter (1982) are significant background studies; Connor's study of Dickens (1985), grounded in varieties of structuralism, post-structuralism and Marxism, offers a useful range of approaches to fiction of this period.

# Exercises

1 What are the implications for the role of the reader stemming from the growing range of types of narratorial intrusion and manipulation in late Romantic and Victorian prose fiction? Consider examples of first and third person narration (e.g., in Mary Shelley, Charlotte Brontë, Hawthorne, Poe, Dickens, Thackeray, Trollope, George Eliot, Hardy, Melville, James) which demonstrate something of the range, and analyse how the triads of textuality are manipulated to bring out the impact of the narratorial presence. Then go on to consider the narratee/reader relationship in each case.

2 How are varying presuppositions about the Self's relationship with external stimuli (natural and man-made) and with Other encoded in the language of nineteenth-century literary texts? Find examples in prose and verse (e.g. the novelists already suggested, and others; poets such as Tennyson, Browning, Dickinson, Whitman, Arnold, Hopkins, Hardy), which show something of the range of variants. Look specifically at instances where women writers use their language to encode a female viewpoint.

3 Compare and contrast the following passages from Walpole's *Castle of Otranto*, Ch. 1, from Austen's *Northanger Abbey*, Ch. 20, from Peacock's *Nightmare Abbey*, Ch. 1, and from Emily Brontë's *Wuthering Heights*, Ch. 1, to bring out the differences in the presentation of point of view as it relates to atmosphere, reason/emotion/sensory appeal, and symbolism:

(i) The lower part of the castle was hollowed into several intricate cloisters; and it was not easy for one under so much anxiety to find the door that opened into the cavern. An awful silence reigned throughout those subterraneous regions, except now and then some blasts of wind that shook the doors she had passed, and which, grating on the rusty hinges, were re-echoed through that long labyrinth of darkness.

(ii) As they drew near the end of their journey, her impatience for a sight of the Abbey — for some time suspended by his conversation on subjects very different — returned in full force, and every bend in the road was expected, with solemn awe, to afford a glimpse of its massy walls of gray stone, rising amidst a grove of ancient oaks, with the last beams of the sun playing in beautiful splendour on its high Gothic windows. But so low did the building stand that she found herself passing through the great gates of the lodge, into the very grounds of Northanger, without having discerned even an antique chimney.

(iii) The tower which Scythrop inhabited stood at the south-eastern angle of the Abbey; and, on the southern side, the foot of the tower opened on a terrace, which was called the garden, though nothing grew on it but ivy, and a few amphibious weeds. The south-western tower, which was ruinous and full of owls, might, with equal propriety, have been called the aviary. This terrace or garden, or terrace-garden, or garden-terrace (the reader may name it *ad libitum*), took in an oblique view of the open sea, and fronted a long tract of level sea-coast, and a fine monotony of fens and windmills.

(iv) Wuthering Heights is the name of Mr. Heathcliff's dwelling. 'Wuthering' being a significant provincial adjective, descriptive of the atmospheric tumult to which its station is exposed in stormy weather. Pure, bracing ventilation they must have up there at all times, indeed: one may guess the power of the north wind blowing over the edge, by the excessive slant of a few stunted firs at the end of the house; and by a range of gaunt thorns all stretching their limbs one way, as if craving alms of the sun. Happily, the architect had foresight to build it strong: the narrow windows are deeply set in the wall, and the corners defended with large jutting stones.

4 Compare and contrast how the cohesion/congruence/
  coherence triad functions in Tennyson's 'Morte D'Arthur',
  36–79, and in Browning's 'Fra Lippo Lippi', 323–59. What
  part is played by the narrative line in influencing reader
  participation in each?

5 Compare and contrast Keats's 'Ode on Melancholy',
  Tennyson's *In Memoriam*, section 56, Dickinson's poem 510
  ('It was not Death'), and Hopkins's 'Carrion Comfort' to
  bring out how the interaction of the syntagm, the paradigm
  and the signifier/signified destabilizes the signification of
  meaning. Which aspects of the triads of textuality carry most
  weight in each poem?

6 Compare and contrast Whitman's 'On the Beach at Night',
  Arnold's 'Dover Beach', and the following passage from
  Dickens' *David Copperfield*, Ch. 55, to show the extent to
  which the anthropomorphizing of nature is presupposed by
  the language use:

> Coming near the beach I saw, not only boatmen, but half
> the people of the town, lurking behind the buildings;
> some now and then braving the fury of the storm to look
> away to sea, and blown sheer out of their course in trying
> to get zigzag back.
> Joining these groups, I found bewailing women, whose
> husbands were away in herring or oyster boats, which
> there was too much reason to think might have foundered
> before they could run in anywhere for safety. Grizzled old
> sailors were among the people, shaking their heads as
> they looked from water to sky, and muttering to one
> another; shipowners, excited and uneasy; children huddling
> together, and peering into older faces; even stout
> mariners, disturbed and anxious, levelling their glasses at
> the sea from behind places of shelter, as if they were
> surveying an enemy.
> The tremendous sea itself, when I could find sufficient
> pause to look at it, in the agitation of the blinding wind,
> the flying stones and sand, and the awful noise,
> confounded me. As the high watery walls came rolling in,
> and, at their highest, tumbled into surf, they looked as if
> the least would engulf the town. As the receding wave

swept back with a hoarse roar, it seemed to scoop out deep caves in the beach, as if its purpose were to undermine the earth. When some white-headed billows thundered on, and dashed themselves to pieces before they reached the land, every fragment of the late whole seemed possessed by the full might of its wrath, rushing to be gathered to the composition of another monster. Undulating hills were changed to valleys, undulating valleys (with a solitary storm-bird sometimes skimming through them) were lifted up to hills; masses of water shivered and shook the beach with a booming sound; every shape tumultuously rolled on, as soon as made, to change its shape and place, and beat another shape and place away; the ideal shore on the horizon, with its towers and buildings, rose and fell; the clouds flew fast and thick; I seemed to see a rending and upheaving of all nature.

# 5 The twentieth century: struggles with the word

Man has loved nature too much.
It is time to love man. And woman.

And the works of each. We must hurry
While the colours last,

As emptiness and redundancy
Approach head-on like trucks.

(John Ash, 'In the Street', 1–6)

## Rethinking the syntagm and paradigm relationship

As our overview of the history of literature has shown, period styles are determined by the kinds of syntagmatic and paradigmatic choices that prevail at any synchronic moment. The twentieth century has been characterized by an unusual self-consciousness about the process of choice, and in literature written during the earlier part of the century this is evident both in extensions of previous trends and in reactions against them.

It is a twentieth-century notion that language determines what can be written. Previously, writers have generally believed that language is the servant of art, and that if it proves inadequate there are strategies of augmentation – lexical, grammatical, figurative – that can correct the deficiency. But much of the writing in our century has sought to extend the range of syntagmatic/paradigmatic options with the object of subverting the axes, of escaping their tyranny. The effect of this may be more apparent as it bears upon the syntagmatic axis, but it also involves a renewed tendency in this century to push out the boundaries of what may be the acceptable range of choice for the paradigmatic slots. As F. W. Bateson has pointed out (1973, 76–83), Victorian poetry had developed a kind of semantic vagueness, a split between the language of the heart and the language of the head, with the two languages rarely seeming to come together; but by the end of the nineteenth century, in writers such as Hardy, there emerges a movement back on the one hand towards a precision in the use of language, and on the other towards a language of poetry which is again coextensive with the language within which it occurs, so that any kind of language becomes possible for use in poetry. The language of poetry once again becomes highly denotative, in an ongoing reaction particularly against, for instance, the Pre-Raphaelite poets, such as the Rossettis and Swinburne, who had cultivated a language which was very highly connotative.

Poetry begins to aspire to a language which is simple and direct, though that doesn't necessarily mean that the poems themselves are simple. Along the syntagmatic axis, one important factor is the discarding of the Victorian habit of generating the syntagmatic line by building some kind of story element into the poems. This earlier habit is opposed most obviously by, say, the Imagist poets, of whom it might be said that in their attempt to concentrate on the image they attempted to abolish the syntagm almost entirely and to work instead largely with the paradigmatic axis. This, of course, is impossible to do completely, since there can hardly be meaning without the syntagmatic chain, though one axis can be weighted more heavily than the other. These issues are encapsulated in Ezra Pound's 'In a Station of the Metro':

> The apparition of these faces in the crowd;
> Petals on a wet, black bough.

The grammatical (syntactic) relationship between these two lines is quite suppressed, the only link between the paratactic clauses being that implied by the impression that the second clause involves some kind of ellipsis – perhaps of a verb (there is no verb in the first, either, so the clauses share a grammatical absence), or of a simile-marking connective ('like' or 'as'). The connection is wholly visual and exophoric; one particular visual scene is presented, and then followed by a second which the first in some sense conjures up. One of the key things in the poem, of course, is that paradigmatic choice of 'apparition' in the first line, which does largely determine how we read the whole. 'Apparition' as opposed to, say, 'appearance', is not just the strictly visual but an allusion to something more ineffable, for it effects an instant movement from perceptual to conceptual point of view.

## Maintaining a strong syntagmatic axis: Yeats's 'Easter 1916'

Despite its self-conscious attempt to make a break with the past, Imagist poetry still maintained, and even intensified, the practice of interpreting phenomena subjectively and anthropomorphically. The problem of solipsism, to be confronted shortly by Stevens, and by Joyce in fiction, seems not to have been felt, so that in one way there is less of a gap than there appears to be between this kind of poetry and writing which continued to employ older modes. Beside the Pound we can usefully place the last paragraph of Yeats's more public-oriented 'Easter 1916':

> Too long a sacrifice
> Can make a stone of the heart.
> O when may it suffice?
> That is Heaven's part, our part                           60
> To murmur name upon name,
> As a mother names her child
> When sleep at last has come
> On limbs that had run wild.
> What is it but nightfall?                                  65
> No, no, not night but death;
> Was it needless death after all?
> For England may keep faith
> For all that is done and said.
> We know their dream; enough                               70
> To know they dreamed and are dead;
> And what if excess of love
> Bewildered them till they died?
> I write it out in a verse –
> MacDonagh and MacBride                                    75
> And Connolly and Pearse
> Now and in time to be,
> Wherever green is worn,
> Are changed, changed utterly:
> A terrible beauty is born.                                80

This appears to be a very simple kind of poetic; it is rhymed, ballad-style, on an alternating *abab* pattern, and the rhymes themselves are often only such 'half-rhymes' as 'death/faith' or 'enough/love', which to some extent hold rhyme back from achieving the emphatic function of consistent full rhyme; the syntax is generally right-branching; there is little in the paradigmatic choices to draw attention to them as intrusive in a speech-based language (perhaps 'excess of love/Bewildered them' stands out, but this is a syntagmatic effect, a combination of words not in themselves especially unusual); there is an absence of syntactic inversion, so the order is that of speech; there is a tendency towards colloquialism in the syntax – deletion of the verb *to be* in 'our part/[is] To murmur' or '[it is] enough/To know', for example, creates an effect of colloquial speech. And yet the language is really patterned quite heavily, so that the appearance of prose syntax is only an appearance. While the lines occasionally run on, they don't do so very often, and usually the syntactic unit is the same as the line unit. In line 60–1, for example –

That is Heaven's part, our part
To murmur name upon name

– the repetition of 'part' and the 'Heaven:our' contrast mark the integrity of the line unit in the face of the pull of the syntax against it. A couple of lines later, in

When sleep at last has come
On limbs that had run wild

the running-on is very weak, as the line-end coincides with the break between verb and complement. Yeats generally liked using questions, and question–answer units, and this is another device which is used here to pattern the discourse as an inner dialogue building up to the final, unanswered question with its simple but effective syntagmatic ambiguity:

And what if excess of love
Bewildered them till they died?

While there seems to be an underlying iambic metre, it is not insistent enough to assert the predominance of one function word over another – that is, there is nothing to determine whether the 'what' or the 'if' should be more heavily stressed, and yet it makes a large difference to the sense, with the latter suggesting a more defiant utterance. There is also a lot of cohesive repetition through the passage (name/names; nightfall/ night; death/death and dead/died; etc.). Thus a text which doesn't have 'story' in a strong way nevertheless develops quite a strong syntagmatic axis, at the same time as poets like Pound are looking for ways to disrupt that axis.

## (Over-)weighting the paradigmatic axis

By comparison, prose fiction of the same period may weight the paradigmatic axis more heavily than the syntagmatic. The following extract was published within about four years of the Yeats poem:

> It was evident she had a strange passion to dance before the sturdy, handsome cattle.
>
> Ursula began to sing, in a false quavering voice:
> 'Way down in Tennessee–'
> She sounded purely anxious. Nevertheless, Gudrun, with her arms outspread and her face uplifted, went in a strange palpitating dance towards the cattle, lifting her body towards them as if in a spell, her feet pulsing as if in some little frenzy of unconscious sensation, her arms, her wrists, her hands stretching and heaving and falling and reaching and reaching and falling, her breasts lifted and shaken towards the cattle, her throat exposed as in some voluptuous ecstasy towards them, whilst she drifted imperceptibly nearer, an uncanny white figure, towards them, carried away in its own rapt trance, ebbing in strange fluctuations upon the cattle, that waited, and ducked their heads a little in sudden contraction from her, watching all the time as if hypnotized, their bare horns branching in the clear light, as the white figure of the woman ebbed upon them, in the slow, hypnotizing convulsion of the dance. She could feel them just in front of her, it was as if she had the electric pulse from their breasts running into her hands. Soon she would touch them, actually touch them. A terrible shiver of fear and pleasure went through her.
> (D. H. Lawrence, *Women in Love* (1920))

This might be thought of as modernist writing in its development of a kind of stream-of-consciousness technique, but on the one hand Gudrun's psycho-sexual relationship with the cattle is in effect a quintessential example of the solipsistic Self's interpretation of some external Other (or, less kindly, a demonstration of what Lawrence saw as the destructive female urge to appropriate people and things), and on the other hand both the paradigmatic selection and the syntagmatic drift seem essentially Romantic. Very pertinent for the relationship of the axes here is the implicit dominance of narrator over narratee in a way symptomatic of Lawrence's fiction. While the discourse may often be presented from the point of view of one of the characters, there is a constant tendency to blur the difference between character and narrator point of view in order to grasp the narratee by the scruff of the emotions. In other words, there is very heavy narrator-directing without there being an overt or obtrusive narrator.

Neither narrator nor narratee has an obtrusive presence here, as the text drifts point of view amongst narrator, narratee, characters, and even the cattle. The effect is very similar to the way Romantic poets and novelists cultivate (or tolerate) semantic and syntactic drift, while exploiting the paradigmatic axis and syntagmatic recursion to amass a large number of words within three key lexical sets:

| 1 | 2 | 3 |
|---|---|---|
| arms | outspread | strange palpitating |
| face | uplifted | spell |
| body | lifting | frenzy of unconscious sensation |
| feet | pulsing | voluptuous ecstasy |
| arms | stretching | strange |
| wrists | heaving | uncanny |
| hands | falling | rapt trance |
| breast | reaching (× 2) | hypnotised |
| throat | falling | hypnotising convulsion |
| | lifted | |
| | shaken | |
| | exposed | |

The first column contains a paradigmatic accumulation of parts of the body. The second column contains a set of gestural terms which are all participles – of particular note here is the frequency of the present participle, which Lawrence habitually uses to link sentence elements together: such linking does away with the kind of formal subordination which conjunctions create, and tends also to efface temporal difference, to imply that a number of things are going on simultaneously; present participles are also more 'exciting'/immediate than past participles, because they convey actions occurring in a discoursal present. The third group consists of terms which are, in effect, comment – a large set of words which denote strangeness, magic, ecstatic states, mental aberration. The method of underlining this strangeness is to disrupt such syntagmatic line as there is, most notably in the segment following 'Whilst she drifted . . .' where the double focus on the narrator's commentary and the motion of the dancing figure is maintained by intercutting two lexical sets in a way that breaks up any possibility of a straightforward syntagm. The disruption is achieved primarily by embedding subject modifiers within the predicate. In effect, the subject is, 'she, an uncanny white figure, carried away in its own rapt trance' and the predicate is 'drifted . . . nearer, towards them, ebbing in strange fluctuations'. It is only with 'strange' that the lexical set of commentary shifts from subject into predicate, and is joined with the set whose node is 'motion towards'. The effect for the reader, clearly enough, is a heightening of suspense, tension, and excitement.

## Disrupting the syntagm in verse:
## T. S. Eliot (1888–1965)

Comparable strategies for disrupting the syntagmatic axis are employed by T. S. Eliot in sections of 'The Waste Land' (1922), as in this example:

The river bears no empty bottles, sandwich papers,
Silk handkerchiefs, cardboard boxes, cigarette ends
Or other testimony of summer nights. The nymphs are
    departed.
And their friends, the loitering heirs of city directors;     180
Departed, have left no addresses.
By the waters of Leman I sat down and wept . . .
Sweet Thames, run softly till I end my song,
Sweet Thames, run softly, for I speak not loud or long.
But at my back in a cold blast I hear     185
The rattle of the bones, and chuckle spread from ear to ear.
A rat crept softly through the vegetation
Dragging its slimy belly on the bank
While I was fishing in the dull canal

On a winter evening round behind the gashouse                190
Musing upon the king my brother's wreck
And on the king my father's death before him.
White bodies naked on the low damp ground
And bones cast in a little low dry garret,
Rattled by the rat's foot only, year to year.               195

The syntagmatic axis here is rather elusive. It might be noted at the outset that with Eliot, as with a lot of modern poetry, discussion of the syntagm may also involve discussion of rhetorical schemes, since a rediscovery of rhetoric in the early twentieth century prompted a revived interest in rhetorical organization of texts. Otherwise, the syntagm is disrupted here in two ways: first, by the element of recursion, the piling up of paradigmatic accumulations in the one slot; second, by building up a discourse which appears to consist largely of randomly collected pre-texts, a stream of 'misquotations' from Spenser, Marvell, Shakespeare, the Bible, and so on. Also found within this kind of piling up of paradigmatic elements is a very unpoetic collection of things – empty bottles, sandwich papers, and the like. The movement to a somewhat higher register with 'testimony of summer nights' is palpably ironic because it is contextualized within the more sordid elements. What happens to a silk handkerchief when it is located between a sandwich paper and a cardboard box? It is an obvious point, but the syntagmatic context generates connotations which override the normal denotations of such words. To put this another way, the handkerchief is pulled into the lexical set which is the dominant one around it. This happens with words of other kinds as well – with 'softly' and 'vegetation', for example, which may be thought of as neutral or even positive in their associations ('softly' quite pleasant; 'vegetation' even quasi-scientific), but in the context of

A rat crept softly through the vegetation
Dragging its slimy belly on the bank

they are pulled into the range of the more unpleasant terms, the whole utterance really taking its cue from the socially conditioned revulsion evoked by the signifiers 'rat' and 'slimy'. Items which might possibly have filled these paradigmatic slots, but which have not been selected – say, 'cat' and 'slinky' – readily show how crucial a couple of pivot terms can be in imposing a severe semantic narrowing on other items within the same syntagmatic chain. Another way of destabilizing the syntagmatic axis occurs in 193–5:

> White bodies naked on the low damp ground
> And bones cast in a little low dry garret,
> Rattled by the rat's foot only, year to year.

Forward movement along the chain is heavily dependent on finite verbs; if these are removed the linear movement is deprived of a crucial cohesive factor, and this is not offset by the weaker progression through these three lines from complete verblessness, to the past participle 'cast' (which is agent-free), to the more cohesive 'rattled', with its link backwards to the antecedent 'bones' and forwards to the agent in the next phrase. Verbs are also vital for imparting temporality to a text, in a way the vaguely continuous 'year to year' cannot effect.

Since the essence of the syntagmatic axis is its power to express relations of, and in, space and time, without which humans are unable to perceive meaning in existence, the stripping away of one of these factors is of paramount importance. In this example, the connections from line to line are made largely by the less overtly cohesive device of repetition: of signifiers, 'low/low' (although the *signified* shifts from, say, 'low-lying' to 'having a low ceiling'); of terms belonging to a lexical set, as with 'bodies/bones' (properly meronymy) or with the oppositional pair 'damp/dry'; and of sounds, as with the 'd' and 'g' repetitions and the complex patterning in 'little . . . rattled . . . rat's . . . foot'.[1] All this cohesiveness, however, only serves to promote the experience of disorientation felt when reading the text. This perhaps originates in the larger (hyper-)syntagm, in that there is a lack of both overt content relation and paradigmatic congruence between various parts of the text. This seems most obvious at line 185, where the lack of relation is exacerbated by the use of the adversative 'but' to begin the line; at the same time, lines 185–6 are so markedly a (mis-)quotation from Marvell that they enforce the impression that the syntagm is essentially a collection of fragments.

## Extremes in syntagmatic/paradigmatic deviation: Dylan Thomas (1914–53)

Still more extreme in its handling of syntagm and paradigm is the poetry of Dylan Thomas, even in his less complicated poems, such as 'The Force that through the Green Fuse Drives the Flower', where he does not make use of the word-coinages, the strange compounds, or the unusual periphrases characteristic of such a poem as 'A Refusal to Mourn'. Thomas is a more romantic poet than Eliot – his poems do not contain accumulations of distasteful lexical sets, or the sense of loss generated by the interpolated substitution of weakened, mundane, or even pejorative paradigmatic options within cited pretexts (e.g., 'fishing in the dull canal' which replaces Shakespeare's 'sitting on a bank' in line 189, above). In 'A Refusal to Mourn' the syntax is very complicated, as the first sentence illustrates:

> Never until the mankind making
> Bird beast and flower
> Fathering and all humbling darkness
> Tells with silence the last light breaking
> And the still hour                                             5
> Is come of the sea tumbling in harness
>
> And I must enter again the round
> Zion of the water bead
> And the synagogue of the ear of corn
> Shall I let pray the shadow of a sound          10
> Or sow my salt seed
> In the least valley of sackcloth to mourn
>
> The majesty and burning of the child's death.

This sentence is an extensive left-branching structure, with the main verb and subject, 'Shall I', deferred until line 10 because of a series of three temporal clauses (in lines 1–4, 5–6 and 7–9). But further, the paradigmatic development within the first of these clauses is remarkable. The subject of the clause consists of the structure

{deictic   adjective   noun}
the   . . .   darkness.

A paradigmatic slot filled by an adjective does readily allow for a multiplying of signifiers within that slot. The Eliot extract discussed above has a simple example:

$$\{\text{deictic} \qquad \text{adjective} \qquad \text{noun}\}$$

$$\text{the} \qquad \left\|\begin{array}{c} \text{low} \\ \text{damp} \end{array}\right\| \qquad \text{ground}$$

Thomas, though, has heaped up three elliptical compounds (built on present participles) to fill this slot:

$$\{\text{deictic} \qquad\qquad\qquad \text{adjective} \qquad\qquad\qquad \text{noun}\}$$

$$\text{the} \quad \left\|\begin{array}{cc} \text{mankind} & \text{making} \\ \text{bird beast and flower} & \text{fathering} \\ \text{all} & \text{humbling} \end{array}\right\| \text{darkness}$$

The second compound has within itself yet another paradigmatic accumulation (*bird beast flower*). Once the whole combination has been sorted out, it is found to be further complicated by the deviation of the final participle, 'humbling', within what had seemed to be a paradigmatic set accumulating around the node *engendering*. That is, we might have expected a development parallel to that of the 'species'-set, such as, let us say, 'making/fathering/*creating'. It is an excellent example of how a paradigmatic choice can evoke certain possibilities which were *not* selected. The effect on the syntagm of this piling up of elements within a single paradigmatic slot is that of extreme retardation of the reader's comprehension.


THOMAS'S PARADIGMATIC AXIS

What is generally characteristic of Thomas – as has often been observed – is the appearance of unexpected items in paradigmatic slots. This trait is to a great extent Hopkins's legacy to the twentieth century, and is evident in other mid-century poets such as George Barker and David Gascoyne. We will illustrate it from 'The Force that through the Green Fuse Drives the Flower'. The stanzas of this poem are so heavily organized and patterned that each has the same syntagmatic structure, and in such a context, the paradigmatic location of the linguistic strangeness becomes obvious (though such an observation must always be qualified by the *caveat* that paradigmatic effects can only be realized within syntagmatic contexts). Readers have an expectation of what kind of items usually appear at certain paradigmatic slots along the syntagmatic chain – what kind of adjectives, what kind of verbs, etc. – and of what constitutes a 'normal' collocation (Leech, 1969, 42–6). The notion of collocation points immediately to the interrelation of syntagm and paradigm, since it is the syntagmatic combination which marks a paradigmatic choice as in some way aberrant. In these senses, the opening one and a half lines appear immediately deviant at several places:

The force that through {the green fuse} {drives the flower}
{Drives my ‹green age›} . . .

Here the {deictic adjective noun} structure which might have yielded *'The [ . . . ] force' has been transformed by the standard operation of rank-shift; that is, a relative clause has replaced the adjective. This clause links two nouns (and, incidentally, reinforces the link by sound patterning as well as by grammatical linking), but they are nouns which are difficult to associate: *fuse:flower*. The first has denotative connections with electricity, or, more probably (especially because of one possible signified of 'blasts' in line 2), explosives, neither of which has much to do with flowers. It is not difficult to see how 'green' and 'flower' collocate, and only a little more difficult to make the metaphoric jump to 'green age', but the notion of life exploding into being, which is the apparent connotation of 'green fuse', demands a much more imaginative leap. At the same time, the verb-slot in this relative clause is filled by a word which is congruent with its antecedent, 'the force', but incongruous with its direct object, 'the flower'. Put together, all the combinations are so unexpected and hard to assimilate that meaning becomes largely a matter of subliminal association. So while the utterance is grammatically strong, syntagmatic combinations highlight significant paradigmatic deviation.

There are a number of other types of paradigmatic innovation in this poem, of which those in lines 16–18 are particularly interesting:

The lips of time leech to the fountain head;
Love drips and gathers, but the fallen blood
Shall calm her sores . . .

One of the important aspects of syntagm/paradigm relations here is that strangeness of paradigmatic choice leads to figurative expression. This figurativeness is further promoted by the mixing of abstract and concrete terms. Both are readily evident in the combination 'the lips of time', for example, which is then easily read as the concrete bodily part converting the abstract 'time' into a personification. But the signified deduced from this in turn complicates the inherently more problematic 'leech', because although this signifier occupies the grammatical position and function of a verb, Present English has no verb denotation available which makes sense in the syntagmatic context ('to heal' is archaic, and does not form a compound verb with 'to'). Moreover, although the immediate frame of reference concerns fluids, the homophone *leach*, 'to percolate; to remove soluble substances by percolation', seems no more apt (again because of the directional 'to'). So the signifier is probably to be interpreted as a shift in word-class (noun to verb), giving the sense 'to cling to like a leech', and is thus marked {+ pejorative}. Even then, the sense of the whole line (clause) remains fairly opaque. There is a paradigmatic congruence between 'time' and 'fountain head' if the latter is taken in a figurative sense, 'origin', but this only underlines how the free play of association across the signifiers impedes a forward syntagmatic movement.

Such impeding by retrospective connection is more evident still in the next lines, where a much more accessible sense is produced if the subjects of the two clauses are interchanged:

*‹the fallen blood› drips and gathers, but
*‹Love› shall calm her sores.

The impulse to make this switch has a twofold origin: on the one hand, the transposed sentence reflects a traditional religious concept, and on the other it redistributes abstract and concrete terms into more familiar configurations (blood drips; love calms). Much of the complexity of the utterance derives from the implicit awareness that signifiers *have* been assigned to paradigmatic slots in rather arbitrary fashion, and in such a way (once again) as to alert the reader to the options not assigned. Such extreme strategies are particularly products of the twentieth-century struggle against the syntagm, but they also represent a striving to draw analogies between individual human experience and either the natural world or cultural tradition, in a period when facile relationships between the Self and such Others cannot be assumed.

## Syntagm/paradigm and the representation of mental processes

JAMES JOYCE (1882–1941)

A study of prose fiction yields yet other kinds of syntagmatic/ paradigmatic relations. The following extracts from Joyce's *Ulysses* seem especially pertinent to our study, since a number of scholars have argued that Joyce's own theory of language involved a conception of the paradigmatic and syntagmatic axes which at least closely paralleled Saussure's (Scholes, 1972; Michels, 1982; McArthur, 1986). In the extracts, which depict the response of a consciousness to external stimuli, the narrating agency, Bloom, is observing events; the text is presented through a complex mixture of third person narration, dialogue, and free direct thought. This has important implications for paradigmatic choice, since what is presented as going on inside Bloom's head is not necessarily in the vocabulary of his speaking idiom – indeed, it is not in speech idiom of any kind:

> The carriage steered left for Finglas road.
>     The stonecutter's yard on the right. Last lap. Crowded on the spit of land silent shapes appeared, white, sorrowful, holding out calm hands, knelt in grief, pointing. Fragments of shapes, hewn. In white silence: appealing. The best obtainable. Thos. H. Dennany, monumental builder and sculptor.
>
> (1960 edn, 125)

Two kinds of point of view are being mediated through Bloom's thoughts: the paragraph is framed by simple perceptual point of view, the external world being re-presented uninterpreted ('The stonecutter's yard on the right . . . . Thos. H. Dennany, monumental builder and sculptor'); within the frame, the funerary sculptures are interpreted through a lexical set centring on the concept of grief ('silent, white, sorrowful, calm, grief'), in a way that presents an interesting problem about the relationship between sign and thing. Why, we might ask, is the sequence so evocative, given that it is describing the standard gestures of funerary art? One obvious answer lies in the selection of syntagmatic option, in that the humanizing 'crowded' precedes subject and verb, 'silent shapes appeared'. Then the kernel of the sentence, subject and verb, involves three resonant paradigmatic choices: 'silent' strongly conjures up the absence of its opposite, 'speaking'; 'shape' is denotatively indeterminate, suggesting undefined forms, silhouettes, phantoms; and 'appeared' can denote not just 'came into view' but 'manifested themselves'. The element of indeterminacy is furthered by a syntagmatic ambiguity in the following paradigmatic accumulation – the gestures are distributed amongst a number of shapes (it is a list of impressions) but the syntagmatic chain tends to imply that more than one gesture or epithet applies to any single shape. The shifting and uncertainty promote an awareness of the pretexts which the configuration conjures up – classical texts in which the dead in Hades appeal to the living visitor (*Odyssey*; *Aeneid*).

This kind of discourse stands in contrast to the dialogue amongst some of Bloom's companions shortly afterwards:

Mr Power pointed.
– That is where Childs was murdered, he said. The last house.
– So it is, Mr Dedalus said. A gruesome case. Seymour Bushe got him off. Murdered his brother. Or so they said.
– The crown had no evidence, Mr Power said.
– Only circumstantial, Martin Cunningham said. That's the maxim of the law. Better for ninety nine guilty to escape than for one innocent person to be wrongfully condemned.

(ibid, 125)

This is a mundane exchange, but highly cohesive through its use of deictics, and through its binding together of a number of incomplete sentences by ellipsis (for example, the response to 'The crown had no evidence' merely states a clarification of 'no', and assumes the rest of the utterance: '[The crown had] only circumstantial [evidence]'). Beside this kind of cohesion, Bloom's following meditation seems discontinuous, as once again he moves from perceptual point of view to association, this time by fragmenting the discourse of others – his companions, popular lore, newspaper reports, Shakespeare, Chaucer:

They looked. Murderer's ground. It passed darkly. Shuttered, tenantless, unweeded garden. Whole place gone to hell. Wrongfully condemned. Murder. The murderer's image in the eye of the murdered. They love reading about it. Man's head found in a garden. Her clothing consisted of. How she met her death. Recent outrage. The weapon used. Murderer is still at large. Clues. A shoelace. The body to be exhumed. Murder will out.

(ibid)

Structure now lies elsewhere than in the grammatical ordering of the syntagmatic axis, which has been dissolved into mere linearity, no longer functioning as a connector of paradigmatic choices. We need go no further than the two occurrences of 'they' to illustrate the breakdown of that kind of cohesion: the first refers back to the occupants of the carriage, but the use of the second appears to be the colloquial indefinite. On the other hand, there is substantial paradigmatic congruence amongst the items which make up the discourse on the theme of 'Murder', so that there is still a perceivable hypersyntagmatic structure.

## VIRGINIA WOOLF'S *MRS DALLOWAY* (1925)

Joyce's prose illustrates one kind of disruptive strategy. A roughly contemporary text, Virginia Woolf's *Mrs Dalloway*, employs a different strategy again:

Sir William himself was no longer young. He had worked very hard; he had won his position by sheer ability (being the son of a shopkeeper); loved his profession; made a fine figurehead at ceremonies and spoke well – all of which had by the time he was knighted given him a heavy look, a weary look (the stream of patients being so incessant, the responsibilities and privileges of his profession so onerous), which weariness, together with his grey hairs, increased the extraordinary distinction of his presence and gave him the reputation (of the utmost importance in dealing with nerve cases) not merely of lightning skill and almost infallible accuracy in diagnosis, but of sympathy; tact; understanding of the human soul. He could see the first moment they came into the room (the Warren Smiths they were called); he was certain directly he saw the man; it was a case of extreme gravity. It was a case of complete breakdown – complete physical and nervous breakdown, with every symptom in an advanced stage, he ascertained in two or three minutes (writing answers to questions, murmured discreetly, on a pink card).

(1958 edn, 105–6)

This paragraph is heavily paratactic; there is little subordination, and there are a lot of parenthetic statements which create a double focalization, since they seem to be attributable to Sir William, the character being described. But one of the difficulties which confronts the reader lies in determining what is the important information in a text presented so paratactically. Do we have anything to fall back on apart from, say, the end-focus which is our last resort even in paratactic sequences which fall within a larger subordinating structure, as with the concluding series of 'the reputation . . . not merely of lightning skill and almost infallible accuracy in diagnosis, but of sympathy; tact; understanding of the human soul'? Are 'sympathy', etc. just a series, or are they in an ascending order? Such questions remain broadly indeterminable.

The problem of sequencing comes up clearly a little later in the dialogue between doctor and patient, where Woolf has intermingled direct speech, reported speech, and free indirect thought:

'You served with great distinction in the War?'
The patient repeated the word 'war' interrogatively.
He was attaching meanings to words of a symbolical kind.
A serious symptom to be noted on the card.
'The War?' the patient asked.

(ibid)

Information is presented here in, as it were, a loop in syntagmatic sequence. A question is asked in direct speech, and the reply is rendered as indirect speech, heavily marked for point of view. It is Sir William who perceives Septimus as 'the patient', and presumably the quasi-technical description of the actual utterance – 'repeated the word . . . interrogatively' – is also Sir William's, paving the way for the extrapolation of an extraordinary conclusion from a simple utterance. When the text then loops back to re-render Septimus's reply as direct speech, the disruption of syntagmatic order drives home the irony directed against Sir William's 'sense of proportion', even as the text represents two crucial types of failure to perceive the existential reality of Otherness as separate from the acts of perception which seek to comprehend that Otherness. (For a complementary analysis of Sir William's language, see Armstrong, 1983, 355.)

## Total revolt against the tyranny of 'The Word': William Burroughs's *The Naked Lunch* (1959)

*The Naked Lunch* represents perhaps the ultimate in twentieth-century syntagmatic disruption. The following extract is from the 'Preface', which, coming as the concluding chapter of the book, openly flaunts hypersyntagmatic non-linearity:

> Now I, William Seward, will unlock my word horde . . . My Viking heart fares over the great brown river where motors put put put in jungle twilight and whole trees float with huge snakes in the branches and sad-eyed lemurs watch the shore, across the Missouri field (The Boy finds a pink arrowhead) out along distant train whistles, comes back to me hungry as a street boy don't know to peddle the ass God gave him . . . Gentle Reader, The Word will leap on you with leopard man iron claws, it will cut off your fingers and toes like an opportunist land crab, it will hang you and catch your jissom like a scrutable dog, it will coil round your thighs like a bushmaster and inject a shot glass of rancid ectoplasm . . . And why a *scrutable* dog?
>
> The other day I am returning from the long lunch thread from mouth to ass all the way the days of our years, when I see an Arab boy have this little black and white dog know how to walk on his hind legs . . . And a big yaller dog come on the boy for affection and the boy shove it away, and the yaller dog growl and snap at the little toddler, snarling if he had but human gift of tongues: 'A crime against nature right there.'

Extreme parataxis is now emphasized by continual use of ellipsis (as dot sequences). About half of the novel is a catalogue of sense-impressions and mental fantasies, going well beyond the point Joyce reached in *Ulysses*, loosely strung together by the ellipses. There are extreme register-shifts: in a short section appear Black English, medical jargon, grammatical solecisms, tabu words, words which are class-shifted, mixed in with such diverse pre-texts as Tarzan movies and (just after the quoted extract) *Antony and Cleopatra*, disrupting paradigmatic congruence as much as syntagmatic cohesion. Conceptually, the text also disrupts time and space. The 'scene' conjured up in the opening paragraph spans the world spatially, from Scandinavia to Africa, from Missouri to South America. The excruciating pun on 'word horde' (which plays the anarchic notion of a barbarian 'horde' against the Anglo-Saxon poet's creative shaping of his 'word hoard') sets modern anti-logocentrism,[2] the sense of the tyranny of language, against the logocentrism of the past.

The effect is repeated in the contrast between the Victorian and Modern novel implicit in 'Gentle Reader, The Word will leap on you with leopard man iron claws, etc.', and then in the glance at the arbitrariness of language which enables a word marked by a negative prefix, 'inscrutable', to be in common usage while its positive counterpart is rare, and even seems comic. These are all ways of creating disruption, of escaping the tyranny of the syntagm, and the tyranny of The Word itself, working from the presumption that language is restrictive and oppressive, and can prevent perception as readily as enable it. The responsibility in such a text is thrown heavily upon the reader, whose task it is to make the connections normally made by the syntagmatic axis.

## Syntagm/paradigm relations in the later twentieth century

Characteristics of the literary landscape since the middle of the twentieth century are too vastly differentiated for us to aspire to more than a sampling of what appear to be some main trends in the shaping of syntagm/paradigm relations. A full account would have to include not just the various competing traditions within fiction and poetry of both England and America – and the two countries have proceeded independently, with only minimal and occasional mutual influence – but also other literatures written in English around the world, in Africa, Asia, Australia, Canada, the Caribbean, New Zealand, the Pacific . . . .

The extent to which particular cultural traditions and concerns differing strongly from the traditional Anglo-American concerns may shape variations in the ways syntagm and paradigm are treated is a fascinating but vast subject, lying well beyond the scope of our present study; the following comparison offers, perhaps, an *extreme* difference. In an earlier chapter (Chapter 2), we designated a particular type of prose as 'naïve realism' because in it story and signified take precedence over discourse and signifier. The following example, from one of the 'New Literatures', is particularly interesting, since it falls within the category of naïve realism, even though the novel it comes from has a complex hypersyntagm (a series of flashbacks situated within overlapped accounts of two journeys, in opposite directions, between the urban 'centre' of Wellington and the protagonist's Maori 'centre' of Waituhi):

> I was never afraid of being alone even if the day was clouded with rain. I'd wander through the scrub or along a small stream or among the shadowed ravines. Dad was there, I had no need to fear.
>
> But once I wandered too far and couldn't find my way back. I wanted to cry. Night was coming. But boys aren't supposed to cry. So I waited and watched the stars springing into the sky. Then I heard Dad calling.
>
> – Tama! Tama!
>
> I yelled back. Dad rushed down to me and crushed me in his arms. Afterward he growled me for wandering too far away. I didn't care even though a grave tear trickled down my face. Dad was there. I knew that I could never be lost because father would always be there to find me.
>
> Sometimes I'd have to stay at the whare. Those were lonely times because I liked being with Dad.
>
> (Witi Ihimaera, *Tangi*, 1975, 50–1)

Described by its publisher as 'a poetic drama in prose' (and so by implication praised for transcending supposed genre limitations?), the book's claim to this description rests on paradigmatic choices and hypersyntagmatic relationships. The smaller-scale syntagmatic axis is presented through short units organized chiefly by parataxis or co-ordination. There is some subordination, all right-branching in this brief extract (elsewhere in the text, conditional or concessive clauses result in some left-branching sentences, though these are infrequent). The protagonist's register, largely fixed by local idioms ('growled me') or Maori words ('whare'), is poeticized by intrusive lexical choices such as '*clouded* with rain', '*shadowed* ravines', or 'the stars *springing*', choices which unbalance the prose by throwing sudden emphasis upon signifiers in a context in which signifier–signified relationships generally lack complication. The result of such self-conscious choices is thus to emphasize the 'naïve realism' which is the essence of this prose.

Within the older literatures, the British and American, the heritage of Modernism, in its various facets, has a much stronger influence than in much written in the New Literatures (but see Bhabha, 1984), and inevitably has some rather different effects on the ways in which writers handle the syntagmatic/paradigmatic axes. The following extract from Donald Barthelme's *Views of My Father Weeping* shows how the differences might be restated:

> There is my father's bed. In it, my father. Attitude of dejection. Graceful as a mule deer once, the same large ears. For a nanosecond, there is a nanosmile. Is he having me on? I remember once we went out on the ups and downs of the West (out past Vulture's Roost) to shoot. First we shot up a lot of old beer cans, then we shot up a lot of old whiskey bottles, better because they shattered. Then we shot up some mesquite bushes and some parts of a Ford pickup somebody'd left lying around. But no animals came to our party (it was noisy, I admit it). A long list of animals failed to arrive, no deer, quail, rabbit, seals, sea lions, condylarths. It was pretty boring shooting up mesquite bushes, so we hunkered down behind some rocks, Father and I, he hunkered down behind his rocks and I hunkered down behind my rocks, and we commenced to shooting at each other. That was interesting.
>
> (1978, 22–3)

Despite its mainly paratactic style, the Ihimaera is cohesive because of cause-and-effect relationships, semantic links, and temporal adverbs. The result is coherently to evoke memories of childhood as something within which firmly to ground the narrator's being. But in the Barthelme, memory is immediately disjunctive and the discourse leans towards lack of coherence. Try as the reader might, there is no satisfactory, determinable relationship between the present tense question, 'Is he having me on?' and the anecdote confidentally beginning, 'I remember once'. All that seems to be charted is separation and absence.

The reification of the father in the opening sentences is effected by syntagmatic order and by the ellipsis of function words which might personalize, such as verbs or pronouns other than 'my'. Thus the initial focus on the bed renders it more important than the father, so that the segment begins by foregrounding acts of perception; dejection is impersonalized by representing it as an observed pose in a description stripped of personalizing pronouns, though now an interpretation is placed upon the object seen; but then the next stage, the empathetic gesture implicit in the memory of a lost quality (once 'graceful', a traditional attribute of deer) is sequentially undercut by the unexpected focus on 'the same large ears'.

The text is a process of making strange, and this is continued in the invented, pseudo-scientific words 'nanosecond' and 'nanosmile' (the former, being $10^{-9}$ of a second, is almost unthinkable). Register shifts almost violently from here to the idiomatic 'having me on', and the extract is marked by a number of comparable disruptions, generating a paradigmatic incongruence vastly different from the relatively simple register-mixing of *Tangi* – 'ups and downs' defines shapes of mood rather than topography; 'came to our party' is a collapse into the literal of the figurative idiom 'come to the party' ('fall in with one's plans'); 'commenced to shooting' mixes two grammatical structures; 'condylarths' is more pseudo-science (apparently a blend of *arthropod* and *condylopod* – presumably these creatures failed to arrive because they no longer had any feet (-*pod*)!; in an earlier memory, with similar linguistic panache, the narrator and his father were shooting *peccadillos*, a hybrid of 'the collared peccary and the nine-banded armadillo').

Such games challenge the way language is structured, and in doing so question the way language structures reality. This also occurs on the syntagmatic and generic levels. Temporals sequence events, but don't organize them meaningfully; on the contrary, to introduce the notion of Time is to help alert the reader to the anachronism between the implicit genre, the western, and the modern rubbish littering the landscape (cans and car-debris – though the figures may also be in a landscape which is the cultural debris of a John Ford western).[3] Genre here is simultaneously flaunted and destroyed, blurring boundaries in typical postmodern fashion (see Hassan, 1987, 446); beside it, would-be critical formulations such as 'poetic drama in prose' seem extraordinarily innocent.

We are not proposing that for any of the above reasons one or other of the texts is better; they are really almost too different to compare.[4] The Ihimaera is, so to speak, 'about' a primal relationship and what that signifies in respect to concepts of Self and Place; in Barthelme, the father–son relationship is merely contingent to a construction of perceptual process, an illustration that the spirit of *bricolage* pervading high Modernism is closely akin to incoherence, and a recognition of the displacement of imagination by memory in Modernist practice (Craig, 1982, 65–71).

## The assault on the syntagm in Modernist verse

While Barthelme's playfulness with language multiplies signifieds, and even invents signifiers, the impulse behind it is suspicion of a literary language over-dependent upon the connotative power of words. We have previously remarked that intertextuality might be regarded as a key aspect of literary language, but since about 1950 various schools of poetry, in particular, have espoused the desire for a language rinsed clean of associations. This desire has, of course, profound implications both for paradigmatic choice and for syntagmatic form: if signification is either multiplied by associations generated by syntagmatic relationships, or diminished because syntagmatic strings discourage focus on what occupies particular slots, then ways must be found to counteract that effect. In America, the poetry of William Carlos Williams, not strongly influential until the later 1940s, seemed to offer a way forward:

> *Poem*
> As the cat
> climbed over
> the top of
>
> the jamcloset
> first the right                    5
> forefoot
>
> carefully
> then the hind
> stepped down
>
> into the pit of                   10
> the empty
> flowerpot

In its simplicity, this poem appears to have affinities with Imagist poetry and the haiku which influenced them, but is neither figurative nor expressive of some transcendent vision. What the poem rather expresses is, in Anthony Libby's words, 'the particularity of individual things'.[5] It does this chiefly by using the verse line to break up the continuity of the syntagmatic axis, counterpointing line units made up of as little as one word against the structure of what is a carefully patterned, hypotactic two-clause sentence (a temporal clause in lines 1–4, and principal in lines 5–12), and to a lesser extent by ellipsis to compact two clauses at deep structure level into the single principal clause. Here is the poem set out in such a way as to show the parallel grammatical and semantic elements (slashes mark the original line-ends, and dashes the ellipses):

1   As the cat/ climbed over/ the top of/ the jamcloset/

2   first the right/ forefoot/

------- ---- carefully/                    [*stepped down*]

then the ----- hind----/                   [*right -foot*]

stepped down/

into the pit of/         the empty/ flowerpot

Objects and actions are not only separated out by the visible effect of line division but, as this setting-out quickly indicates, also by differentiation through opposition: the two verb-groups, 'climbed over ‖ stepped down'; the locatives, 'the top of ‖ the pit of'; the cat's limbs, 'forefoot ‖ hind[foot]'. The verb ellipsis creates the impression that the modifier 'carefully' has been positionally shifted and it is accordingly foregrounded. Its increased isolation as it comprises the whole of line 7 further enforces the apprehension of the essence of being careful. The modifier 'empty' in the last phrase is a kind of deviation, breaking the parallelism between lines 3–4 and 10–12 in terms both of grammar and verse structure, but sharply focusing the starkness of absence at the moment it is displaced by the presence of the cat. It is finally this interplay of presence and absence which penetrates things to the abstract forms within them.

The only word in the poem which might come already charged with associations is 'pit', which in other contexts may denote such concepts as 'animal pen' or 'abyss' (especially biblical – there are nine examples of 'descend into the pit' in the Book of Ezekiel alone); 'pit' does not usually collocate with 'flowerpot', which might have restricted its meaning if it were not for 'empty' and the shadow of such other paradigmatic possibilities as 'empty abyss'. Paradoxically, perhaps, the very strategy of isolating the word within the syntagm has exacerbated the difficulty of restricting its associations. The method has its weaknesses, as well as its strengths.

## Implications of syntagmatic minimalism

The use of such short lines is a break from the traditionalism of such modernist poets as T. S. Eliot, and as such its adoption by later poets – especially Robert Creeley and A. R. Ammons – was deplored in a pugnacious attack by Wyatt Prunty (1985). Discussing Creeley's 'I Know a Man', Prunty recognizes that 'Ambiguity is created because the poem's foreshortened lines frustrate the reader's syntactical expectations' (1985, 81), but rejects such minimalist poetry on two interrelated grounds which have some bearing on our discussion of syntagm and paradigm.

On the one hand, such short lines do away with the possibilities of rhythm/metre counterpoint and an effective use of enjambment, and on the other hand the disruption of speech units creates mere surprise rather than the 'intellectual complication' of irony, paradox and ambiguity (Prunty's critical position is overtly New Critical). In our terms, the issue is a matter of attempting to weight the paradigmatic axis heavily, and to reduce, as far as possible, the power of the syntagmatic axis to restrict meaning.

For the Black Mountain poets – especially Creeley, Charles Olson, and Robert Duncan – this was a deliberate process, of creating what Olson called a 'field' or space within which words, images and sounds existed atemporally rather than linearly. In other words, signifiers are free to float within the paradigmatic axis, a process illustrated, for example, in Duncan's 'At the Loom' (a poem about language and poetry), where the denotative meanings of the key terms, 'warp' and 'shuttle', are laid out etymologically, dictionary-fashion, to articulate their resonance and range. For 'shuttle' he gives:

>          And the shuttle carrying the woof I find
>              was *skutill*   *"harpoon"*  – a dart, an arrow,
>                      or a little ship,
>                  *navicula*          *weberschiff*,
>
>      crossing and recrossing from shore to shore –
>
>          prehistoric *\*skutil*   *\*skut-*

This is a method for laying heavy stress on the paradigmatic axis, if a signifier can liberate any or all of its past or present signifieds and then work back from those signifieds to other signifiers. Duncan, however, further clarified the 'field' idea by stating that the poet 'strives not for a disintegration of syntax but for a complication within syntax, overlapping structures, so that words are freed, having bounds out of bound' (1968, ix). The result of the theory is Duncan's pastiche or collage poems, or such poems as 'The Moon' (Duncan uses a · as equivalent to a musical rest):

>      so pleasing              a light
>              round,      haloed,              partially
>      disclosed,                a ring,
>          night's wedding signet   ·
>
>
>              may be
>      a great lady drawing
>              her tide-skirts up   ·
>                      in whirls
>                  and loosening to the gilt
>                          shore-margins      of her sea-robes
>                                              (lines 1–10)

Once again, as with the Williams, the effect depends on the reader translating visual gaps into syntagmatic silences. Otherwise, these lines are a left-branching sentence with a heavy paradigmatic accumulation within the subject and parallel co-ordinate participial clauses following the verb:

> so pleasing a light [etc.]     may be a great lady
> drawing her tide-skirts up . . .
> and loosening . . . her sea-robes

The poem's impact derives largely from the reader's freedom to find congruences between and to generate visual and emotional associations from the members of the paradigmatic set *before* they are subject to the restricted meanings imparted retrospectively by 'may be a great lady'. Through the compounds and polysemes, the figurative complex of lady–skirts (vehicle) and moon–sea (tenor) is firmly sustained throughout the predicate of the sentence, despite the (self-reflexive?) attempt to loosen the grammatical relationships in 'loosening . . . of'. Up to a point, then, the attempt once more to break the tyranny of the syntagm is successful – but only up to a point, since Duncan's choice of a hypotactic structure allows it to make a strong and persistent return.

## An extended example: A. R. Ammons (1926– ) and Adrienne Rich (1929– )

As we have shown earlier, the difference between predominantly hypotactic and paratactic styles obviously affects the paradigmatic/syntagmatic axes. A more paratactic style in itself tends to reduce the power of the syntagm to control signification. To illustrate this from contemporary poetry, we will use A. R. Ammons's 'Pet Panther' (1983):

> My attention is a wild
> animal: it will if idle
> make trouble where there
> was no harm: it will
>
> sniff and scratch at the                                    5
> breath's sills:
> it will wind itself tight
> around the pulse
>
> or, undistracted by
> verbal toys, pommel the                                     10
> heart frantic: it will
> pounce on a stalled riddle

and wrestle the mind numb:
attention, fierce animal
I cry, as it coughs in my                                                15
face, dislodges boulders

in my belly, lie down, be
still, have mercy, here
is song, coils of song, play
it out, run with it.                                                     20

An obvious feature of this poem is the low level of
correspondence between the syntactic and the verse-line units.
There are twenty lines and within them twenty clauses, but line-
end and clause-end coincide only seven times (lines 2, 6, 8, 12,
13, 14, 20); that most of these fall at even lines constitutes the
poem's strongest formal characteristic. There are some weak
enjambments, such as subject/verb (3, 18) and verb/object (17,
19), but Ammons mainly enjambs strongly by breaking up
phrases so that he ends a line with a definite article (5, 10), a
personal pronoun (15), or a preposition (9), or else he separates
auxiliary from lexical verb (4, 11), or adjective from the noun it
modifies (1). The disruption of the traditional correlation
between syntactic and line units, as well as the lack of other
line-end markers such as rhyme or sound-patterning, both
emphasizes the difference from traditional verse form and
loosens the usual certainty of signification that derives from the
syntax, especially when so many of the clauses are short. This
uncertainty is most obvious in line 14, where 'Attention' can be
either the abstract noun repeated from line 1, and so a vocative
in apposition with 'fierce animal', or else an imperative, being
then the first in the set of verbal imperatives in 15–20.

Along the syntagmatic axis, the paradigmatic slots are filled by
signifiers seemingly chosen to allow the opening metaphor to
be extended at some length. But the signified concept declared
by the poem's title is not clarified but rather made less and less
determinable as the syntagm extends. The set of verbs
apparently chosen as the vehicle of the extended metaphor,
and grammatically paralleled by common dependence on the
repeated 'it will', singularly fails to point to 'panther' as its node
(though may in some way apply to 'attention', the real tenor of
the metaphor); instead, the associations which mark each
member of the set point away from the concept 'panther', and

even from 'wild animal', as the series moves from the generalized 'make trouble', to 'sniff and scratch' {+ dog}, to 'wind itself tight' {+ snake}, to 'pommel' {+ human}, to 'pounce' {+ cat}, to 'wrestle' {+ human, again}.

The adjectival-noun/verb combinations also function to prevent determination of the signifieds, as when the riddle is stalled, the adjective suggesting a motor-vehicle; and pommel-ing the heart and wrestling the mind are associated with 'frantic' and 'numb' respectively. The formal syntactic markers of appositional relationships (as in the repeated 'it will') signal links between concepts which cannot be linked. This applies also to the apposition of 'song' and 'coils of song' in line 19, where 'coils' refers to something tangible and physically apprehended, while 'song' is oral and aurally perceived. The sensory combination tends to render the signified indeterminable, and this destabilization of signification is exacerbated by the effect of the appositional imperatives on either side, insofar as the two sets, 'lie down, be still, have mercy' and 'play it out, run with it', are mutually exclusive; the last two further complicate the poem's chain of associations when the sporting associations of 'run with it' {+ football, and even, perhaps, + kite-flying} re-mark 'play it out' as {+ fishing} instead of/as well as {+ musical}, thus effectively emphasizing the vehicle of this new metaphor over its tenor.

The strategies adopted in the poem to refuse signification have the effect of focusing attention on the play of the signifiers themselves, and then the poem's own references to language in the phrases 'verbal toys', 'stalled riddle', and 'coils of song' foreground its self-reflexive meditation on such problems as the arbitrary relationship between linguistic signs and things, or on one of its more tangible manifestations, the frustrating symbiosis between poetic inspiration and writer's block.

From the outset, 'attention' has been an odd paradigmatic substitution (the slot might be 'better', or more conventionally, filled by *imagination* or *inspiration*) which has located the poem to one side of a sub-genre ('poems on the imagination'). But the substitution works well as part of the poem's overall focus on the characteristic late twentieth-century emphasis on the gaps in language, rather than on the relationships, so that by decon-structing and subverting notions of what 'my attention' could 'mean', Ammons puts in its place a radical uncertainty about how language functions.

Whereas 'Pet Panther' explores the difficulty of formulating signifiers to express pre-verbal thought in the face of the problem that meaning is corrupted at the moment it is realized through signifiers, Adrienne Rich's 'A Valediction Forbidding Mourning' (1970) still more radically disrupts the syntagmatic axis, on the assumption that language signifies too well but according to a hidden agenda, and therefore has to be reshaped in an attempt to refloat signifier–signified relationships. The title repeats that of a well-known poem by Donne, challenging intertextual consideration of the interplay of repetition and difference, and of the power of the past to determine the shape of the present; in essence, Rich's poem strives to refuse a patriarchal hegemony over literature and language:

My swirling wants. Your frozen lips.
The grammar turned and attacked me.
Themes, written under duress.
Emptiness of the notations.

They gave me a drug that slowed the healing of wounds.     5

I want you to see this before I leave:
the experience of repetition as death
the failure of criticism to locate the pain
the poster in the bus that said:
*my bleeding is under control*.                                          10

A red plant in a cemetery of plastic wreaths.

A last attempt: the language is a dialect called metaphor.
These images go unglossed: hair, glacier, flashlight.
When I think of a landscape I am thinking of a time.
When I talk of taking a trip I mean forever.                     15
I could say: those mountains have a meaning
but further than that I could not say.

To do something very common, in my own way.

Ammons played syntagm against paradigm in order to destabilize the tenor–vehicle relationship of metaphor. Rich engages in both syntagmatic and hypersyntagmatic disruptions in order to create a metaphorical situation within which literal and figurative are interchangeable; that is, the failure of a relationship is a metaphor for a sociolinguistic problem *at the same time* as a failure of language acts as a metonymy for failed relationships. The poem's title once again acts as an important cue. One of its further functions is to prompt the reader to expect and look for a human situation in some sense comparable to that of the Donne poem, even though hypersyntagmatic story is as fractured as syntagmatic discourse. It is possible to construct from the poem's fragments a narrative situation in which a woman explains to her partner why she is leaving him (so inverting the sex roles found in Donne, and making the separation permanent rather than temporary); this has its own inherent force and logic, but partly because yet another function of the title is to invoke the notion of literary precursors, this little narrative is primarily a metaphor for the poet's secession from what is perceived as a patriarchal literary tradition.

Omission of finite verbs, other than as clear cohesive ellipsis, disrupts syntagmatic continuity, and this happens seven times in the poem, throwing weight on other cohesive devices. The two word-strings in the first line lack both verbs and connectives, but are tightly bound together by their common structure – possessive pronoun/adjective/noun – and by the immediate opposition of 'My/Your'. At a further stage of complexity, 'swirling' and 'frozen' have a key area of opposition; as terms of topographical description they apply to water in particular states of motion or stasis, but are also commonly applied to human emotions. Finally, because 'lips' is a metonym for *speech*, 'wants' and 'lips' relate oppositionally as *need:response*. The deviancies of truncated grammar and figurative language make strange, and therefore re-focus, a commonplace problem, often expressed as conflict between female emotionalism and male reserve (and our rephrasing immediately illustrates the underlying language problem, since 'emotionalism' is {+ pejorative} and 'reserve' {+ ameliorative}). The return to normal grammar in line 2 is paradoxically used to express the destructive impact seen in 'grammar', a metonym for male-dominated speech in which signifiers *are* linked to signifieds, but by male authority; for women they are empty signs ('Emptiness of the notations').

The poem is deeply concerned with signs and their interpretation, and, recognizing the arbitrariness of signifier–signified links, asserts the value of that recognition. Take the following sequence:

1   the poster in the bus that said:
    *my bleeding is under control.*

2   These images go unglossed: hair, glacier, flashlight.

3   I could say: those mountains have a meaning
    but further than that I could not say.

How to interpret the first of these is partly determined by its syntagmatic placement as last in a list of covertly repressive factors (the others concern seeing the past as a model, an analysis which unwittingly accepts or confirms the status quo), and then the lines demand triple decoding: the words themselves must be recognized as referring to an advertisement for tampons; then the implication must be read off, that there is something unclean about female sexuality and it must be kept hidden; and finally, the stigmatization of women is seen as an instrument of male dominance.

The process of decoding the sign retraces the process whereby the coding of the sign is implicitly weighted against women, or, in other words, it is a pattern of the way signifier–signified relationships can be inimical to female experience. One response is the second of the above examples, the refusal to gloss a series of three semantically disparate signifiers. And yet the lure of language is such that the mind will impose connectedness even where it is not syntagmatically indicated. We have just decoded one group of signifiers and found an advertisement; the principle of 'repetition' will enable us to do it again, even against the explicit directions of the text. Hair – a sexual emblem; glacier – a background evoking coolness; flashlight – a photograph. An advertisement for menthol cigarettes, perhaps, exploiting female sexuality for commercial gain? To follow this process of encoding is to walk into the trap the poet has laid: signs are so burdened with culturally-determined conventions that signifier–signified relationships are an intellectual prison. But the speaker finds different associations for 'a landscape' by remaking the spatial concept as a temporal one; she repeats the process when *trip* 'a short-term journey' (or 'a drug-induced experience') becomes 'forever'. The final gesture, in lines 16–17, is to refuse signification, to reach out (as Williams tried to do in his poetry) for the *haecceitas*, the 'thingness', of phenomena.

Rich has thus given a new, urgent, feminist slant to the late twentieth-century anxiety about language, detecting a silent but powerful ideological factor within the arbitrariness of signifier–signified relationships, and demanding a heightened awareness of the process whereby the gaps in language are filled. The poem also acts as a very interesting practical comment on syntagmatic disruption, in that it emerges as a neutral tool; on the one hand, the kinds of disruption employed mark the text as non- or even anti-traditional; on the other hand, Rich demonstrates that semantic links can be powerfully syntagmatic, enforcing cohesion where more obvious kinds of links have been deleted. Our analysis of how problems of language and gender are confronted in one poem might also have been used to raise these problems more generally. For a survey of the issues and a substantial bibliography readers can consult McConnell-Ginet (1988).

## Philip Larkin (1922–85) and the problem of solipsism

The relationship between surfaces and essences, and so by extension between Self and Other, which is an issue central to the American poetry we have been discussing, also concerns British postmodern poets, but the dominant trend has been to employ more traditional forms and to pay less direct attention to the issue itself. British poets have been more interested too in the way the relationship of signs to things bears on the problem of solipsism, still felt to be bedevilling poetry almost a century after Darwin. Contemporary British poetry has been largely shaped by the so-called Movement poets, poets who, seeking significances which lie outside the Self and the Self's apprehension of phenomena, have stressed the reality of surfaces, and who deliberately eschew the kind of poetic strategies which Ammons or Rich employ to open up a difference between explicit and implicit meaning.[6]

The best-known, and most accomplished, of these poets is Philip Larkin. The following poem, 'A Study of Reading Habits', is in many ways typical Larkin, and makes a pertinent comparison with the previous poems discussed, in its uses of intertextuality, its implicit awareness of the culturally deterministic role of sign-systems, and its treatment of solipsism:

When getting my nose in a book
Cured most things short of school,
It was worth ruining my eyes
To know I could still keep cool,
And deal out the old right hook                    5
To dirty dogs twice my size.

Later, with inch-thick specs,
Evil was just my lark:
Me and my cloak and fangs
Had ripping times in the dark.                      10
The women I clubbed with sex!
I broke them up like meringues.

Don't read much now: the dude
Who lets the girl down before
The hero arrives, the chap                          15
Who's yellow and keeps the store,
Seem far too familiar. Get stewed:
Books are a load of crap.

The central strategy of this poem pivots on the syntagmatic
presentation of time and the restriction of the paradigmatic axis
within two registers which construct a speaker readily separable
from the poet himself, and thereby inviting superiority and
some humour at his expense.

The title of the poem is once again vital for establishing the
reader's bearings, this time declaring the poem to be something
like a case-study dealing with one of Larkin's important
recurrent themes, the crippling effect of 'habits' on human life.
The first of the registers which construct the speaker is made up
of a large number of idioms and colloquialisms which place
him, albeit not very specifically, according to social class and
education: 'getting my nose in a book'; 'specs'; 'the old . . .';
'my lark'; 'ripping times'; 'get stewed'; and the grammatically
incorrect use of 'me' as a sentence subject in line 9. Readers
may feel some unease, or else they may find humour in the use
made of this register, in that it tends to disclose the essentially
middle-class stance of Movement poetry with its habit of
implying a reader who shares the poet's privileged and superior
insight and his amusement over the speaker's inferiority.

The other register carries the poem's intertextuality, in that it consists of words which evoke the language of the books referred to in the first two stanzas: 'dirty dogs'; 'cloak and fangs'; 'dude'; 'yellow'; 'the store'.[7] Register-mixing is widely used by Larkin, whether mixing registers from different types of discourse, as here, or from different levels, moving, for example, between plain words of one syllable in simple sentences and more elevated rhetorical language (more unusual words, complex syntax). Its effect in this poem is to establish a dialectic between a somewhat satirized romantic desire and the real world. The formal device of rhyme is used subtly and cleverly to underline this dialectic, as in the rhyming of 'book/right hook' and 'school/keep cool' in the first stanza. Rhyme can be regarded as a specialized syntagmatic device, with the capacity to pull disparate concepts into functional cohesion. Here, the 'book/right hook' rhyme interpolates a disjunction into the familiar collocation of 'book' and 'school' which normally represents what might be thought of as 'higher' cultural values, or at least part of an educative process. But what the rhymes emphasize is that the use of books by the speaker was instead degenerative, giving him only an escapist Walter Mitty-type fantasy life.

The passage of time, and of the speaker's experience, is marked by temporal markers at the beginning of each stanza ('When/Later/now'). In the first stage he identified with heroes (stanza 1); in a second stage, marked by fantasies of *sexual* violence, with villains (stanza 2). The rhyme-link of 'inch-thick specs' and 'sex' generates a more mordant, more unkind irony than the comparable rhymes in stanza 1, and signals the link between temporality and degeneration along the syntagmatic axis. In the present time of the third stanza the speaker can only identify with the non-hero, the characters who fill minor and ignoble roles. Books have failed him, so he has rejected them in favour of the mind-numbing escapism of getting drunk. A change of quality in the speaking voice is effected by a change in the relationship between syntagm and verse form: in the first two stanzas there are no mid-line breaks and the rhymes are all nouns, apart from the adjective 'cool', so that each individual line is firmly delineated. This is especially so in stanza 2, where every line except the third is followed by a strong pause. In the third stanza there are clause boundaries within half the lines, and the strong running-on past line-ends, with the use of a function-word like 'before' in rhyme position, breaks down the firm patterning and can be said to reflect the self-conscious loss of confidence experienced by the speaker.

Generally speaking, Larkin's poems move towards moments of revelation, but what is revealed can either be an illumination which transcends everyday experience, taking the speaker out of himself so that he sees the world in a different way, or the revelation of a void, an emptiness lying beneath the surface of human life. Poems of the second kind, such as 'A Study of Reading Habits', can seem to be permeated with rather black humour, which slides into melancholy, but they can also encourage a consideration of what might fill the absences created within them. This in turn points on to an examination of the values thus implied. The habit of reading which the poem is about is symbolic of a larger failure to come to grips with external reality – the speaker in this poem has made a crucial choice early in life which conditions his possible later choices. The poem is implicitly framed by acts of choice: in the first two lines the speaker chooses escapism as a 'cure' for life's ills (though significantly not all of them). In the last two lines he chooses between alternative escapist possibilities. The void remains, because in opting for these kinds of choices he has relinquished the possibility of positive life-choices.

The attitude to women in the second stanza, in particular, represents an important loss: by fantasizing male–female relationships in terms of violence, dominance and exploitation, he has been left with the emptiness which comes when *love*, the realization of the reality of another, has been made impossible. The human need is to dismantle stereotypes, do away with hero-cults, and discover how one relates to a world external to the self – how one escapes solipsism. The speaker's reading is an emblem of his solipsism, for, where books might have represented an external apprehension of the world, he has used them only as an extension of himself, and has allowed that self to be conditioned by limiting cultural values. Once his reading has turned on him, as it were, he has nowhere to go but to seek oblivion. The escape from solipsism through the discovery of moments which move beyond confinement within the self is an important aspect of the endings of Larkin's poems, and is represented in this poem by its antitype.

Crozier has pointed out that the majority of Movement poems revolve around an art object, a cultural site, or a moment of experience, and that it is the concentration on surfaces which separates these poems from 'the tradition of enfeebled Romanticism' (1983, 204–5). The relationship of speaker to object, site, or moment, however, involves the creation of a small fiction. It seems almost inevitable that a consequence of attempting to shift emphasis from the paradigmatic to the syntagmatic, and so to produce poems which have simpler surfaces, is a reinscription of narrative as an implicitly central aspect of the syntagmatic axis. Over half the poems in *The Whitsun Weddings* volume, where 'Reading Habits' appeared, have an overt narrative frame or component.

## Drifting point of view in realist fiction: Olga Masters's *Loving Daughters* (1984)

The equivalent of such poetry in fiction is the continuing tradition of realism. It is hard to think of many novels which have managed to exclude narrative, though its ordering has often been subjected to violent disruptions in some modernist and postmodernist novels. On the other hand, traditional narrative has remained as a constant alternative to more experimental forms. We conclude this discussion with a piece from a recent Australian novel, Olga Masters's *Loving Daughters* (the central character here is a young Englishman, Colin Edwards, Anglican rector of a small country parish):

> 'Dear Mother,' he wrote, 'I have been thinking a lot about you today, possibly because I'm wearing the grey jumper you knitted me, which I thought would be too warm for this climate, but that is not so.'
>
> The words, very high on the page, ran quickly into the    5
> shadows. Dull, puny things escaping in their shame! He felt the need to escape too and went to look out on Wyndham merging into the dusk.
>
> But it was grey too, all grey, the war memorial a blackish grey, the posts holding up the roof over Grant's    10
> store verandah, a washed out grey, the sky a nothing colour, but grey when you looked at it for any time, his staggering fence posts grey too, and the wattle tree where Una's horse had been tethered not the silvery grey of daytime, but cut out dark and sharp with hard    15
> decisive scissors, a guard for the road. A grey, grey road leading to nowhere.

He sat on his couch with his back to it. He
remembered Una's small round buttocks settling onto
the saddle. She had shaken them down as you would      20
shake seed to the bottom of a bag, and made her back
very straight as she pulled on one rein to turn her horse
around.
   He got up and went to the table, flicking his pen so
that it rolled off his pad, leaving it a white and gleaming   25
thing, relieving the dark, pleasing him as a soft light
would.

(1984, Ch. 20)

The style here depends mainly on parataxis. There are many
single-clause sentences, and the rest are loosely co-ordinated –
the series of present participle clauses in lines 24–7, for
example, is chained along the syntagm in such a way that each
of the first three refers back to a subject in the immediately
preceding clause but then the fourth is grammatically parallel
with the third:

He . . . flicking

   it [the pen] . . . leaving

      it [the pad's whiteness] . . . ‖ relieving the dark
                                      ‖ pleasing him

Of course this only reflects the chronological, cause-and-effect,
'story' order of the details; the last two, however, are more
'discourse'-oriented, presenting simultaneously felt perceptions,
but exhibiting a tension between simultaneity and syntagmatic
linearity – that is, while 'relieving' and 'pleasing' are common
collocables and so reinforce the impression of simultaneity, the
simple fact of order and the 'dark:light' opposition do imply
causality. There is no difficulty in grasping the meaning of the
sentence, especially since such syntactical linking is quite
speech-like, but 'pleasing him as a soft light would' is really
quite loosely related to the rest of the string. Such syntagmatic
looseness enables Masters to slip into the character's perceptual
point of view; in retrospect, it has happened in this sentence
with 'white and gleaming'. As is usual in fiction, a slip into the
presentation of a character's thoughts does not demand a shift
into language appropriate to that character. The extract clearly
shows this in the contrast between Edwards's epistolary style

and the recording of what he sees outside his window: the first is hypotactic and formal in comparison with the serial style of the second.

The scene is built up with a lot of attention to physical particularity, as might be expected in a text in the realist tradition. It also shares with other realist texts the technique of getting below the surfaces of things by manipulating point of view and by the use of the figure of metonymy. In Chapter 4 we pointed to similar strategies in *Middlemarch*, though there the point of view was not shifting as rapidly as here, and the signifiers carrying extra implicit signification did so more by associations than as metonymy. Edwards's grey jumper, though, is metonymic. He is a naïve young man, with no experience of women beyond his childhood home, who has just become sexually awakened; the connection between the jumper and his mother links his present and his past life, his adolescence and his marginal maturity. His writing to his mother about his jumper is the prelude to a meditation on the young women who have aroused his desire, and as such it becomes a symptom of his essentially undeveloped understanding of relationships and sexuality.

The stilted prose of his letter also marks the pull between his conditioning and his desire. Lines 5–8 reflect on what he has just written, slipping quickly from narrator reporting into the character's mind. They reflect on language itself, on the capacity of language to mask signification, as words are used for little more than phatic communication. The 'shadows' into which the words disappear have overtones of a need to hide, as is spelled out when the words are fully personified in the next sentence, 'escaping in their shame', retroactively confirming both literal and figurative meanings for 'very high', 'ran', and 'shadows'. The repetition of 'escape' explicitly connects Edwards's impulse for a literal escape with the failure of language to express what he wants to say.

The jumper has a further metonymic function as an emblem of the culture shock Edwards is experiencing as actuality fails to match his expectations. His personality is too small to be able to cope with the demands made on it by life in a rural community quite alien to anything he has known in the past – whereas the jumper, a trivial object, turns out to be suitable for the climate, the other baggage of the man's Englishness renders him untranslatable. The text plays out the gap in the next paragraph, when Edwards is presented surveying the Australian scene from his window (the shift to perceptual point of view is marked by 'went to look out' and strongly reinforced by 'when you looked at it', especially as the indefinite 'you' locates narratee at the same place as the character).

From the outset, the meaning of *grey* is extended beyond its colour-denotation to include its pejorative emotional connotation, as Masters explicitly links the greyness of the landscape with the greyness of the jumper – 'it was grey *too*, all grey' – so that the precise physical details, the war memorial, the verandah posts, and so on, are overtly pushed beyond verisimilitude to become also metonymic of Edwards's feelings, specifically of his sense of lack and of absence, as he projects these on to the landscape. His depression is expressed particularly by the set of negations: 'washed out', 'a nothing colour', 'not the silvery grey', 'leading to nowhere'. The barrier to his desire is expressed by the transformed wattle tree, associated with Una but now 'cut out dark and sharp with hard decisive scissors', in which metaphor is coloured by four adjectives with strong subjective associations. The vehicle itself, though, is essentially domestic, as is the comparison in the next paragraph between Una's 'small round buttocks' and the seed shaken to the bottom of a bag.

The text has now shifted from perception to memory, so that conceptual point of view becomes more important. The comparison surprises – it seems very visual, and might have fertility overtones, but is the reader to visualize a packet of seed purchased in a shop, or a large quantity bagged on a farm? The simile is much less precise than the physical, but objective, 'small round buttocks' (the words are carefully chosen here, as a few paragraphs later the same referent is transformed, in a dramatic register-shift, into a 'beautiful little bum').

Generally, then, the presentation of realistic detail, as focalized through Edwards's perceptions and conceptions, reveals how he solipsistically remakes the world, projecting his mood on to the landscape and reifying the human figure he places in it. As it turns out, Edwards can only function in a world where woman is refashioned according to a fantasy based on his own limited past experience.

Our overview has traversed rather vast tracts of time and space to come to this point, a description of a marginalized character in an isolated town, in a novel written in one of the physically remoter literatures in English. Our choice was deliberate, a way of stressing the absence of a central tradition in late twentieth-century literature. Moreover, the present situation of literature allows our overview no ending, for all it can be is a position from which to look back over the long, and often wayward, history of literary English. To conclude our study, we wish to turn to an aspect we have frequently alluded to, but not yet examined in any detail, the place of figurative language in literary English. [8]

# Notes and further reading

1   For a measure of the relation between semantics and sound-patterning, compare this line with Wilfrid Owen's 'the stuttering rifle's rapid rattle' ('Anthem for Doomed Youth', line 3), in which an onomatopoeic effect is readily perceived because the framing terms, 'stuttering' and 'rattle', signify auditory concepts which are then further defined by 'rapid'.

2   The term 'logocentrism' originates in the writings of Jacques Derrida, and the concept has been widely discussed in post-structuralist thinking. Briefly, it refers to the desire in western thought to find some 'centre' of meaning to explain existence, and takes the notion of the originating 'Word' as a primary example. For fuller discussion see, for example, Culler (1983, 92–4 and 99–111).

3   For a full account of Barthelme's evoking and destroying of generic expectations in this story, see Clark (1983).

4   A text from the Anglo-American tradition more readily comparable with *Tangi* would perhaps be Elizabeth Smart's *By Grand Central Station I Sat Down and Wept* (1945), though in this work loss is not recuperated as it is in *Tangi*.

5   Our discussion here is generally indebted to Libby's excellent account of Williams (1984, 31–46). See also Moore's discussion of Williams's syntax (1986).

6   For an overview of these poets, see Morrison (1980); and for a more hostile evaluation, see Crozier (1983).

7   This is an Americanism here, belonging to a lexical set appropriate to Westerns; the normal British signifier for the signified here is *shop*: *store* has a specialized application in British English quite distinct from a *shop*, in that a *store* refers to a large establishment selling a variety of goods

usually for cash and at low prices, and conventionally not patronized by the 'better' people.

8   Further reading: Leech (1969), ch. 3; Libby (1984); Hassan (1987); MacCabe (1978), for the politics of language and Joyce's changing of relations between reader and text; McGann (1987), on (mainly) syntagmatic 'derangement' in contemporary American poetry.

# Exercises

(Given the range and diversity of twentieth-century literature, no specific texts have been nominated for these exercises; we suggest that several should be selected from that vast range for each exercise, while some exercises call for an even wider diachronic selection. Each exercise could also be considered as a comparison/contrast with earlier periods.)

1   Find several examples of twentieth-century literary texts which seem to attempt to defy the tyranny of the syntagm and/or the constraints of the paradigm; what strategies are used to do this? To what extent do such texts also attempt to subvert signification of meaning?

2   How is the problem of solipsism (the view that the Self is the only object of verifiable knowledge) encoded in twentieth-century literary texts? To what extent does that attitude impinge upon and interact with the alienation and disorientation so frequently expressed in the texts? How does the use of language convey such concepts?

3   Compare and contrast the self-conscious textuality of twentieth-century literary texts with the self-consciousness of eighteenth-century literary texts. How does the use of the elements of textuality differ between the two periods, especially in conveying the different presuppositions of each period?

4   Compare and contrast the treatment in literary texts of all periods from the fourteenth to the twentieth century of nature, and especially its relationship with the viewer. How are twentieth-century attitudes similar to and different from those of earlier periods?

5   Compare and contrast methods of presenting protagonists'
    speech and thought in prose fiction of the eighteenth,
    nineteenth, and twentieth centuries, and analyse the effect
    upon the status of the narrator (and so upon the narratee/
    reader relationship).

6   To what extent do some modern literary discourses (such as
    those written by women, those written in post-colonial
    areas) displace older traditions of literary discourse? Do
    the elements of textuality (especially the two triads of
    syntagm/paradigm/signifier–signified   and   cohesion/con-
    gruence/coherence) provide means for coming to terms with
    such texts?

# 6 'This mad *instead*': figurative language

And then I wondered why this mad *instead*
Perverts our praise to uncreation, why
Such savor's in this wrenching things awry.
(Richard Wilbur, 'Praise in Summer')

## Figurative language as a product of the paradigmatic/syntagmatic axes

Wherever figurative language has appeared in our earlier chapters, it has been treated primarily in terms of its function within the interaction of syntagm and paradigm. Like other elements of a literary text, however, figurative language, an area of primary concern to literary criticism, is in its own right strongly affected by the syntagmatic axis, and can be regarded as one more product of the way signifiers are combined syntagmatically. It would have been impossible to discuss certain texts and certain periods in our earlier chapters without some mention of figurative language, but we have not dealt with it systematically. This chapter will attempt to do that. We will begin by considering how the relationship between paradigm and syntagm generates figurative effects, and then we will go on to examine some of the ways figures are sustained or extended. The chapter also seeks to incorporate some sense of how the relative importance of tropes varies from period to period, and of how socio-linguistic context affects figurative signification. Our examples will be drawn mainly from poetry, but we will conclude the chapter with a brief discussion of some uses of figurative language in prose.

Put simply, the syntagmatic axis connects signifiers in such a way that in certain combinations unusual *chains* of reference are generated within the connected paradigmatic entities. What characteristically initiates figurative movement along such a chain of signifieds can be described as a dislocation of surface meaning, of the obvious relationships between signifiers. Another way to say all this is to observe that in tropes the syntagmatic axis makes an assertion which is a violation of the audience's sense of empirical reality, or sense of what is 'true', as in the opening lines of this Campion lyric:

There is a garden in her face
Where roses and white lilies grow . . .

The first line remains a logical absurdity until the ordinary core signified of *garden*, 'a piece of ground used for cultivating plants', is replaced by some further signified which the usual cultural associations of *garden* suggest – let us say, 'a place of beauty', or perhaps 'a site (or sight) which gives pleasure'. Other possibilities, such as 'a place to grow vegetables', are retrospectively precluded by the specification of flowers in the extension of the trope in line 2. At the same time, the location of this garden 'in her face' pushes signification past the immediate signifieds of *roses* and *lilies* to some ancillary associations centred on colour. The move is facilitated by the fact that for at least two hundred years preceding Campion English poetry had used roses and lilies, denoting redness and whiteness, as clichés in the evocation of female beauty. The place of cultural conventions in figurative language is a topic of interest for a number of reasons. For example, selection of vehicles is markedly subject to diachronic change, as in this example (since the roses-and-lilies convention, with its biblical origin,[1] has now lapsed), but also in other ways, reflecting changes in world-view, technology, socio-cultural values, and so on; it also may be vitally connected with the question of the kind of claims that can be made for the cognitive power of tropes – are they special or are such referential chains purely conventional, a product of the way a culture organizes reality, as Goodman (1981) claims?

## Simple and complex metaphors

The Campion lyric illustrates one of the simplest kinds of syntagmatic arrangements which results in *metaphor*, the declarative 'A=B' structure where '=' is realized by some part of the verb 'to be'. There is, however, also an element of cognitive complexity inherent in such a structure, and which pertains generally to metaphor, simile and personification (and which distinguishes these tropes from others). While one entity is proposed as analogous with another on the basis of some perceived or imagined isomorphism (as faces and gardens might offer comparable visual delight derived from pleasing combinations of colour), the two entities remain *semantically* heteromorphic: a face and a garden are not comparable in size, shape, texture, substance or odour.

The kind of decoding operation which the audience must carry out is, nevertheless, more complex in the Campion example than in, say, the contemporary cliché with which Bartholomew Griffin begins a sonnet, 'My Ladies haire is threeds of beaten gold'. There is a clear difference in the two examples between the extent and type of gap between signifier and signified, which suggests the possibility of differentiations within tropes of the same kind, and also proves significant in differentiating various tropes such as metaphor and metonymy. Thus extension into a third dimension is again crucial in any application of the intersecting syntagm/paradigm axes to an examination of figurative language.

Our emphasis on the multi-dimensional structuring of figurative language leads us to question theories of metaphor which hold that, because metaphor operates at the level of the sentence and not of the word, the signifier/signified relationship remains stable within a metaphoric utterance (see, for example, Harrison, 1986). Our approach reveals such a position to be an oversimplification because of its implicit restriction of language to two dimensions. Underlying all notions about figurative language are crucial presuppositions about the relationship between language and phenomena: if it is accepted that there is an arbitrary relationship between verbal signs and referents, and that the world is constructed through culture and language,[2] tropes will be perceived as an element which enables language to construct ideas about the world, and criticisms with a materialist basis may choose to deny to metaphor any status as a quasi-mysterious cognitive process, a key to transcendent Truths, and to resituate it as a sub-code of rhetoric. A related issue is whether such constructing is creative or functions as a tool of ideological constraint.

# The historical valuing of particular tropes

Such presuppositions affect the relative status accorded various tropes, and explain such major changes as the post-structuralist downward revaluation of the importance of metaphor and the privileging of metonymy. Metaphor had been established by Coleridge as the queen of the tropes, and metaphor and symbol subsequently had become the privileged figures for the New Critics, with high claims being made for their power to penetrate to deep inner truths by their ability to bring together unstated resemblances with great immediacy. The separation of figurative from literal language insisted upon by New Criticism implied that there was a difference of kind between the two, though I. A. Richards's earlier work on metaphor had already made it clear that there was a grey area between the black and white of literal and figurative, as with so-called 'dead' metaphors such as 'the *leg* of the table'. And since New Criticism dealt mainly with poetry, where the most heavily foregrounded metaphors often occur, metaphor was regarded as a marker of poetic ability, and its handling very much a part of the evaluative criteria fundamental to New Criticism. The Romantic/New Critical view is still current in some quarters, and underlies as recent a study as Harrison's (1986), where it is claimed that the point of some lines from Shakespeare's Sonnet LXXIII is 'to restructure the reader's feelings by opening, between commonplace words, channels of analogy through which feelings attached to one set of words and what they mean may flow and embrace other words, and what *they* mean' (51). Significantly, at a crucial stage of his analysis Harrison has resorted to a concatenation of figures (architecture, and irrigation and sex as figures for human communication) to evoke the mystery of feelings created by metaphor. That is, the commentator's own use of metaphors loaded with values approved within his culture has obscured any difference there might be between the ideology of the culture within which the text was produced and that within which it is being read.

In contrast, structuralists and post-structuralists have tended to concentrate much more on metonymy and, to a lesser extent, on allegory. The post-structuralist challenge to the habit of thinking in binary opposites, especially through arguments about the indeterminacy and deferral of meaning, not only sets out to deny the metaphor/metonym opposition, but also the literal/figurative distinction, arguing that the indeterminacy of the signifier/signified relationship prevents any clear-cut division between the literal and figurative uses of language.

Such a readjustment amongst the hierarchy of figures is not a modern phenomenon but part of a long process within which shifts in cultural and literary values affect the selection of predominant figures. In form, though not in the significance given to that form, the late twentieth century has returned to an earlier, albeit implicit, position. That is, the nineteenth-century stress upon metaphor can be viewed as a reaction against an eighteenth-century privileging of metonymy and synecdoche. This privileging may not have been enunciated in eighteenth-century theory, but the practice of a poet such as Pope makes it apparent that metonym and synecdoche were of primary importance, and Augustan poetic diction, especially periphrastic phrasing, is heavily dependent on them. The question of what metonymy is will have to be addressed shortly, so we will return to some Augustan examples then.

## 'Tenor', 'vehicle' and 'ground'

Some terms we have chosen to retain for discussing figurative language are those coined by I. A. Richards to describe the two parts of a metaphor: the *tenor* for the literal concept, the *vehicle* for the figurative one. Hrushovski (1984, 16–25) has proposed abandoning these terms, for the very good reason that they imply 'a limitation of metaphor to a one-directional substitution theory', whereas in the process of their interrelationship *both* elements of a metaphor are subject to change. The criticism is an important one, but use of the now traditional terms has not in practice precluded the possibility of interchange between them, so we see no need to discard them in favour of new and less elegant terms.[3] The difference between the two elements of a metaphor – and the potential for interchange – is particularly clear where both are spelled out in noun form and are then subjected to retrospective modification, as for example in the opening stanza of A. R. Ammons's 'Pet Panther':

> My attention is a wild
> animal: it will if idle
> make trouble where there
> was no harm. . . .

In simple declarative figurative structures of the kind exemplified in the first two lines, the noun tenor ('My attention') is stated to be the same as the noun-plus-adjective vehicle ('a wild animal'). The figurative element comes into being here when it is asserted that two signifiers (or signifying phrases) occurring along the one syntagmatic axis express the same underlying signified. This may be represented, as in Figure 6.1, as a roughly equilateral triangle, the apex of which should be conceived as lying behind the basal points in the third dimension.

**(Signified)**

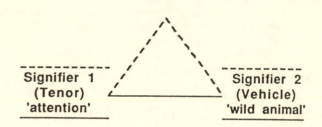

Figure 6.1

Leech (1969, 151–6) has termed this common signified the *ground* of the metaphor, and has defined its function as being to posit the area of relationship shared by tenor and vehicle. The ground is not necessarily stated within the text, though in this example the rest of the stanza does indicate a ground (in fact, the first in a series of grounds). To put this another way, it can be said that the combined signifiers 'wild animal' conceptualize a signified made up of such semantic elements as

-domesticated  +savage
-human        +bestial.

But the process of referral does not end here, for the syntagm retrospectively asserts that this newly created signified, for which there is no simple signifier, no phonemic or graphic representation, must now function as a signifier pointing on to a further signified (which will be in some way isomorphic with the signified pointed to by 'attention'). Simultaneously, within the metaphorical structure, this signified pointed to by 'attention', normally comprising such positive associations as {+cognitive, +disciplined, +alert}, is, under the combined influence of vehicle and ground, made to slide away from its signifier and to develop negative connotations associated with 'wild animal', the second signifier along the syntagmatic axis.

The three-dimensional model of chapter 1 (p. 15) will readily accommodate this further paradigmatic complication, since it merely needs to be modified by the addition of one more unit to the plane receding behind the paradigmatic axis, as in Figure 6.2:

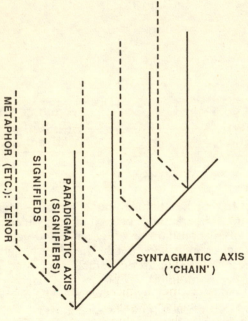

Figure 6.2

The simile and the symbol are variations in degree upon the triangle frame by which metaphor was represented in Figure 6.1. The simile is closely related, but overtly declares itself as a statement of similarity by the presence of its introductory prepositions, 'like' or 'as'. The symbol, however, virtually rotates the triangle so that the vehicle occupies apex position in the two-dimensional text, with the tenor and ground both lying in the third dimension behind it.

# Metonymy

We have suggested that in at least two periods metonymy has been primary amongst tropes. It is also the most problematic of the tropes, as far as reaching a consensus definition is concerned. The conventional discrimination between metaphor and metonymy has been to define the former as a device of *substitution*, the latter as a device of *contiguity*.[4] A metaphor substitutes for something else implied in its context, while a metonym deletes something from its context; it takes out the main thing, and provides some aspect, or part, of the whole concept, something from which that whole can be inferred, given the aspect that is stated; there is a process of overlap between the part and the whole. The notion of 'contiguity' is, however, much too broad, with the result that metonymy becomes a catch-all for anything that can't be classified as something else. This loose notion of metonymy has pursued the term throughout its history, and even Leech, whose work on metaphor was so subtle, still reverts to it – 'in practice, metonymy is treated as a residual category including all varieties of transference of meaning apart from those separately classed as synecdoche or metaphor' (1969, 152). Our proposal for clarifying the nature of metonymy derives from what we have been constantly stressing, that is, that tropes are created by the interaction of syntagm and paradigm, not by either of them functioning on its own.

Such an approach also answers a need for clarification which emerges from the post-structuralist argument that the distinction between metaphor and metonymy cannot always be sustained, since the ground for metaphoric relationships often, though not always, resides in some metonymical connection (see Culler, 1981, Ch. 10). Since a shared property has to be the ground for the comparison between the two things, then to that extent the two overlap, and are linked by metonymy, and thus the metonym becomes the basis for the metaphor. If this is the case, it is argued that the larger claims for the status of metaphor become subverted, because the similarities it discovers turn out to be accidents of tradition and culture. But as our later discussion shows, while the hard and fast distinction between different tropes cannot be maintained, the extent of multi-dimensionality differs as between metaphor and metonymy.

Problems of a different kind emerge from an examination of

what is perhaps the most impressive recent attempt to resolve the nature of metonymy, that of Hugh Bredin (1984b). On the basis of a list of metonymical relations culled from a variety of rhetorical sources, Bredin seeks to escape the idea of metonymy as a rag-bag for unclassifiable tropes and to determine its constituent modes of operation. A crucial strategy in his closely-wrought argument is to dismiss the structuralist separation of sign and referent (and with it the signifier/signified gap), in order to remove metonymy from the ambit of *linguistic* relations, insisting instead that 'metonymical relations are relations between things, not between words' (52). The theory then adduces an analogy between figurative relations and 'modalities of consciousness' (55), specifically the analytic and synthetic operations of cognition, with synecdoche linked to the analytic and metonymy falling within a group, including metaphor, linked to the synthetic. It is an elegant theory, but emphatically two-dimensional and essentially syntagmatic in its assumptions about language, and it might be objected that its effect is to replace the substitution:contiguity opposition with the analytic:synthetic opposition (which may not be very different), and to redistribute the tropes in a different configuration. Metonymy is different from metaphor, in this system, in that it is 'a transfer of names between objects which are related to each other extrinsically and simply' (57) or, in other words, a product of conventional cultural coding (as most traditional views of metonymy have recognized): 'metaphor *creates* the relation between its objects, while metonymy *presupposes* that relation . . . metonymy can never articulate a newly discovered insight' (57).

DIFFERENTIATION OF METONYMY AND METAPHOR

While Bredin's conclusions are sensible and unexceptionable, we do not see them as a conclusive solution to the problem of metonymy, precisely because his argument has discarded the third dimension of language brought in by the paradigmatic axis. Let us now see how the analytical frame used throughout this book applies to the problem. The following lines, from a popular song by Carly Simon ('Two Hot Girls', 1987), afford an illuminating example of a metonymic figure which is obviously culturally determined, in that the key term is heavily marked along its paradigmatic axis; the figure is a simple one, but cannot be 'correctly' decoded in its place within a text unless the audience has access to essential cultural information about the semiotics of female clothing:

> It happened last night,
> We were feeling adventurous,
> We put on our heels
> And went out for a walk

The principal effect in line 3 of the synecdochic *heels* (the part standing for the whole high-heeled shoe) is what we perceive to be metonymic signification, as it conveys 'dressed up' and contains the further implication (suggested by the song title and later confirmed syntagmatically) of sexual attractiveness and availability.[5] This process of signification is not metaphoric, however: high-heeled shoes have such associations conventionally, but also retain a literal function since the associations have been acquired from the actual physical effect such shoes have on the visual impact made by their wearer (lengthening legs, tightening calf muscles, modifying the walk). The audience of the text can thus be expected to draw on cultural knowledge and visual memory to decode the signification of *heels*.

The difference between metaphor and metonymy is further clarified in an examination of paradigmatic choice in the opening lines of Howard Nemerov's 'The Blue Swallows':

>     Across the millstream below the bridge
> (1)  Seven blue swallows divide the air
>     In shapes invisible and evanescent . . .

The clause frame in the second line – swallows divide the air (1) – is an apparently simple declarative statement turning on a metaphor, here a verbal rather than a nominal figure such as that in the Ammons example. The paradigmatic choices involved in its construction are: a selection of a particular class of bird; a selection of a signifier to express movement; a term to denote location in space. The result, obviously enough, is different from (2)*'birds fly through the sky' (where other paradigmatic choices have been substituted), but a comparison of (1) and (2) brings out how the verb of (1) has been selected because it carries a sense which is not literal with respect to swallows: 'divide the air' indicates that the birds fly through it, but 'shapes' and 'divide' constitute a lexical set relating to geometry.

By a further paradigmatic substitution, metonymy (here also periphrasis) may be introduced into the statement and metaphor removed: (3)*'the harbingers of summer fly through the air.' This time an attribute of swallows has been substituted for the birds themselves. Regardless of the migratory habits of swallows, there is a literary and cultural convention which assumes that swallows signal the onset of summer, and that (3) will therefore be read as a metonym made possible by the whole cultural context and formally produced by deletion of the actual referent 'swallows'. The metonymy is merely a cultural cliché or stereotype derived from the accidental observation of natural phenomena, and the reader is not encouraged to linger over the signifier group but rather is encouraged to discover the signified behind it, and mentally to supply another unmarked signifier generated by that signified. Metonymy thus becomes (with the more easily identifiable synecdoche) a trope which differs in structure from the frame within which metaphor, simile and symbol operate (Figure 6.1): since the concept conveyed by the signifier(s) of the vehicle is always *in some sense* literally true of the tenor – whereas the vehicle of the other tropes is never true of the tenor – metonymy operates without a *ground* and within a chain of readily determinable signification, because metonymic relationships are predetermined by socio-cultural coding of language; as such, it is a figure with limited depth and is not inventive or particularly creative. Metaphor, on the other hand, in asserting that different signifieds at a deep level of cognition signify the same *thing*, enters an area of much less determinable meaning. The Nemerov example clearly illustrates the difference between the two tropes, for where the metonymy we have supplied is merely a cultural cliché, a stereotype derived from the accidental observation of natural phenomena, the metaphor of 'divide' encourages a fresh way of looking at the swallows' flight through an unusual connection; it is *expressive*.[6]

This is much the same conclusion as Bredin reached, though the route has been different, for we are arguing that metonymy lacks that combination of multi-dimensional isomorphism and hetermorphism which characterizes metaphor.

SLIPPINGS BETWEEN TROPES

We remarked earlier that Augustan poetic diction was based on
the metonym and synecdoche, but even here there is an
element of slipping between the various tropes, as in the
following:

> To fifty chosen Sylphs, of special note,
> We trust the important charge, the petticoat;
> Oft have we known that sevenfold fence to fail,
> Though stiff with hoops, and armed with ribs of whale.
> Form a strong line about the silver bound,
> And guard the wide circumference around.
>
> (*The Rape of the Lock*, II.117–22)

The subject, 'the petticoat', is both stated simply and by means
of periphrases which re-present it through spatial or contingent
connections. The last two, 'the silver bound' and 'the wide
circumference', have deleted all other aspects of the base
signified except, respectively, the ornamented edge and a sense
of the space the garment occupies. The first might be taken as
synecdoche, since it seems to be part standing for whole, but as
'bound' also belongs to the lexical set of military terms,
whereby the petticoat becomes a defence of female chastity, it
is also metonymy; the second is more clearly metonymic,
substituting space for the object contained within it. More
complex are the first two, 'the important charge' and 'that
sevenfold fence'. In the first of these, an abstract replaces the
concrete, as responsibility for an object stands for the object
itself, and the figure becomes strongly attitudinal in presenting
the speaker's (Ariel's) point of view. In the second, a metonymy
alluding intertextually to a shield[7] is transferred to the petticoat;
it seems to remain metonymic, in a user:instrument relationship,
in that as a shield is a 'fence' for a warrior, so a petticoat is a
'fence' for a virgin. At the same time, the implicit analogy
between warrior and virgin in the context of a lexical set of
military terms can be seen as tipping the figure into metaphor.
Beyond this again, the petticoat, in a container:contained relationship to its wearer, becomes a metonym for virginity, though
it might also be tempting to say that it symbolizes virginity. The
breakdown of hard-and-fast differentiation between the tropes
is very apparent. Much of the complexity of this example
derives from intertextuality (the epic shield) and cultural coding

(the association of petticoats and sex). These elements extrinsic to linguistic structure are not confined to metonymy, though, but also affect metaphor.

Finally, whereas in a metaphor there is always some gap between tenor and vehicle, in a metonym the same basic concept is present whether it is referred to by the conventional unmarked culturally-coded signifier or by the metonym that has displaced it in its particular context. In other words, the process of paradigmatic referral lacks depth because it turns out to be reflexive: the signifier chosen to replace the signified within the syntagm merely points the reader back to the original signifier, as 'sevenfold fence' points back to 'petticoat'. In a sense, the metonym is the obverse of the symbol, for while the metonym's signifier points to two different signifieds which remain aspects of the one concept, with the symbol the syntagm (often the hypersyntagm) prevents (usually only gradually and cumulatively and retrospectively) acceptance of the conventionally coded signified(s) normally connected with that signifier. Like metaphor, the symbol depends at least in part on disparity between signifier and signified; like metonym, it is not represented within the discourse by a double signifier, that is, both a vehicle and a tenor (whether as two signifiers or as a single but polysemous signifier). What the text provides initially is the literal element, which is displaced to be the vehicle for conveying something else, and so there is a conflation of the tenor/vehicle relationship at the textual level, as what appears to be tenor becomes retrospectively vehicle for another tenor that is signified behind the symbol, in another type of arbitrary relationship, but this time built up by the larger hypersyntagmatic contextual framework.

## Tropes in earlier literature

We have already in this chapter drawn attention to the varying status amongst tropes which depends on the critical position, and beyond that the world-view, of readers, but this finally only reflects the hierarchies into which tropes have been organized within the literary practice of different periods. It is to this variation, and its implications, that we now turn our attention.

At the beginning of the earliest of our periods, figurative language is conditioned by a number of factors interrelated within the macrocosm–microcosm model. Because the world is perceived as a system of signs pointing upward and outward from microcosm to macrocosm, discourse favours those tropes which best facilitate the movement from visible phenomena to the invisible or abstract. The result is that metaphor, the trope modern readers most readily associate with figurative language, is of negligible significance prior to the last quarter of the sixteenth century, and tends to be embedded within the ruling tropes, which are allegory, symbol (with conventionally pre-determined significance), and types of analogy (simile, 'epic' simile, comparison). The following stanzas from Chaucer's *Troilus and Criseyde* illustrate some aspects of this relation of tropes:

> Who myghte tellen half the joie or feste
> Which that the soule of Troilus tho felte,                    345
> Heryng th'effect of Pandarus byheste?
> His olde wo, that made his herte swelte,
> Gan tho for joie wasten and tomelte,
> And al the richesse of his sikes sore
> At ones fledde; he felte of hem namore.                    350
>
> But right so as thise holtes and thise hayis,
> That han in wynter dede ben and dreye,
> Revesten hem in grene, when that May is,
> Whan every lusty liketh best to pleye;
> Right in that selve wise, soth to seye,                    355
> Wax sodeynliche his herte ful of joie,
> That gladder was ther nevere man in Troie.
>
> (III.344–57)

The second stanza is a clear example of an epic simile: as is usual with this figure, the boundaries of the vehicle are marked by the indicators of comparison ('right so as . . . Right in that selve wise'), and vehicle and tenor are both spelled out; in most epic similes, as here, vehicle precedes tenor, so that the audience's linear reception of the text means a transition through the sensory phenomena of landscape and season and their impact ('every lusty liketh best to pleye') to the more abstract 'joie'. Line 354, which both makes the impact explicit and anticipates the tenor, also reflects a tendency for epic similes to be expanded in their own right, without necessarily achieving the thematic linking evident here. Further, the simile's associative effect is increased by *revesten*, 'reclothe': to describe the return of leaves to the trees as a reclothing is a metaphor, but its actual function here is to embed a small personification allegory within the simile, with the result that the anthropomorphosed landscape more readily anticipates the human emotion which is the tenor of the vehicle. Even when that tenor is given, it is still further expanded by the comparison implicit in the use of the rhetorical 'outdoing topos' which concludes the movement – 'That gladder was ther nevere man in Troie'. In these ways, a network of inter-reflecting relationships is established between the individual experience, the natural world, and society. When the tenor, Troilus's access of joy, is given, it turns out not only that it has been explicitly anticipated within the vehicle but also that it is a restatement of a topic from the preceding stanza, in which personification is already suggested as a trace by the anthropomorphic qualities in the verbs *wasten* and *fledde*. The former, indeed, functions as a kind of conceit, since it recodes the language conventionally applied to the lover (love being represented as a wasting disease) to describe the process which frees him from the sorrow of love-longing.

## Epic simile

As a type of extended trope, the range of the epic simile is restricted virtually to the long narrative poem and to the period before 1700 (though its use continues in parodic form in Augustan mock-heroic and satire). We will here illustrate the trope with an example from Milton's *Paradise Lost* (I.766–76):

> the spacious Hall . . .
> Thick swarm'd, both on the ground and in the air,
> Brusht with the hiss of russling wings. As Bees
> In spring time, when the sun with *Taurus* rides,
> Poure forth thir populous youth about the Hive       770
> In clusters; they among fresh dews and flowers
> Flie to and fro, or on the smoothed Plank,
> The suburb of thir Straw-built Cittadel,
> New rub'd with Baum, expatiate and confer
> Thir state affairs. So thick the aerie crowd       775
> Swarm'd and were straitn'd . . . .

As in the *Troilus* example, the boundaries of the simile are formally and clearly delineated by the correlative connectives 'As . . . So', but the marking is here intensified by the near repetition of the ground of the comparison, 'Thick swarm'd' (767, 775–6), with the return to the main subject. (The repetition is not precise, since in 775–6 word-order has been varied to place the subject of the clause between 'thick' and 'swarm'd', and 'swarm'd' is used with a different denotation.) As we have remarked before, what is perhaps most notable about epic simile is the tendency to extend the vehicle of the comparison for its own sake, without maintaining a pertinent analogy with, or reference back to, the main subject. This tendency is first seen here in the decorative, cosmological gloss on 'spring time' (769), and then in the long digression beginning in line 771, which in part simply describes the bee-community, but mixes literal information – 'New rub'd with Baum' – with an embedded trope comparing the hive and its activities with human communities: 'suburb . . . State affairs', and especially the elevated register of the doublet 'expatiate and confer', terms which apply human labels to non-human activity. This last point is of particular interest, since it illustrates both how tropes can be used in general (i.e. ahistorically) to reorganize reality, and how a cultural assumption such as the microcosm/macrocosm idea functions to construct that reality. The beehive as a figure for communal order is itself a convention in western literature; Milton's use of it here derives specifically from Homer and Vergil, but it is a widespread classical *topos*, as Whaler (1932, 545–52) demonstrated. The intertextual effect underlines the immediate point that epic similes embrace contrast and disparity as well as comparison (Ricks, 1963), and then, especially if the effect is mock-heroic (Broadbent, 1960, 105–6), further suggests the irony that the fallen angels still act according to universal models of behaviour.

## Extended tropes

A kind of extended trope that has survived more persistently than the epic simile is that which sustains a figure along the syntagmatic axis by means of a series of signifiers relating variously to tenor or to vehicle or to both at once, and which maintains a congruence between vehicle and tenor. Andrew Marvell's 'A Dialogue Between the Soul and Body' contains some excellent examples (although it also, as in stanza 3, uses quite drastic shifts of vehicle from trope to trope). The 'prisoner in a dungeon' figure is sustained throughout the opening stanza; we will take the first six lines:

> O who shall, from this Dungeon, raise
> A Soul inslav'd so many wayes?
> With bolts of Bones, that fetter'd stands
> In Feet; and manacled in Hands.　　　　　　　　　4
> Here blinded with an Eye; and there
> Deaf with the drumming of an Ear.

The opening question distributes its extended trope amongst elements which variously represent tenor (x) and vehicle (y) of a metaphor. The whole figure is (re-)constructed as the reader combines the specific details and pursues chains of reference within related paradigmatic slots, as follows:

*Dungeon* [vehicle] ⟶ x (the unstated tenor, i.e. 'body')
*Soul* [tenor] ⟶ y (vehicle 'prisoner' implied by the verb, *inslav'd*)

An enrichment of the verbal complex here lies in the process whereby the chain of reference not only proceeds from vehicle to tenor in order to generate the metaphor but also proceeds from tenor to vehicle. That is, although the point of the argument hinges on the state of the soul, the intertwining of vehicle and tenor signifiers encourages readers to work backwards, as it were, from the key thematic signifier 'Soul' to the unstated vehicle element *'prisoner'. Such a double movement is an important aspect of extended metaphors because it maintains the presence of tenor, vehicle *and* ground for the duration of the figure. It is particularly important in this example because the poem's self-consciousness about its own figurative processes is a primary means of alerting the reader to the fallacies of its speakers' arguments. The argument in the opening stanza of the poem – that the physical is inferior to the spiritual – is expressed by the series of conceits which represent locomotion and the senses not as powers giving access to the world but as impediments which trap the soul. Thus in 'blinded with an Eye', the effect of the paradox that the organ of sight prevents the Soul from seeing what it craves is to promote the referential movement in 'blinded' from the literal and physical 'deprived of the power of sight' to the figurative 'deprived of spiritual capacity'. Immediately afterwards (in lines 7–8) the ground of the extended metaphor is more overtly foregrounded by the summative

A Soul hung up, as 'twere, in Chains
Of Nerves, and Arteries, and Veins.

The parenthesis 'as 'twere' draws attention to the figurative sense of 'hung up' and simultaneously functions as a reminder that the soul is to be conceived of as occupying the same space as the body, but as not sharing the same substance. This doubleness of reference serves to undermine the idea of the soul's entrapment, with a resulting deconstructive effect on the force of its argument. In a comparable way, the adjunct to 'Chains', linked to it by the genitival *of*, simultaneously explicates the text's basic trope by rendering it thoroughly overt, and draws further attention to the gap in referential 'truth' at the centre of the Soul's argument. A further effect is thus to mark the physically-oriented emotive words – 'inslav'd, manacled, blinded', and so on – as mere functions of the rhetoric of argumentation. The extended trope quite clearly operates on the *intellectual/emotive* axis of figurative language, but with the intellectual ultimately predominant.

What we have been arguing here is that the text becomes opened up to a deconstructive reading through a propensity for the signifieds generated within paradigmatic chains to lead to semantic contradictions. This is an aspect of tropes which can be regarded as characteristically seventeenth-century.

## Allegory

Allegory, perhaps the best-known form of extended trope, is to be distinguished in kind from the extensions we have so far discussed. It arose principally as a didactic mode, in which obvious disjunctions in the 'truth' relation between vehicle and tenor are effectively neutralized by the operation of a controlling, inherited typology (Abrams, 1965, 556). The existence of this typology also means that, given the highly conventional relationship between vehicle and tenor within the trope, the notion of *ground* becomes virtually irrelevant to analysis. These features can be readily demonstrated in George Herbert's small allegory 'The World', which begins

*Love* built a stately house; where *Fortune* came,
And spinning phansies, she was heard to say
That her fine cobwebs did support the frame,
Whereas they were supported by the same:                    4
But *Wisdome* quickly swept them all away.

Nowhere in the poem after its title is the tenor–vehicle relationship of 'house'='World' explicitly articulated. The title is sufficient to enable the reader to link the text to a pattern of conventional significations whereby *Love* refers to God the Creator, and *buildings* refer to some microcosm within the created universe – the Earth, or a human society on Earth, or a human body within that hierarchy. The decoding of the trope is then further facilitated by the tendency in allegory of this kind to make heavy use of personification and to structure its discourse through grammatical relationships which consistently recur. Thus in the above stanza the grammatical subject of most of the clauses is an abstraction, or a pronoun anaphorically linked to an abstraction (*Love*, *Fortune*, *Wisdome*), and the verbs and predicates refer to actions or objects; only the subordinate clauses of lines 3–4 have subjects which are not abstractions, and these clauses are adjuncts to a preceding clause's predicate ('to say'). The abstractions are, in fact, personifications: as Morton W. Bloomfield long ago pointed out (1963), personification is primarily created by the effect upon abstract nouns of verbs denoting human activity (though adjectives, to a lesser extent, may also personify); subjects are literal, but predicates figurative. After the cue given in the title, this distribution of parts of the trope between subject and predicate makes it an easy matter to read off the allegorical sense, with perhaps more admiration going to the cleverness of the extension of the correspondences than to their aptness.

Allegory, however, need not depend on personification in this way, and where the subject is also the vehicle of a trope, other cues for decoding the allegory are built into the syntagmatic axis. Herbert's 'Redemption', for example, while again using its title to orient any reading of the poem, overtly explains its allegory about God the landlord and man the tenant in line 5: 'In heaven at his manor I him sought.' Such obvious cues necessarily control the parameters of re ling, in accord with the custom of allegory to eschew ambiguity.[8] This principle still applies in modern allegories such as James Tate's 'The Blue Booby', in which male–female relations in modern materialistic society are presented allegorically (and comically) through a description of sea-birds:

> The blue booby lives
> on the bare rocks

of Galapagos
and fears nothing.
It is a simple life:                                          5
they live on fish,
and there are few predators.
Also, the males do not
make fools of themselves
chasing after the young                                      10
ladies. Rather,
they gather the blue
objects of the world
and construct from them

a nest . . . .                                               15

In lines 10–11, and later in lines 32–4 ('When she returns/ from
her day of/ gossip and shopping'), the behaviour of the birds is
described in a language gently satirizing certain modes of
human behaviour: the very intrusiveness of this language
indicates how to begin unravelling the allegory in order to grasp
that the birds figure human life, not vice versa. The polysemy of
*booby* is retrospectively activated ('a stupid person' as well as a
seabird), and then the associations of 'Galapagos' evoke the
work of Charles Darwin, with all its implications for human
development. The materialistic morass into which human
transactions have sunk can thus be allegorized in terms of a
description of the booby's evolutionary development:

in the past
fifty million years
the male has grown
considerably duller,                                         25
nor can he sing well.
The female, though,

asks little of him—
the blue satisfies her
completely . . . .                                           30

The poem thus develops into a comic yet still trenchant criticism
of a culture in which the male is under no pressure to remain
physically attractive or intellectually or verbally stimulating to his
partner as long as he can provide her with the material goods

she desires (which 'the blue/objects of the world' have come to signify). An important aspect of this allegory is that while the reader must re-read earlier parts of the poem once its allegorical meaning has begun to emerge, the poem never decodes as a complete set of one-to-one relations, but some of the early details, such as 'they live on fish', are as much elaborations within the trope's vehicle as are the elaborations found in epic simile. The effect is that such details have a general attitudinal suggestiveness, such as that stimulated by reference to a limited and boring diet, rather than a specific figurative referent. This development within the vehicle also reflects the nature of allegory to unfold primarily as a narrative form (which can also be seen in the Herbert examples), a form in which meaning emerges predominantly as an aspect of the syntagmatic and hypersyntagmatic axes. There is little that might be described as paradigmatic complexity, and a consequence is that the texture of meaning is not particularly dense.

## Indeterminate meanings: the Romantic use of tropes

When the function of figurative language becomes less obviously a branch of rhetorical argument, the signifying relationship between vehicle and tenor may become looser, and the process of figurative extension itself becomes more amorphous. Both tendencies can be seen in the following elaborated simile from Wordsworth's *The Prelude* (1850):

> The immeasurable height
> Of woods decaying, never to be decayed,                625
> The stationary blasts of waterfalls,
> And in the narrow rent at every turn
> Winds thwarting winds, bewildered and forlorn,
> The torrents shooting from the clear blue sky,
> The rocks that muttered close upon our ears,            630
> Black drizzling crags that spake by the way-side
> As if a voice were in them, the sick sight
> And giddy prospect of the raving stream,
> The unfettered clouds and region of the Heavens,
> Tumult and peace, the darkness and the light –          635
> Were all like workings of one mind, the features
> Of the same face, blossoms upon one tree;

Characters of the great Apocalypse,
The types and symbols of Eternity,
Of the first, and last, and midst, and without end.          640
                                                     (VI.624–40)

The hypersyntagmatic structure of the extract is very simple, since what it asserts, in a heavily left-branching sentence, is merely that 'All [x] were like all [y]': everything preceding line 636 is a paradigmatic elaboration of [x], the subject of the sentence and apparently the vehicle of the trope, and everything from line 636 on is an elaboration of [y], the predicate and ultimately the tenor. The items piled up in the one paradigmatic slot are in themselves various, and include not just noun phrases such as 'The stationary blasts of waterfalls' (626), but also duplication of signifieds through near-doublets ('sick sight and giddy prospect') and near-repetitions (629 seems to describe the same phenomenon as 626), and also units within which modifiers are represented by rank-shifted clauses (the extreme example is in 631–2). Further, several of the paradigmatic units incorporate some element of inner contradiction or binary opposition: 'decaying, never to be decayed' (625); 'stationary blasts' (626); 'tumult'/'peace', 'darkness'/'light' (635); and the complex interplay of literal and figurative in 'crags that *spake* . . ./As if a voice were in them', where the personifying force of the verb is immediately diminished by the qualifying 'as if' clause. This last example is, indeed, symptomatic of how throughout the sentence paradigmatic accumulation works against determinable signification, and promotes a sense that despite the development of scenic detail the signifieds invoked point on to other meanings. Even such uncertainty as to whether 'thwarting', 'bewildered' and 'forlorn' function as personifying agents expressing emotional responses or are principally archaisms ('crossing the path of', 'lost in pathless places', and 'lost', respectively) contributes to the literal/figurative indeterminacy. Again, the differing interpretative demands made by the noun phrases in 'the sick sight . . . of the raving stream' (in which 'sick' is a transferred epithet expressing the response of the speaker while 'raving', presumably, is not, but belongs in a set with 'muttered' and 'spake') suggest either a lack of concern to handle the tropes in a consistent manner or an exploitation of different figurative types and of semantic drift to destroy determinable meaning. Finally, meaning is further set adrift by the incorporation within the vehicle of the trope of the series of abstract oppositions in line 635. When the predicate of the sentence is finally arrived at, it is found to consist initially of a further series of tropes (636–7), before the entire group is declared to be a series of signs, namely 'Characters . . . types and symbols', which, combining diversity into unity, signify the transcendent tenor 'Eternity'.

Such a figurative process contains within it its own undoing, since the risk a writer takes in dismantling material significance in order to assert transcendent significance is that the result may be a gap in, rather than a transfer of, meaning. There is a general tendency for Romantic period writers to employ figurative language of this kind, and it is perhaps significant that simile is prominent amongst the tropes, since the nineteenth century marks the beginning of a major shift from a conceptualization of the world as bound by cause and effect relationships to a more cautious notion of analogical relationships. Amongst the later Romantic poets, Byron shows a clear awareness of the implications for (un-)meaning in the structure of such tropes, as can be seen in the following example, in which a natural phenomenon, a rainbow, introduced into the text ostensibly as a sign of hope for Juan and his ship-wrecked comrades, is reduced to a mere starting-point for a game with tropes:

> It changed, of course; a heavenly chameleon,
> > The airy child of vapour and the sun,
> Brought forth in purple, cradled in vermilion,
> > Baptized in molten gold, and swathed in dun,  4
> Glittering like crescents o'er a Turk's pavilion,
> > And blending every colour into one,
> Just like a black eye in a recent scuffle
> (For sometimes we must box without the muffle).  8
>
> > > (*Don Juan*, Canto II.xcii)

In contrast to Wordsworth's paradoxical stasis in change, this passage asserts the inevitability of change, even of dissolution, and represents it by a dissolution of the describing language. *Change* is the ground of the relationship between tenor and vehicle: it is stated at the outset, and sustained in 'chameleon', but then only partly sustained in the paradigmatic overlay 'airy child'. There is no obvious congruence between 'chameleon' and 'child', so their occupation of the same paradigmatic slot depends on their separate signifieds being recoded, through the ground of the trope, to signify comically disparate aspects of the rainbow. But the internal extension of the 'child' figure, first with its embedded and then with its appended tropes, shifts focus away from the concept of *change*. Lines 3–4 do this in two ways. First, the order of the events which develop the vehicle – 'brought forth . . . cradled . . . baptized . . . swathed' – is empirically and intertextually wrong, resulting in disorder rather than change or progression. This then foregrounds the way the colour series, 'purple' etc., goes awry: apart from culminating anticlimactically in 'dun', the series is fraught with literal/figurative instability. The first item, 'purple', denotes royal state and dress as well as a colour, and is thus potentially a conventional trope which supports the intertextual allusion to Christ; 'vermilion' doesn't have such associations (it is unlikely that the archaic sense 'scarlet wool' would be available here – last recorded 1641), so seems an uncomplicated trope; 'baptized in molten gold' requires a stronger disjunction between tenor and vehicle, since the literal sense is such an absurdity. This isn't merely to be explained as another example of a comic deviation from empirical 'truth' which is the nature of tropes, since Byron's purpose here is to draw attention to that deviation in order to suggest that tropes may simply deconstruct reality rather than expressing some transcendent something beyond 'reality'. Lines 5–8 are a still more obvious comment on Romantic practice, as first the ground of the trope is shifted, with 'crescents', from process to shape, and then the similes become increasingly and hilariously inappropriate, to culminate in a palpably irrelevant extension of the final one. The use of a register much more colloquial than Wordsworth's helps show up how far the figure has drifted from its starting-point in line 1.

## Sensory/emotive tropes

Broadly speaking, from the Restoration to the end of the Victorian period a ruling notion about the characteristics of figurative language was that such language would positively enhance its object and context, that tropes would be, if not beautiful, at least not ugly or excessively subtle. This is not universally reflected in practice, of course, and satiric and comic writing such as Pope's and Byron's affords many exceptions. The twentieth century has tended to take the different view that the appropriateness of a trope is determined by its expressive effectiveness. The shift is to some extent explicable in terms of a shift in the relative status accorded to the members of the triad *intellect/emotion/sensory representation*: tropes usually express two of these, but not all three. Romantic and Victorian tropes tended to favour the emotive and the sensory, as in the following brief example from Tennyson's *In Memoriam* ci:

> into silver arrows break
> The sailing moon in creek and cove.

The lines encourage a visualization of moonlight on moving water, and, in their capacity to produce feelings and memories in the audience, have a strong sensory impact; they are figurative in that the familiar visual illusion of the moon 'sailing' on water is treated as a literal event, and the fragmented light is said to be 'arrows', a visual connection only reached after several steps along the chain of referentiality; the two tropes, as object and adjunct of the same clause, are closely linked syntactically, but they are not paradigmatically congruent, since arrows and sailing belong to unrelated semantic fields, and it seems inappropriate to attempt to determine the intellectual relationship between them. Rather, they function as sensory/emotive representations of a visual idea.

For a more worked-out relationship between two tropes, we can stay with Tennyson, examining now lines 18–24 of *Ulysses*:

> I am a part of all that I have met;
> Yet all experience is an arch wherethro'
> Gleams that untravell'd world, whose margin fades
> For ever and for ever when I move.
> How dull it is to pause, to make an end,
> To rust unburnish'd, not to shine in use!
> As tho' to breathe were life!

The two briefly extended and quite disparate figures (the glimpse through the arch; the rusting armour) are here interwoven by an aspect of textual cohesion – the presence of a lexical set which has *shining* as its node: 'gleams, fades, dull, unburnished, shine'; that is, all these terms are marked either as '+ shining' or '- shining'. The first of these figures is extended from the simple metaphor, 'all experience is an arch' (i.e. tenor A = vehicle B), through the verb-metaphors of the following clauses which further explicate the initial metaphor:

the untravell'd world *gleams*
the margin [i.e. that furthest from the viewer] *fades*.

The second of the two main figures, which has as vehicle the notion of armour rusting through neglect or disuse, doesn't spell out its tenor–vehicle relationship as clearly as does the first, insofar as the armour has to be inferred from 'unburnished' and conditioned by such contextual elements as the references to 'battle' and 'Troy'. The link between the two metaphors is the pivotal *dull*, which has a literal tenor-signification 'boring, tedious' and a figurative vehicle-signification, 'not-shining'.

This use of figurative language is aesthetically pleasing: the visual images evoked are pleasant; they engage the reader's intellectual and sensory responses, stimulating a satisfying sense of the gap between tenors and vehicles and yet of the aptness of the connection; pleasure is to be found in the way the two figures are made to cohere and further cultivate that interplay of sameness and difference which is the essence of figurative language. The attitude towards the object is clear and clearly controlled.

## Twentieth-century tropes

With twentieth-century figurative language, especially that of the first half of the century, the situation has changed in two ways: first, there is a tendency to draw on the seamier, less pleasant aspects of life for vehicles; second, there is less tendency to develop extended images than there was in earlier periods – extended figurative structures tend now to be allegory or the kind of extended symbolism whereby a whole work is a vehicle for an undeclared tenor, which is indeed a key aspect of the notorious 'difficulty' of much modern poetry. In addition, and on a more theoretical level, the argument during recent times over the relative status of metaphor and metonymy can be seen, in our view, as a delayed critical response to differing notions about the relationship between *experience* and *the representation of experience in literature*. Extreme positions are occupied here by Ezra Pound and Wallace Stevens, writers in the forefront of an essential bifurcation within Modernism. Pound came increasingly to distrust figures of equivalence, of substitution (i.e. metaphors), preferring figures such as metonymy and synecdoche. Stevens works primarily through symbols, perhaps the most extreme form of substitution. For Stevens, poetry is an access to *Being*; for Pound, it is a sign-system employed for getting a job done.

POUND

In much of Pound's poetry, intensely metonymic figuration is employed very markedly as part of a highly rhetorical structure, as in the following extract from 'Hugh Selwyn Mauberley', IV:

> Daring as never before, wastage as never before.            20
> Young blood and high blood,
> fair cheeks, and fine bodies;
>
> fortitude as never before
>
> frankness as never before,
> disillusions as never told in the old days,            25
> hysterias, trench confessions,
> laughter out of dead bellies.

There are in effect only three paradigmatic slots along the syntagmatic axis here: within the first are clumped the group 'Daring . . .', 'wastage . . .' and 'fortitude . . .'; within the second are the four youth/beauty phrases of 21–2; and the third comprises the various references to *utterance* in 24–7. The repetitions, of grammatical structures, words and sounds, create a haranguing mode of address; the only figures within it are metonymies ('young blood', etc.), but the distance between the metonymic and literal elements of the text is very small. In comparison, the poetic of V is much more figurative:

> There died a myriad,
> And of the best, among them,
> For an old bitch gone in the teeth,
> For a botched civilization,            4
>
> Charm, smiling at the good mouth,
> Quick eyes gone under earth's lid,
>
> For two gross of broken statues,
> For a few thousand battered books.            8

Lines 3–4 employ metaphor, with tenor and vehicle both

stated; the ground is quite complex, because 'gone in the teeth'
activates both meanings of *bitch* 'a female dog; a whore' (NB
*bitch* has undergone semantic shift during the last half-century,
so that its application to humans now primarily refers to back-
biting or selfishness). The individual units of tenor and vehicle
are linked chiastically,

an old bitch    gone in the teeth

a botched    civilization

and the writer's attitude is pushed very hard by the colloquial
adjective in the tenor, 'botched', and its obvious sound-
relationship with the head noun of the vehicle.

The next paragraph begins metonymically, but blends
metonym into metaphor: first in the opposition of 'smiling at the
good mouth' to 'gone in the teeth', where it must be presumed
that line 5 declares something literally true of its tenor and is
therefore metonym; and then more particularly with 'Quick eyes
gone under earth's lid', where the double ambiguity – *quick*
'living'/'lively' and *lid* 'eye-lid'/'cover for a vessel' – begins to
slide the double metonymy into metaphor; that is, 'quick eyes'
are metonymic of the positive and beautiful aspects of the
human spirit; 'earth's lid' is perhaps a metaphor for the grave,
but since 'earth' is literal to burials, and coffins do have lids, the
distance between tenor and vehicle is minimal. Lines 7–8 are
also clear metonymies, the statues and books standing for the
minority, élite culture on whose behalf, the poem argues, the
First World War was fought.

An outstanding feature of the language here is the large
number of pejorative terms built into the figures: the tabu
'bitch', the colloquial 'botched', the mercantile 'gross', the
casual 'a few thousand'. This has come a long way from the
attitude that an important function of figurative language is to
give aesthetic pleasure. Here it is primarily used to stimulate
revulsion, and to propound an argument which is even more
overt than that of the Tennyson with which we began.


STEVENS

Standing at the other end of the figurative spectrum from the
Pound is a poem such as Stevens's 'The Emperor of Ice-Cream'.

This is a poem which almost defies interpretation because it doesn't offer any stated equivalences or substitutions that can be used as entry-points, and no sure way of determining whether we are confronted by a series of figures or an extended development of a vehicle which may then, perhaps, be read as allegory.

> Call the roller of big cigars,
> The muscular one, and bid him whip
> In kitchen cups concupiscent curds.
> Let the wenches dawdle in such dress
> As they are used to wear, and let the boys                    5
> Bring flowers in last month's newspapers.
> Let be be finale of seem.
> The only emperor is the emperor of ice-cream.
>
> Take from the dresser of deal,
> Lacking the three glass knobs, that sheet                    10
> On which she embroidered fantails once
> And spread it so as to cover her face.
> If her horny feet protrude, they come
> To show how cold she is, and dumb.
> Let the lamp affix its beam.                                 15
> The only emperor is the emperor of ice-cream.

That the poem makes little initial sense is an encouragement to attempt to read it figuratively, to make *some* sense of that extended vehicle involving a corpse, a funeral, and a wake. It might be noted that most of the verbs are imperatives, so that someone (for example, the reader) is being urged to act in certain ways, ways that make strange the rituals of living and dying. The way into the poem might be to begin with its most abstract utterance – that is, the most likely declared tenor. This occurs in line 7, 'Let be be finale of seem', though even here *finale* ('the concluding piece of a concert, musical composition, etc.') is figurative. As such, it encapsulates the poem's larger reference to performances and endings. Line 7 suggests that the tenor of all those vehicles has something to do with the idea of *Being* itself, and it might be argued that the poem's concern is with finding an expression for the idea that *Being* and *Not-Being* include not just life and death but also the power of the human imagination to comprehend and encompass them in their essence. The language of signification is used towards the end of the second stanza (line 14, 'to show') to declare that *things* might signify nothing beyond themselves – that any attempts to decode the missing glass knobs and the embroidered pigeons may be an abuse of signification. Of course immediately line 15 exploits the capacity of figurative language to *make* things mean something else, as 'the lamp' signifies the power of the intellect (ultimately a culturally-determined symbol). Stanza 1 in part works by inverting symbolic gestures determined by culture – that people dress up for funerals, and the like; that flowers, themselves put to symbolic functions, are further dressed up for presentation. The implication is perhaps that the sign-systems of language are similarly used to dress up 'reality' so that it doesn't have to be gazed at for what it is.

## AN ATWOOD SIMILE

Twentieth-century writers favour symbol and metonym, which is a significant trend, though this obviously doesn't mean that simile and metaphor are discarded. Brogan has shown how Stevens's frequent use of simile 'forces speculation about the representational nature of language, about the problematic presentation of the "thing itself"' (1986, 108). The following brief poem by Margaret Atwood illustrates a different, but equally effective, use of simile – here, to shock the reader:

'You Fit into Me'

you fit into me
like a hook into an eye

a fish hook
an open eye

This poem is a very complex piece of figurative language, and as such neatly illustrates the power of the syntagmatic axis in constructing and controlling figuration. There is no part of the poem which does not involve some element of transferred meaning. The opening line, which states the overt theme and functions as controlling tenor for the subsequent tropes, pivots on the polysemous *fit into*: while it could be sexually literal it also suggests the transferred senses 'be in close accord with', 'belong together'. The simile of line 2 compares the signifieds of line 1 with something unlike, but the ellipsis of the verb (*\*fits*) makes a strong cohesive link by focusing attention on the ground of the comparison, already stated as part of the tenor. The ground emphasizes the aspect in which tenor and vehicle are isomorphic, while the actual objects compared – 'you . . . me' and 'hook . . . eye' – are essentially heteromorphic. The associations of the analogy selected are everyday, domestic, and marked as {+female} (since a hook-and-eye is uncommon on male apparel). The syntagmatic determination of meaning operates here in an obvious but important way. First, 'eye' is itself a dead metaphor, pointing to a signified at one further remove from the original signified ('the organ of sight'); second, it is the syntagmatic relationship of *hook/fit into/eye* which determines the signifieds indicated by these signifiers. It is because of the strong co-operation of syntagmatic effects, of cohesion, of syntagmatic determination of signifieds, and of extension into figurative signification, that there is such a deep shock effect at the subsequent remaking of the paradigmatic elements of the simile in lines 3–4. Still further ellipsis of linking and grammatical devices strips back the syntax so that the drastic remaking of the simile through the addition of the modifiers 'fish' and 'open' becomes heavily foregrounded. The shock effect principally resides in the returning of 'eye' to its literal signified, a movement on which the contrast between the poem's two similes turns. The reader is compelled to try to sort out the relationship between the two as the second is retrospectively imposed on the first, which now has two inextricable but profoundly opposed meanings, generating an extremely compressed utterance about relationships between person and person, male and female, and hopes and expectations and disappointments.

## Some examples from prose

Much more attention is paid to the figurative language of poetry than to that of prose. This is so partly because poetry tends to have cultivated figurative language as a key instrument for compressing meaning, and partly because prose, and prose fiction in particular, is customarily read with primary attention on its larger syntagmatic effects. Figurative language is used more sparsely in prose than in verse, but for this very reason its presence tends to be self-foregrounding, though the extent to which this happens – the extent to which we can identify self-conscious uses of figurative language – does still vary from period to period and from author to author. A diachronic study of figurative language in prose might be expected to offer some more sharply focused insight into the milieu in which the prose is situated, especially if particular attention is paid to the *function* of the figures and the *kind* of vehicles selected, since these are likely to reveal something about the presuppositions of a period, or of a writer. As with poetry, the effects achieved involve weighting of the parts of the intellectual/sensory/emotive triad, so that the text might determine whether reader response to it, or involvement with it, is primarily mental or primarily emotional. There are major contrasts between, say, figurative language used as part of a process of persuasion and figurative language used as a means of representing human subjectivity.

Any attempt at a comprehensive discussion of tropes in prose would, however, result in repetition of many things already said, so we will confine ourselves to four brief examples.

## FRANCIS BACON

For our first example we have taken another sentence from Francis Bacon's *Aduancement of Learning* (1605):

> . . . if the inuention of the Shippe was thought so noble, which carryeth riches, and commodities from place to place, and consociateth the most remote regions in participation of their fruits: how much more are letters to bee magnified, which as Shippes, passe through the vast Seas of time, and make ages so distant, to participate of the wisedome, illuminations, and inuentions the one of the other?

When we discussed an earlier part of this argument in Chapter 2, we remarked that the essence of Bacon's style was a broad repetition of syntagmatic units which is put to the service of rhetorical persuasion, and the extract here suggests that figurative language is carefully subordinated to this style and purpose. The introductory conditional clause briefly suspends the progression of the logic in order to present the vehicle for the coming trope, and does so in language expressing strong approval ('noble . . . riches . . . consociateth . . . participation of their fruits'); the positive values of human co-operation and, especially for the sixteenth century, of exploration are thus placed before the reader in readiness for the extended comparison that is to be made with 'letters'. As the argument unfolds, not only are the trope's vehicle and tenor fully spelled out but also the ground of the comparison through such synonymies as 'the most remote regions' = 'ages so distant' and 'participation of' = 'to participate of'. This emphasis on the ground blurs the fact that there is a substantial disjunction between the vehicle (which is spatial, and two-directional) and the tenor (which is temporal, and one-directional). But the force of the rhetorical structuring carries the argument over the logical hiatus by focusing attention on the benefits of exchange. It is because the figurative language is subordinated to discursive argument, in a way which is symptomatic of a general tendency in sixteenth- and seventeenth-century writing (and especially prose), that the logical flaw within the *trope* will go unnoticed.

## OLIVER GOLDSMITH

The following extract, from Goldsmith's *The Citizen of the World*, Letter XLI (1762), illustrates a very different manipulation of a trope:

> In this [temple], which is the most considerable of the
> empire, there are no pompous inscriptions, no flattery
> paid the dead, but all is elegant and awfully simple.
> There are however a few rags hung round the walls,
> which have at vast expence been taken from the enemy　5
> in the present war. The silk of which they are composed,
> when new, might be valued at half a string of copper
> money in China; yet this wise people fitted out a fleet
> and an army in order to seize them; though now grown
> old, and scarce capable of being patched up into a　10
> handkerchief.

Goldsmith's prose stands in a direct line of descent from Augustanism, and a key aspect of this to be seen here is that the figurative language has its basis in metonymy. Like Bacon, Goldsmith withholds the tenor of his trope and determines audience response in advance, by means of the pejorative signifier 'rags', but in his case the tenor is never directly stated: the reader must deduce *'flags' from the context and proceed from the simple metonymy *rags* (a term referring to the constituent fabric rather than to the manufactured object) to the implied signified (that of *flag*), and then in turn to the notions of military might and national honour of which a country's flag is a conventional metonymy. This intellectual/emotive chain of signification has, obviously, a satiric effect, as the reader decodes the trope within a given pejorative framework. To achieve this effect the writer controls the chain as carefully as Bacon controls his trope, leaving virtually no scope for alternative meanings or attitudes.

## GEORGE ELIOT

As in poetry, nineteenth-century, Romantic-type uses of tropes in prose tend to incorporate a lot of drift in both tenors and vehicles and to lean towards sensory/emotive effects. *Middlemarch* contains some typical examples, such as this one:

> Lydgate instantaneously stooped to pick up the chain. When he rose he was very near to a lovely little face set on a fair long neck which he had been used to see turning about under the most perfect management of self-contented grace. But as he raised his eyes now he saw a   5 certain helpless quivering which touched him quite newly and made him look at Rosamond with a questioning flash. At this moment she was as natural as she had ever been when she was five years old: she felt that her tears had risen, and it was no use to try to do   10 anything else than let them stay like water on a blue flower or let them fall over her cheeks even as they would.
>     That moment of naturalness was the crystallizing feather-touch; it shook flirtation into love. Remember   15 that the ambitious man who was looking at those forget-me-nots under the water was very warm-hearted and rash. He did not know where the chain went; an idea had thrilled through the recesses within him which had a miraculous effect in raising the power of passionate love   20 lying buried there in no sealed sepulchre, but under the lightest, easily pierced mould.
>
>                                (Ch. XXXI)

The first five lines contain several positive items which create the context for the tropes to follow ('lovely . . . fair . . . perfect . . . grace'), and help to establish the character, Lydgate, as a subjective focalizer at this point of the scene. But focalization is shifting amongst Lydgate, Rosamond (9–13), and the narrator (8–9, and the whole of the second paragraph), and hence between emotive commentary and subjective feeling. The tropes undergo a still more drastic process of drift: beginning with the simile, 'like water on a blue flower' (11–12), there are *six* different figures within a very short stretch, with little attempt being made to achieve any congruence amongst the vehicles. The effect is strongly sensory/emotive, and to analyse mentally the relationship of the figures would perhaps be to convict them of absurdity. A glance at the series 'the crystallizing feather-touch; it shook flirtation into love' (14–15) readily demonstrates the absence of congruence between *crystal* and *feather* on the one hand, and between *touch* and *shook* on the other. On its own, each of the three tropes is quite commonplace; in context, each has its own particular function to perform, to signify, respectively, 'giving shape to', 'adding the final delicate element', and 'transforming'; but the connotations of beauty and delicacy are perhaps more important. Part of the larger emotive effect achieved by the other tropes is that although 'tears', part of the tenor 'eyes filled with tears', is stated, *eyes* is not, and there is a cumulative emotive effect in the movement from the simile 'like water on a blue flower' to the strongly visual and sensory metaphor 'those forget-me-nots under the water'. Finally, the quasi-religious ground for the tropes in lines 20–2 introduces an entirely new concept, and with it another range of connotations. In clear distinction from the handling of tropes in Bacon and Goldsmith, Eliot's method of stringing together a series of vehicles loosely grouped by subjective association around the story-element/tenor, 'Lydgate falls in love with Rosamond when he sees her tears' shifts the function of tropes from the logical aspect of text to the emotive, and encourages a reader-participation in apprehending vehicles (the forget-me-nots, the sepulchre, and so on) which is not subject to the same control exerted by the earlier writers.

VIRGINIA WOOLF

A further important point to be made about the Eliot passage is that the natural objects constituting the tropes' vehicles not only function to represent subjective states of human minds but also appear to determine the outcome of Lydgate's subjective

experience. Thematically, this process is linked with his inability
to construct a strong and independent self. As such, the extract
makes an interesting comparison with an episode in Woolf's
*Mrs Dalloway* in which figurative language plays a major part in
depicting the relationship of characters to the surrounding
world:

But it was later than she [Elizabeth Dalloway] thought.
Her mother would not like her to be wandering off alone
like this. She turned back down the Strand.
   A puff of wind (in spite of the heat, there was quite a
wind) blew a thin black veil over the sun and over the    5
Strand. The faces faded; the omnibuses suddenly lost
their glow. For although the clouds were of mountainous
white so that one could fancy hacking hard chips off with
a hatchet, with broad golden slopes, lawns of celestial
pleasure gardens, on their flanks, and had all the    10
appearance of settled habitations assembled for the
conference of gods above the world, there was a
perpetual movement among them. Signs were inter-
changed, when, as if to fulfil some scheme arranged
already, now a summit dwindled, now a whole block of    15
pyramidal size which had kept its station inalterably
advanced into the midst or gravely led the procession to
fresh anchorage. Fixed though they seemed at their
posts, at rest in perfect unanimity, nothing could be
fresher, freer, more sensitive superficially than the snow-    20
white or gold-kindled surface; to change, to go, to
dismantle the solemn assemblage was immediately
possible; and in spite of the grave fixity, the accumulated
robustness and solidity, now they struck light to the
earth, now darkness.    25
   Calmly and competently, Elizabeth Dalloway mounted
the Westminster omnibus.
                                   (1925; 1958 edn, 152–3)

These perceptions are probably focalized through Elizabeth, or
so it might be deduced from the slipping between free indirect
thought and narration in the opening paragraph.[9] The relationship of the perceiving subject to the natural world is here
playfully anthropomorphizing, in that the subject is able to
maintain a conscious distinction between empirical reality and
trope, even as figurative language is used to make the familiar

strange and thence to render subjectivity. The sheer playfulness is evident in the syntagmatic organization of the sentence running from line 7 to line 13, whereby left-branching syntax is exploited to enable the extension and elaboration of a figure without disclosing what the actual point of it all is: it remains unclear whether emphasis falls on the landscape, the solidity, the colour, or the divine/human analogy. When the main clause comes, at the very end of the sentence, it turns out to be only a kind of tenor for the much earlier trope 'A puff of wind . . . blew a thin black veil over the sun . . .' (4–6). The subject's self-consciousness becomes thematized with 'Signs were inter-changed' (14), since this is precisely what making tropes is all about. The further the game goes, the more fanciful it becomes, but the mind being presented is in control of its material: Elizabeth is able to make a Self and relate to the world – see it, play with it, be aware of it. The elaboration of the vehicle, as it moves further away from the tenor in the 'clouds' section, makes for this differentiation between bits of phenomena and between phenomena and the self. The 'result' is a series of tropes which combine the sensory and the intellectual. Woolf, in the next paragraph, immediately contrasts these perceptions with those of Septimus Warren Smith, who is represented as unable to make distinctions of such a kind, and who, like Lydgate (but more extremely), has a subjectivity governed by sensory/emotive tropes. The paragraph begins thus:

> Going and coming, beckoning, signalling, so the light and shadow, which now made the wall grey, now the bananas bright yellow, now made the Strand grey, now 30 made the omnibuses bright yellow, seemed to Septimus Warren Smith lying on the sofa in the sitting-room; watching the watery gold glow and fade with the astonishing sensibility of some live creature on the roses, on the wall-paper. Outside the trees dragged their leaves 35 like nets through the depths of the air; the sound of water was in the room, and through the waves came the voices of birds singing.
>
> (ibid., 153–4)

The syntagmatic axis in the first sentence is markedly dislocated – the subject of the principal clause, 'the light and shadow', is widely separated from its verb, 'seemed' (31), by the series of four balanced adjectival clauses, and the series of present participles which begins the sentence turns out to be conceptually, if not grammatically, part of the predicate. There are no tropes within this syntagmatically dislocated sentence, but it creates a context for the figurative dislocation which follows. Moreover, the boundaries between literal and figurative are less clear than in the earlier paragraph. In 'watery gold', 'watery' is figurative, even when 'gold' is understood as referring to a colour, but it is conventionally so (the usage is recorded in Middle English); the analogy between the glowing and fading and the 'live creature' is loosely expressed. The passage becomes intensely figurative with the interchange of air and water in '*dragged* their leaves *like nets* through the *depths* of the air', and, while this extended metaphor is readily analysed into tenor, vehicle and ground, the preceding context determines that the sentence will be read not as high imagination but as the mental aberration of a subjective perception within which lateral connections have merged and become confused.

An important aspect of figurative language in prose which emerges from these analyses is that, despite the large differences, all the passages discussed here introduce their major tropes only after careful, non-figurative preparation, so that in most cases interpretation of the tropes is subject to significant control by the hyper-syntagmatic axis. As in poetry, though, this control is again weaker in tropes whose main impact is sensory and emotive.[10]

# Notes and further reading

1   The convention stems originally from *Song of Songs* Ch.2, v.1, and roses and lilies are also associated with female saints such as Saint Cecilia from Old English and earlier Latin sources; there they carry associations of martyrdom and virginity rather than of female beauty.

2   This remains a highly controversial topic. See the discussion of recent scholarship in Hill (1988).

3   The terms Hrushovski substitutes for tenor and vehicle are *BASE* (the frame of reference to which the metaphorical transfer is made) and *secondary fr [frame of reference]* (as with Richards's terms, these are themselves metaphorical). In our view, 'frame of reference' is being used to cover too many disparate elements (for example, both 'vehicle' and 'ground').

4 This distinction was maintained in a study by Roman Jakobson (1971) which has exerted a strong influence on discussions of metonymy. There are major problems inherent in his account, however, as pointed out by Bredin (1984a) and by A. Johnson (1982).

5 Readers might like to compare Umberto Eco's 'Lumbar Thought', a meditation on the semiotics of blue jeans, in *Travels in Hyper-Reality* (London: Pan Books, 1987), 191–5.

6 To do justice to this poem, it should be pointed out that the opening metaphor is immediately deconstructed, and the poem continues on with a rigorous examination of the claims for metaphorical and metonymical perception.

7 The metonymy is created by the combination of the two strands of the periphrasis. On the one hand, *fence* is used in the now obsolete sense of 'a defence, bulwark' (OED *fence*, 4b; cf. the citation from Swift, 'my whole body wanted a fence against heat and cold'); on the other hand, 'sevenfold' is a conventional epithet in epic shield-descriptions (cf. *The Aeneid*, VIII.448–9, where the makers of Aeneas' shield 'septenosque orbibus orbis/impediunt', which Dryden translates as 'Sev'n orbs within a spacious round they close').

8 Even medieval works which cultivate polysemous allegory – for example, *Cleanness*, or certain sections of *Piers Plowman* (as in the allegory of the Good Samaritan) – do not encourage readers to invent their own meanings; all the possibilities are designated and controlled.

9 Further support for this view is offered by David Lodge's comment that Woolf's use of *one* in 'one could fancy' (8) is a 'characteristic upper-middle-class speech habit'. Lodge suggests that this may be a marker of the indulgence Woolf expects her readers to extend to certain of her characters (1966, 85–6).

10 Further reading: the literature on figurative language is vast, but readers should find much of interest and helpfulness in Leech (1969), Ch.9; Goodman (1981); Hrushovski (1984); and the collection of papers edited by Sacks (1979).

# Exercises

1   Examine a range of tropes, drawn from different periods, to show how the very choice and treatment of the tenor/vehicle relationship reflect socio-cultural presuppositions. Look particularly at *which* figures are chosen, and differentiate their impact on reader participation.

2   Analyse the tenor/vehicle relationships in the following figures, and relate them to their context to bring out their larger function in the signification of meaning. Go on to compare and contrast various groupings, diachronic and synchronic:

(a)   Chaucer, *Troilus and Criseyde*, II.764–70 ('But right as when the sonne shyneth brighte')

(b)   Spenser, *The Faerie Queene*, Book III, Canto VII, stanzas 34–5 ('As he that strives to stop a suddein flood')

(c)   Milton, *Paradise Lost*, IX.633–45 ('Hope elevates, and joy/Brightens his crest')

(d)   Shakespeare, *Romeo and Juliet*, I.iii.81–94 ('Read o'er the volume of young Paris' face')

(e)   Shakespeare, *Antony and Cleopatra*, I.iv.10–13 ('I must not think') and 43–7 ('And the ebb'd man')

(f)   Donne, 'A Valediction: Forbidding Mourning', lines 25–36 ('If they be two')

(g)   Herbert, 'Prayer'

(h)   Pope, *Rape of the Lock*, Canto II, 19–28 ('This Nymph, to the destruction of mankind')

(i)   Johnson, 'The Vanity of Human Wishes', lines 141–56 ('Are these thy views?')

(j)   Blake, 'A Poison Tree'

(k)   Wordsworth, 'Intimations of Immortality', lines 25–35 ('The cataracts blow their trumpets')

(l)   Coleridge, *The Rime of the Ancient Mariner*, lines 171–94 ('The western wave was all aflame')

(m)   Shelley, 'Ode to the West Wind', lines 1–14

(n)   Byron, *Don Juan*, Canto II, stanza 148 ('And she bent o'er him')

(o)   Tennyson, 'Now Sleeps the Crimson Petal'

(p)   Browning, 'Childe Roland to the Dark Tower Came', lines 151–6 ('Now blotches rankling')

(q)   Dickinson, Poem 712 ('Because I could not stop for Death')

(r)   Hopkins, 'The Windhover'

(s)   Yeats, 'The Circus Animals' Desertion', lines 33–40 ('Those masterful images')

(t)   Robert Frost, 'Range-Finding'

(u)   Wallace Stevens, 'Thirteen Ways of Looking at a Blackbird'

(v)   T. S. Eliot, 'Whispers of Immortality'

(w)   Hart Crane, 'At Melville's Tomb'

(x)   Dylan Thomas, 'Fern Hill'

(y)   Richard Wilbur, 'Praise in Summer'

3   Analyse the tenor/vehicle relationships in the following prose extracts, and compare and contrast them with relevant examples (e.g., synchronic - similarity, tenor, choice of vehicle, type of trope, underlying presuppositions) drawn from verse; are their functions and effects markedly influenced by the prose form in which they appear?

(a)   Imagine then that all this while, Death (like a Spanish Leager, or rather like stalking Tamberlaine) hath pitcht his tents, (being nothing but a heape of winding sheets tackt together) in the sinfully-polluted Suburbes: the Plague is Muster-Maister and Marshall of the field: Burning feavers, Boyles, Blaines, and Carbuncles, the Leaders, Lieutenants, Serjeants, and Corporalls: the maine Army consisting (like Dunkirke) of a mingle-mangle, viz. dumpish Mourners, merry Sextons, hungry Coffin-sellers, scrubbing Bearers, and nastie

Gravemakers: but indeed they are the Pioneers of the Campe, that are imployed onely (like Moles) in casting up of earth and digging of trenches: Feare and Trembling (the two Catch-polles of Death) arrest every one: No parley will be graunted, no composition stood upon, But the Allarum is strucke up, the Toxin ringes out for life, and no voyce heard but Tue, Tue, Kill, Kill; the little Belles only (like small shot) doe yet goe off, and make no great worke for wormes, a hundred or two lost in every skirmish, or so: but alas thats nothing: yet by those desperat sallies, what by open setting upon them by day, and secret Ambuscadoes by night, the skirts of London were pittifully pared off, by litle and litle:

(Dekker, *The Wonderfull Yeare* (1603))

(b) No sooner had Joseph grasped his cudgel in his hands than lightning darted from his eyes; and the heroic youth, swift of foot, ran with the utmost speed to his friend's assistance. He overtook him just as Rockwood had laid hold of the skirt of his cassock, which, being torn, hung to the ground. Reader, we would make a simile on this occasion, but for two reasons: the first is, it would interrupt the description, which should be rapid in this part; but that doth not weigh much, many precedents occurring for such an interruption: the second, and much the greater, reason is, that we could find no simile adequate to our purpose: for indeed, what instance could we bring to set before our reader's eyes at once the idea of friendship, courage, youth, beauty, strength, and swiftness? all which blazed in the person of Joseph Andrews. Let those, therefore, that describe lions and tigers, and heroes fiercer than both, raise their poems or plays with the simile of Joseph Andrews, who is himself above the reach of any simile.

(Fielding, *Joseph Andrews* (1742))

(c) Darkness rests upon Tom-all-Alone's. Dilating and dilating since the sun went down last night, it has gradually swelled until it fills every void in the place. For a time there were some dungeon lights burning, as the lamp of Life burns in Tom-all-Alone's, heavily,

heavily, in the nauseous air, and winking — as that
lamp, too, winks in Tom-all-Alone's — at many
horrible things. But they are blotted out. The moon
has eyed Tom with a dull, cold stare, as admitting
some puny emulation of herself in his desert region
unfit for life and blasted by volcanic fires; but she has
passed on, and is gone. The blackest nightmare in the
infernal stables grazes on Tom-all-Alone's, and Tom is
fast asleep.

(Dickens, *Bleak House* (1853))

(d) At length Clym reached the margin of a fir and beech
plantation that had been enclosed from heath land in
the year of his birth. Here the trees, laden heavily with
their new and humid leaves, were now suffering more
damage than during the highest winds of winter, when
the boughs are specially disencumbered to do battle
with the storm. The wet young beeches were
undergoing amputations, bruises, cripplings, and harsh
lacerations, from which the wasting sap would bleed
for many a day to come, and which would leave scars
visible till the day of their burning. Each stem was
wrenched at the root, where it moved like a bone in
its socket, and at every onset of the gale convulsive
sounds came from the branches, as if pain were felt. In
a neighbouring brake a finch was trying to sing; but
the wind blew under his feathers till they stood on
end, twisted round his little tail, and made him give up
his song.

(Hardy, *The Return of the Native* (1878))

(e) The lights grow brighter as the earth lurches away
from the sun, and now the orchestra is playing yellow
cocktail music, and the opera of voices pitches a key
higher. Laughter is easier minute by minute, spilled
with prodigality, tipped out at a cheerful word. The
groups change more swiftly, swell with new arrivals,
dissolve and form in the same breath; already there
are wanderers, confident girls who weave here and
there among the stouter and more stable, become for
a sharp joyous moment the centre of a group, and
then, excited with triumph, glide on through the sea-

change of faces and voices and colour under the
constantly changing light.

(F. Scott Fitzgerald, *The Great Gatsby* (1926))

(f) Her voice would not cease, it would just vanish. There
would be the dim coffin-smelling gloom sweet and
over-sweet with the twice-bloomed wistaria against
the outer wall by the savage quiet September sun
impacted distilled and hyperdistilled, into which came
now and then the loud cloudy flutter of the sparrows
like a flat limber stick whipped by an idle boy, and the
rank smell of female old flesh long embattled in
virginity while the wan haggard face watched him
above the faint triangle of lace at wrists and throat
from the too tall chair in which she resembled a
crucified child; and the voice not ceasing but vanishing
into and then out of the long intervals like a stream, a
trickle running from patch to patch of dried sand, and
the ghost mused with shadowy docility as if it were the
voice which he haunted where a more fortunate one
would have had a house.

(Faulkner, *Absalom, Absalom* (1936))

# Conclusion

'It's time and arithmetic I want to know. Time and arithmetic and sense.'

(Alan Garner, *The Stone Book*)

## The social construction of 'meaning'

As an epigraph and lead-in to this final chapter of our broad overview of literary English from the time of Chaucer to the 1980s, we have chosen an utterance which is a reminder that 'sense' is a product of 'time' and 'arithmetic', that is, a point at which temporality, measurement and relationship intersect. Every text is an heir to and a product of past time, and each passes on to others some representation of its own present. The reader's experience of literature involves a constant quest for 'sense', and hence a need to grasp both how meaning is produced by syntagmatic interrelationships and how history, culture and ideological presuppositions precondition the available paradigmatic choices. Most contemporary literary critical practice stems from the assumption that the mind and its products are constructed not only by individual processes but also by historical and cultural processes, one of which is language. This observation inevitably has major implications for those branches of literary study that pay particular attention to the production and reception of certain effects in language. 'Sense', meaning, significance – whatever one likes to call it – is a product of Time and Space, the ultimate units of measurement. That the two are always interacting seems an obvious point, but take these away, and take away from the reading of texts the contexts of the time, place and culture of their production and their reception, as did some critical practices of the mid-twentieth century, and those texts lose much of their power to signify except insofar as they are covertly relocated within the reader's own cultural dimensions. From such a limited perspective, however, all texts tend to become, or to be regarded as, homogeneous, and texts which are resistant to this reductiveness are rejected from the literary canon or what is considered to be the central tradition.

We attempted back in Chapter 1 to represent in Figure 1.2 what we regard as the broad elements of textuality (p. 12). One of the suggestions made by our diagram is that everything that writers and readers do, and everything about the texts which are their meeting ground, is constituted within historical periods and particular societies, in relation to available and even hypothetical literary and cultural intertexts, and within a language whose signifier–signified relationships and possible syntagmatic and paradigmatic choices are already largely predetermined. Put more succinctly, writers and readers, and the parameters within which they function, are to a considerable extent socially constructed, and all are subject to constant temporal and historical change. The broad sharing of codes that allows some type of 'sense' or communication to pass between individuals and societies also has implications for the methods by which writers seek to influence or manipulate readers, and much of our examination of literary language in the preceding chapters has been in effect a documentation of these methods. In our view, readers are never as free as some recent reader-response criticism would like to assume; the pertinent issues are, rather, how aware are readers of the processes of textual manipulation, and to what extent should that awareness be cultivated – something we have tried to do throughout the book.

The circumstances within which individual writers and readers communicate via the text are conditioned by the fact that neither writing nor reading can escape its historical, social, ideological and linguistic context. In the course of the preceding six chapters, we have from time to time touched on the socio-historical contexts of various texts. Often we have done this only very lightly, and sometimes not at all. A writer's historical context and ideological presuppositions are not necessarily fully present in every text, nor in every part of a text, and so examples chosen for one purpose will not serve all purposes. However, we want now in conclusion to consider a few important areas from a retrospective standpoint.

## Socio-historical influences on the author/text/reader transaction

First, we have shown that what constitutes the normal, acceptable lexis of literary language varies historically: in some periods it is heavily restricted, and this reflects an attempt by a particular social group (usually 'polite' society) to strengthen its control over literature and language. This is especially notable in some literary genres of the eighteenth century, with its ideological disapproval of 'low' words in non-satiric literature and of dialect or non-standard vocabulary in language (see MacCabe, 1984, 76). In other periods, notably in the fourteenth, seventeenth and twentieth centuries, and in eighteenth-century satire, literary language has a much more broadly based lexis, though this is still more likely to be a reaction against an earlier process of narrowing than a reflection of a penetration of literary discourse by hitherto excluded social groups. Non-standard language forms (dialects or the speech of sub-cultures) have occasionally been exploited by individual writers (Chaucer, Shakespeare, Hopkins, Hardy, for example), but only rarely has such usage functioned as a challenge to the discourse of the dominant group. Joyce's novels remain the major example, but even these, for most of the century, have been appropriated by the literary establishment.

Second, we have stressed the importance of the syntagm because its interaction with paradigmatic choice largely determines and fixes signification. Loosening of the syntagm is especially significant when the fifteenth-century passion for lexis led to a consequent loss of syntagmatic strength, and when the cultivation of chaotic syntagmatic chaining in Romantic writing resulted in a free play of paradigmatic connotation. These remained the most extreme examples of writers' attempts to subvert or defy the tyranny of the syntagm until a comparable phenomenon appeared in late twentieth-century texts and criticism, where the obsession with the *logos* in deconstructive criticism has resulted in a pervasive disregard of the power of the syntagm to determine signification.

Third, the variation between speech-based and more formal prose varieties has social implications which need further consideration. As early as the late fourteenth century, when English was beginning to assert itself as the pre-eminent language of England, John Trevisa's comments on the English language assume that the best contemporary English is that of the Court and the urban south-east, and, although a national literary standard English doesn't emerge for almost another two hundred years (see Leith, 1983, 38–44), Trevisa exemplifies the perennial tendency to link social judgements with adherence to and deviation from linguistic 'norms'. Between the English Renaissance and the rise of Romanticism, Latin-based rhetorical prose was frequently privileged, but even the rival speech-based prose usually reflected the conversation of an educated élite only. A text's situation in society and culture invites a sharing of basic social assumptions and literary codes between writer and audience, and generally a choice between prose styles is a choice of rhetorical strategies for manipulating the audience. With the watershed advent of Romanticism, the stronger and more obvious projection of a subjective Self, in both poetry and fiction, resulted in a focus on the writer, both as a person privileged to be able to feel and express special, heightened experiences and then as Shelley's 'unacknowledged legislator'. Such assumptions have important consequences for the social and ideological matrix within which writer and reader relate. Now, at the end of the twentieth century, the profound influence of Romanticism is still apparent, partly in the unconscious acceptance of, and partly in conscious reactions against, such presuppositions. The emphasis on the autonomy of the 'text itself' in the mid-twentieth century was an attempt to dethrone the author, who was eventually declared dead by Barthes (1968), and the elevation of the role of the reader shows how the pendulum has swung to the other extreme. Such perspectives tend to ignore the complicated transaction which forms the author/text/reader relationship within the contexts we have sketched.

## The socio-historical construction of the mind: Alan Garner's *The Stone Book*

The textual analysis practised in this book has focused principally on the devices by which texts signify, and does not pretend to be an analysis of culture. However, its power to describe modes of meaning and author–reader relationships (especially with respect to focalization and types of narratee constructed within texts) has much to contribute to an analysis of the relationship between the writing or reading subject and his/her cultural and ideological context.

The concerns of our present discussion – history, society, ideology, representation, interpretation, language and writing – all coincide as the themes of Alan Garner's brief work, *The Stone Book* (1976), and to this we will now turn as a final example. We will begin with a brief summary of its 'story'. The first of an interlocked quartet of stories, it is set in rural England in the nineteenth century. It is focalized through a young girl named Mary, and begins as her father, a stonemason, finishes off the spire of a church he is building. Mary asks him to be allowed to learn to read, and, when this request is refused, she asks for a prayer book to carry to church and to use for pressing flowers. Instead, her father leads her down a mine and then sends her alone into a narrow crevice; at its end she finds herself in a small chamber, where, painted on the wall, are a dying bison, an arrow which she identifies as her father's mason mark, and the outline of a small hand; the floor retains the impression of innumerable footprints. Since time immemorial, the first child of the family has been brought, once, to view these signs. Later, her father carves a prayer book out of stone, opening the stone to reveal two fossilized plant fronds. In this book Mary reads 'all the stories of the world and the flowers of the flood'.

A basic assumption underlying Garner's story is that the mind constructs and is constructed by cultural and historical processes, amongst which language is central. Since the story is also about 'real' people, much of what Garner does as encoder of the story is predetermined. For their part, decoders (the readers) have to maintain a double focus in the process of decoding: on the one hand are the story's treatment of events, history, society, and so on, and on the other hand are its discoursal existence *in* history and its own implicit attitudes and ideology.

The book's generic status is rather ambiguous. Its syntagms are deceptively simple, and it is typeset and marketed as a children's book. As such it has been very successful, though Aidan Chambers (1985, 31) has suggested that, among other features, its 'consciousness of language' and 'the layered density of the narrative' make it 'a touchstone by which to redefine the limits and possibilities of literature for the young'. The book is also presented as a type of family history: the dust-jacket of the 1983 collected edition juxtaposes a photograph which affirms the historical existence of the characters and a review citation which stresses their relationship to the author (though the child of the last story, set during Garner's own childhood in the 1940s, is not Garner himself).[1] On the other hand, *The Stone Book* is also a detailed narrative, with a large proportion of direct-speech dialogue, and in that respect is obviously a work of fiction. Like so much contemporary narrative, the story refuses to discriminate between fact and fiction, but instead seeks to articulate how the individual always exists within time and empirical reality, and is always already constituted within an on-going story; each life is both a repetition and a reconstitution. Garner's task as a writer is to remake the story (which itself 'explains' why he is writing about West Country rural people in the particular language he does), and to refashion the language into the text's discourse.

One outstanding example of the linguistic process occurs on page 14, when, responding to her question, 'what about the Governor?', Mary's father shouts to her from the scaffold on the steeple, 'I'm the Governor of this gang!' A full semantic explication of the two nouns here, both historically and culturally, would be very elaborate, and would need to include both the 'high' culture irony that Father answers the question posed by the Green Knight in the fourteenth-century *Sir Gawain and the Green Knight* (224–5: 'Wher is. . ./The governour of this gyng?')[2] and the reference to 'popular' culture versions of the children's game 'King of the Castle'; it would need to consider semantic shift and drift in *governor*, here a colloquialism for 'employer' (dating from the early nineteenth century), but also shifted, since Father is both a worker and alone on the scaffold. In less drastic ways, the language of the story extends both paradigmatic and syntagmatic choices beyond standard English to include dialectisms ('I've brought your baggin'; 'Doesn't it fear you up here?'; 'She's no church, and she'll not be'; and so on). This is not only a matter of 'realism' or 'local colour', but another example of a tendency we have pointed to several times in the preceding pages, the tendency at certain historical moments to expand the boundaries of literary English. Now, in the late twentieth century, this is happening all over the English-speaking world, especially as post-colonial literature written by non-English authors in English undermines notions of a normative standard English, and an awareness deepens of the extent to which English literary language has long been subject to particular political, social and linguistic ideologies (see, for example, MacCabe, 1984). By privileging empirical knowledge over book-learning, and the knowledge of the ordinary, practical people over that of the gentry, Garner's story rejects the hegemony of upper/middle-class politics, religion, education and language, although at the same time its own historical situation and mode of discourse must paradoxically assume of its reader the ability to read that is denied Mary.

The following extract offers an example of Garner's meta-linguistic examination of the social construction of signification:

> Father had picked the site for the quarry at the bottom of the Wood Hill. Close by the place, at the road, there was stone to be seen, but it was the soft red gangue that wouldn't last ten years of weather. Yet Father had looked at the way the trees grew, and had felt the earth and the leaf-mould between his fingers, and had said they must dig there. And there they had found the hard yellow-white dimension stone that was the best of all sands for building.
>
>   The beech trees had been cleared over a space, and two loads of the big branches had saved them coals at home for a year. It was one of the first memories of her life; the rock bared and cut by Father, and silver bark in the fire.
>
>   Now the quarry seemed so small, and the church so big. The quarry would fit inside a corner of the church; but the stone had come from it. People said it was because Father cut well, but Father said that a church was only a bit of stone round a lot of air. (13)

There are two kinds of construction represented in this extract. At a simple narrative level, it brings together within the discourse a number of experiences, memories and observations, as Mary's mind links the beginning and ending of the construction of the church. Within that frame are the more complex elements of her Father's comments on signification, and the further interaction of these with natural phenomena and socio-economic conditions and mental associations to make up some of the processes which go towards the construction of Mary as a social being as well as an individual. Her father's roles here allegorize the relationships between signifiers and signifieds, in that his selection of the quarry site stems from his ability to decode from the peripheral signs of the tree-growth and the leaf-mould a presence beneath the unpromising immediate masking sign of the red gangue, and his comment on the completed church reveals how signs have to be imbued with signifying power by their use in society. In between is placed Mary's memory of that earlier time, apparently determined by patterns of cause and effect (clearing the trees resulting in both the cut rock and the firewood); the paratactic structure of the phrases, the repetition of /b/, /k/ and /f/, and the front- and end-focus given to the elemental 'rock' and 'fire', suggest a strong relationship between the phrases, though in fact the relationship is primarily that each records an impression that is both sensory and aesthetic, and each is a sign waiting to be filled with significance. The linguistic features we have pointed to only function as rhetorical links:

> the rock bared and cut by Father
> and silver bark in the fire.

That is, the impressions themselves are unsignifying signs, while on either side of them signs are interpreted, albeit in various or contradictory ways. The task facing Mary, as facing any child (or, indeed, any person), is to learn to interact with family and community in order to discover how to make the best sense of the signs which make up their lives. Even such an apparently material and unequivocal sign as a church can have altered the significance which space and time might be expected to have imparted to it, when it is signified as 'a lot of air'. Heed has to be paid not just to the conventional meanings of contemporary culture but also to tradition, historical process and logic (not necessarily majority logic) to be able to decode signs. As Mary's father later expresses it, in the epigraph we have chosen for this chapter, attention must be paid to 'Time and arithmetic and sense'.

Mary also wishes to leave her artisan/farming family to go into service with the gentry. Her experience underground (in the womb of the earth) and the stone book he carves for her are her father's responses to this desire. Throughout the stories that make up the *Quartet*, young people are depicted in search of a vocation. This search most clearly embodies the text's ideology – the idea that a vocation lies at the intersection of the innate talent of the individual and the kinds of work society enables and needs (or even no longer needs). This doctrine resolves the apparent contradiction between the stonemason's rejection of book-learning and the production of this particular text which both gives him his continued being and transforms him into a sign, since writing, in its turn, is a craft, a mode of representation, and a process of making an object which survives within time even though its meanings may change (just as the prehistoric arrow becomes the stonemason's mark). Therefore, without overtly examining the processes of language or of writing itself, Garner is able to suggest the inextricable interconnectedness of history, society, ideology, representation, interpretation, language and writing.

To push the hypersignification of the discourse a little further, it might be observed that one effect of Garner's writing is to question the Saussurean binary dichotomy between archetypal *langue* and its realization in *parole*. Of some pertinence to this point is Allon White's perceptive comment that critical approaches based on metaphysics (such as deconstruction) treat texts 'not as specific performances within a social discourse, but as abstract repertoires of competence' (1984, 140); White goes on to argue that the main social function of such underlying theories of language 'is to act as sophisticated agents of cultural unification and centralization' (ibid.). Garner explores a complementary and yet in some ways contradictory perspective when he uses the signs of the arrow and the hand in *The Stone Book* to exemplify the complex, two-way relationship between *parole* and *langue*:

> Mary saw Father's mason mark drawn on the wall. It was faint and black, as if drawn with soot. Next to it was an animal, falling. It had nearly worn itself away, but it looked like a bull, a great shaggy bull. It was bigger than it seemed at first, and Father's mark was on it, making the mark like a spear or an arrow.
>
> . . .
>
> She lifted her own [hand] and laid it over the hand on the wall, not touching. Both hands were the same size. She reached nearer. They were the same size. She touched. The rock was cold, but for a moment it had almost felt warm. The hands fitted. Fingers and thumb and palm and a bull and Father's mark in the darkness under the ground.     (43–4)

Mary's 'error' here is to misread an arrow as a mason's mark, reversing the historical transmission of meaning. But of course it never *was* an arrow: in the prehistoric time of its origin it was already a stylized sign, representing an arrow, there, we surmise, to have a magical relationship with, and effect on, real phenomena.[3] It is possible to read Mary's experience as an apprehension of the transcendent signified, the *langue* of which she is a momentary projection into *parole* (with the footprints in the clay being traces of other, vanished bits of *parole*), but this really only applies to the close 'fit' between phenomenal hand and represented hand, whereas the arrow/mason's mark demonstrates differentiation and the formative impact of *parole* on *langue*. The mason's mark does not cause the stones to assemble into a building, any more than an arrow flies of itself – preceding each is the human agent. Likewise, the signifier does not have transcendent significance: this is imposed by social interaction within historical time, and hence the signifier may be appropriated and changed, and even become obliterated, like the bull wearing itself away in time.

## Further directions

*The Stone Book*, together with our reading of it, is another way of getting at the assumption underpinning our analyses throughout our study, and which we would like to see taken much further in subsequent work. Any critical practice which proposes to incorporate a socio-linguistic component is committed to a theory of present and effective signification because it must also be committed to the belief that 'meaning' is socially constructed and constituted. To us, this means that signification lies at the *intersections* of the paradigmatic and syntagmatic axes, that is, at the points where context defines the social, historical and intertextual markings of signifiers.

We remain aware that we have not gone nearly far enough, and that much remains undone, but the kind of intensive and extensive study of the socio-linguistic dimensions of individual signifiers and of how the syntagm functions to control those dimensions that we would like to see lies beyond the scope of this brief historical perspective; it is, indeed, an area so discouragingly vast, with such a large corpus of data necessary to elucidate the signifying parameters of even just key words, that we suppose that at best it will always be an operation that will have to be carried out as part of studies of specific texts. The size of the task, nevertheless, should not prompt a recourse to the deconstructionists' 'infinite extendability of context' (Culler, 1983, 215), and hence infinite deferral of meaning, which students of socio-semantics would in general regard as an evasion. In our view, the socio-semantic dimensions and syntagmatic contexts of a signifier can be described in enough detail to imbue it with a practical or functional signifying presence. For a demonstration of how to do so, we point readers to the excellent study by Christine Richards (1985).

Finally, we do not wish to claim that the preceding chapters have offered a theory and practice of textual analysis that generates 'new' interpretations of literary works, and, indeed, we see little point in the pursuit of novel interpretations for their own sake. But we hope that, from time to time, we have enabled literary works to communicate with a force and clarity that is not always their lot in critical interpretation. Much of what we have pointed out is already known; what we have tried to set out is an account of literary English which, joining together a strong analytical method and a sense of the cultural and historical context of particular texts, may enhance a reader's awareness of and capacity to engage more comprehensively with processes of textual signification, and in turn to describe those processes with increased delicacy and power.

## Notes

1   Compare also the entry in *The Oxford Companion to Children's Literature*, p. 200: the stories 'portray members of Garner's own family in their Cheshire village at four points in time, from the mid-19th to the mid-20th cents.'

2   Garner has remarked how on his first contact with this poem its language seemed to be at one with the West Country dialect he spoke as a child ('Achilles in Altjira', lecture delivered in Edmonton, May 1983, and printed in *Children's Literature Association Quarterly*, 8:4, 1983, 5–10). Though cognate with *gang*, *gyng* is not the same word, but refers to a 'company' or 'gathering of people', a 'retinue' or 'household' (*Middle English Dictionary*). It appears to have fallen together with *gang* early in the seventeenth century.

3   Garner's intertexts here are obviously the cave paintings of Altamira, Lascaux, etc., and, perhaps more importantly, the interpretations which modern people place upon them.

# Glossary

**Apposition** (see also **Co-ordination**): the syntactic parallelism, without overt linking, of elements of equal grammatical status, especially a sequence of nouns or noun phrases, as in the appositional variants in the following lines from Lawrence's 'Bavarian Gentians':

> torch-flower of the blue-smoking darkness, Pluto's dark-blue daze,
> black lamps from the halls of Dis, burning dark blue, . . .

**Coherence**: the effect achieved by a concord of **Cohesion** and **Congruence**, at a hypersyntagmatic level. (This concept is much more subjective and less definable than the two that follow.)

**Cohesion** (**Cohesive ties**): devices (including substitutions and ellipses) which link segments along the (hyper)syntagmatic axis, both within and beyond the sentence. Cohesion links what might seem elliptical dialogue in *Antony and Cleopatra* IV.v.6–8:

> *Antony*: Who's gone this morning?
> *Soldier*:                                        Who!
>    One [who was] ever near thee: call for Enobarbus,
>    He shall not hear thee.

Cohesive ties include the repetition by the two speakers of 'who', first as question, then as exclamation; the ellipsis of '[who was]'; the different references to Enobarbus, 'Who!', 'One', 'He'; the opposed pairs, '[i]s gone/[was] near', 'call for/shall not hear'. See pp. 18–21.

**Congruence**: the relationship between paradigmatic choices, including lexical sets and register; where that relationship is breached, **Incongruity** results, as in the last three lines of Lowell's 'For the Union Dead':

giant finned cars nose forward like fish;
a savage servility
slides by on grease

where the lexical set to do with cars is conflated with the lexical set to do with fish, while the Romance and Latin-derived terms of the middle line clash with the native terms preceding and following, foregrounding each group by their contrast. See pp. 20–1.

**Co-ordination**: (see also **Parataxis**) the chaining of phrases and/or clauses of equal syntactic status, usually with *and, but, or*. Co-ordinate phrases and clauses (together with *Apposition*) are illustrated in one stanza of Gray's 'Ode on a Distant Prospect of Eton College' ll. 61–4 which runs:

These shall the fury Passions tear,
    The vultures of the mind,
Disdainful Anger, pallid Fear,
    And Shame that skulks behind;
Or pining Love shall waste their youth, . . .

**Correlatives**: words, phrases, or clauses can be correlated when they are mutually linked, as by *either/or* or *not only/but also*, or *not/nor*. Pope in *Rape of the Lock* IV.3-8 has six correlated lines beginning with 'Not'.

**Discourse**: the term has both broader and narrower meanings, depending on the context in which it is used. In contradistinction to the inferred textual elements of **Story** and **Hypersignification**, **Discourse** is the primary textual level, the syntagmatic chaining of signifiers, from which the reader decodes the other members of the triad.

In its broader sense, **Discourse** is a much less precise term, and alludes to the concept of a general communicative sign system, delimited mainly by its syntagmatic context, as in uses such as, 'dramatic discourse', 'critical discourse', or 'twentieth-century discourse'. See pp. 6–10.

**Doublet**: a paradigmatic slot may be filled by two signifiers which have a similar meaning or belong to the same associative field. Where the meaning of the two words is virtually identical, the doublet is said to be **intensive**; where the second word introduces further meaning, it is **extensive**. Often, especially in earlier periods, the two words may be drawn from different registers (e.g., formal:colloquial; native:foreign).

**Ellipsis**: the omission of words needed to complete the syntactic construction of a phrase or sentence. T. S. Eliot's *Waste Land*, II.134–6 includes dialogue with understood (elided) subject and verb:

'What shall we ever do?'
    [We shall have] The hot water at ten.
And if it rains, [we shall have] a closed car at four.

As this example shows, ellipsis is an important device for promoting cohesion between sentences, since the gap is easily filled from the previous sentence.

**End-focus**: The final position in a syntagmatic unit (sentence or paragraph, or even phrase) carries climactic emphasis, and attracts special attention, often in verse because of heavy rhythmic stress, and also when it occurs before a pause. The last word in a heroic couplet is foregrounded by such means, as in Johnson's 'Vanity of Human Wishes', l.159:

There mark what ills the scholar's life assail,

where the inversion also focuses attention on the last word.

**Hypersignification** (see also **Discourse, Story**): if the decoder takes the question, 'What is the text about?' at a higher level than that of abstracting the **Story**, and moves on to the wider unexpressed signification of meaning, the implicit thematic levels implied both by the **Story** and by its encoding in the **Discourse**, s/he is taking up the **Hypersignification**. See pp. 8–10.

**Left-/Right-branching**: terms used to point to the position of the verb of the principal clause relative to the qualifying phrases or clauses; if the bulk of the sentence occurs before the verb, it is left-branching (visually to the left of the main verb), while if it occurs after the verb, it is right-branching (visually to the right). The first six lines of Dryden's *Absalom and Achitophel* are a long left-branch before the principal clause of line 7, the verb of which does not occur until the last word of line 8.

**Meronymy**: a type of cohesive tie which functions by naming parts of an entity (as 'leg' and 'arm' refer to parts of a whole 'body'). For example, Spenser's *Epithalamion*, ll. 171–80, lists eyes, forehead, cheeks, lips, shoulders, etc., and finally 'body'. See also Marvell's 'A Dialogue Between the Soul and the Body', cited on p. 230.

**Paradigm (Paradigmatic axis)** (see also **Syntagm, Signifier**): the paradigmatic axis is the vertical axis of signifiers which intersects the linear **Syntagm** or **Syntagmatic axis** of discourse. Each paradigm consists potentially of any member of the word-class able to occupy its particular position (noun/pronoun, verb, adjective, etc.). The possibilities appear to be infinite, but are normally limited by the other signifiers in the syntagmatic string. In the opening sentence of Katherine Mansfield's *The Garden Party* – 'And after all the weather was ideal' – the syntax and sense require the final paradigmatic place to be filled by an adjective, and the context indicates that this will be selected from the set of adjectives used for commenting on the weather; the initial semantic choice is then between sets expressing 'good' or 'bad', and the final choice involves degree ('tolerable', 'fine') and **Register**. This example, in which 'ideal' appears to be an unexpected outcome (see p. 20), also clearly illustrates that paradigmatic choices are contrastive, evoking an awareness of signifiers not selected.

The triad of paradigm/syntagm/signified–signified (like the triad of discourse/story/hypersignification) is a key aspect of textuality.

By analogy, the **Hyperparadigm** functions at the discourse level of the text, with some items rather than others selected for encoding. See pp. 11–18.

**Parataxis** (see also **Co-ordination**): a term used to refer to clauses which are placed beside one another without a specific indication of their co-ordination or subordination to one another. Burke juxtaposes clauses paratactically in his speech *On Conciliation with the Colonies* when he says: 'She [Spain] complies too; she submits; she watches times.'

**Register**: a loosely defined notion, referring to types of language selected for particular functions in particular situations or contexts. The discourses of advertising, of the law, or of sports commentary provide obvious examples: distinctions between levels of social formality can also be described as differences of register.

**Semantic drift**: the denotative 'meaning' of a word is drifted when its syntagmatic context begins to alter it or render it indeterminate by way of the connotations or associations which it thereby acquires. One stanza of Tennyson's *In Memoriam*, 67, ll. 13–14 begins

> And then I know the mist is drawn
>  A *lucid* veil from coast to coast, . . .

where the dictionary meaning of the adjective *lucid*, 'bright, clear', acquires a much less definite sense when it is associated with a coast-to-coast mist and compared with a veil.

**Signifier/Signified** (see also **Paradigm, Syntagm**): together the signifier and signified make up the sign which arbitrarily represents an object or concept, each language having its own special sign(s) for the thing/concept. The signifier or term chosen for the paradigmatic slot within the syntagm is only linked to its signified by the particular culture's conventional agreement, and shifts (e.g., diachronic shifts) can occur at the level of both signifier and signified. Even synchronically, no two people will link the signifier with exactly the same signified, and the gap between signifier and signified always has the potential for destabilizing signification. Each epithet in Chaucer's *General Prologue* description of the Knight, 'He was a verray, parfit, gentil knight' (72), is a signifier whose signified was not only floating for the fourteenth-century audience but has also shifted its signified quite markedly for the twentieth-century reader. See pp. 13–18.

**Story** (see also **Discourse, Hypersignification**): if the question 'What is the text about?' is posed, one likely reply will concern what the decoder draws from the discourse about what happens to whom, when and where; it deals with what the decoder perceives as the chronological progression of events befalling the main protagonist(s) located in a temporal-spatial setting. The **Story** differs from the discourse, being the individual decoder's own abstraction from that discourse, and may well vary from reader to reader, depending upon what the individual considers to be important incidents.

If the question is posed a second time, then the decoder may well move on to the **Hypersignification** which is an abstraction at a higher level, taking up what **Story** and **Discourse** together signify in thematic terms.

**Subordination** (see also **Co-ordination**): the hierarchizing of clauses which contain information not considered primary. Where the main information will be encoded in the principal clause, the supplementary information is placed in subordinate clauses, and their relationship to that main clause spelled out by the introductory subordinator, which indicates time, place, manner, purpose, reason, cause, condition, concession and so on. Relative and noun clauses are by and large the commonest subordinate clauses, but the adverbial clauses imply more about the relationship of their information to the principal clause. The syntagmatic ordering of the subordinate clause(s) relative to the principal(s) has an important effect upon the signification. The final stanza of Herbert's poem 'Man' has two brief imperative clauses surrounded by a series of temporal, purpose, and manner clauses.

**Syntagm (Syntagmatic axis)** (see also **Paradigm, Signifier**): the syntagm is the horizontal axis which chains together the items of the vertical axis of the *Paradigm*, bringing the paradigmatic choices into a particular relationship and progression. The writer may use normal word-order, or may distort it in some way, and any deviation from the norm foregrounds the signifiers that are out of their usual position. The syntagm controls the order in which the decoder receives the segments of the encoded message, and imposes a progression which usually functions at a less than conscious level. It thus controls (or subverts) the range of associations or connotations which the **Signifier** carries, and can focus more attention upon either the **Signifier** or the **Signified**. The marked disruptions of the syntagm in the first line of Hopkins's 'Carrion Comfort', 'Not, I'll not, carrion comfort, Despair, not feast on thee', foreground the opening negative, which is repeated twice more before the verb 'feast'. Embedded within two of the negative particles are the appositional signifiers for the addressee, with the metaphoric phrase 'carrion comfort' preceding the abstract noun, and so emotively controlling its associations. The normal word order,

*'I'll not feast on thee, carrion comfort' lacks the heavy emphasis upon the speaker's refusal to ingest despair, and hence upon the strength of the desire to do so.

By analogy, the **Hypersyntagm** functions at the broader discourse level of a text, structuring the ordering and progression of the information being encoded. See pp. 11–21.

**Tenor** and **Vehicle**: in analysis of figurative language, the tenor refers to the decoded significance of a figure (what it is 'about') and the vehicle refers to the analogy by which the tenor is represented. The following lines from Hardy's 'The Darkling Thrush' contain two interrelated illustrations:

> The tangled bine-stems scored the sky
>    Like strings of broken lyres

In the first line, *scored*, as a deviation from the paradigmatic set of verbs which might be expected to express a relationship between tree-branches and sky, is a metaphor. Its vehicle (the primary signified) is a process of cutting; its tenor, a derived signified which the reader must infer, is the shapes made by branches in silhouette against the sky; a third element is the **Ground**, the aspect in respect of which tenor and vehicle may be said to resemble each other. The simile of the second line expands the metaphor, introducing a new vehicle and ground, but this time the ground has been explicitly expressed in 'tangled'. See pp. 218–20 and 234–5.

# Bibliography

Abrams, Meyer (1965), 'Structure and Style in the Greater Romantic Lyric', in *From Sensibility to Romanticism: Essays Presented to F. A. Pottle*, ed. F. W. Hillis and H. Bloom, New York: Oxford University Press.

Aers, David (1987), 'The Good Shepherds of Medieval Criticism', *Southern Review*, 20, 168–85.

Amis, George T. (1976), 'The Structure of the Augustan Couplet', *Genre*, 9, 37–58.

Armstrong, Nancy (1983), 'A Language of One's Own: Communication-Modeling Systems in *Mrs. Dalloway*', *Language and Style*, 16, 343–60.

Barber, Charles (1976), *Early Modern English*, London: Andre Deutsch.

Barrell, John (1988), *Poetry, Language and Politics*, Manchester: Manchester University Press.

Barthelme, Donald (1978), *City Life*, New York: Pocket Books.

Barthes, Roland (1968), 'The Death of the Author', in *Image – Music – Text*, trans. Stephen Heath, New York: Hill & Wang, 1977, 142–8.

Bateson, F. W. (1973), *English Poetry and the English Language*, 3rd edn, Oxford: Clarendon Press.

Beer, Gillian (1983), *Darwin's Plots*, London: Routledge & Kegan Paul.

Bhabha, Homi (1984), 'Representation and the Colonial Text', in Frank Gloversmith (ed.), *The Theory of Reading*, Brighton: Harvester Press, 93–122.

Blake, N. F. (1977), *The English Language in Medieval Literature*, London: Methuen.

Blake, N. F. (1983), *Shakespeare's Language: An Introduction*, London: Macmillan.

Bloomfield, Morton W. (1963), 'A Grammatical Approach to Personification Allegory', *Modern Philology*, 60, 161–71.

Bredin, Hugh (1984a), 'Roman Jakobson on Metaphor and Metonymy', *Philosophy and Literature*, 8, 89–103.

Bredin, Hugh (1984b), 'Metonymy', *Poetics Today*, 5, 45–58.

Broadbent, John B. (1960), *Some Graver Subject: An Essay on*

*Paradise Lost*, New York: Barnes & Noble.

Broadhead, Glenn J. (1980), 'Samuel Johnson and the Rhetoric of Conversation', *Studies in English Literature*, 20, 461–74.

Brogan, Jacqueline Vaught (1986), 'Wallace Stevens: "The Sound of Right Joining"', *Texas Studies in Literature and Language*, 28, 107–20.

Brook, G. L. (1970), *The Language of Dickens*, London: Andre Deutsch.

Brown, Laura (1985), *Alexander Pope*, Oxford: Basil Blackwell.

Brown, Paul (1985), '"This Thing of Darkness I Acknowledge Mine": *The Tempest* and the Discourse of Colonialism', in Jonathan Dollimore and Alan Sinfield (eds) (1985), *Political Shakespeare*, Manchester: Manchester University Press, 48–71.

Burnley, David (1983), *A Guide to Chaucer's Language*, London: Macmillan.

Cameron, Deborah (1985), *Feminism and Linguistic Theory*, London: Macmillan.

Carpenter, Humphrey and Mari Prichard (1984), *The Oxford Companion to Children's Literature*, Oxford: Oxford University Press.

Carroll, David (1975), 'Mimesis Reconsidered: Literature, History, Ideology', *Diacritics*, 5, 5–12.

Carter, Ronald and Paul Simpson (eds) (1989), *Language, Discourse and Literature: An Introductory Reader in Discourse Stylistics*, London: Unwin Hyman.

Castiglione, Baldassare (1974), *The Book of the Courtier*, trans. Thomas Hoby, London: Dent.

Chambers, Aidan (1985), 'Axes for Frozen Seas', in *Booktalk*, London: Bodley Head, 14–33.

Chapman, Gerald (1984), 'Burke's American Tragedy', in James Engell (ed.) (1984), *Johnson and His Age*, Cambridge, Mass.: Harvard University Press, 387–423.

Chatman, Seymour (1978), *Story and Discourse: Narrative Structure in Fiction and Film*, Ithaca: Cornell University Press.

Choe, Wolhee (1985), 'Stevens' "An Ordinary Evening in New Haven": The Mind and the Poetic Sequence', *Language and Style*, 18, 277–92.

Clark, Beverly Lyon (1983), 'In Search of Barthelme's Weeping Father', *Philological Quarterly*, 62, 419–33.

Clark, John W. (1975), *The Language and Style of Anthony Trollope*, London: Andre Deutsch.

Cluysenaar, Anne (1976), *Introduction to Literary Stylistics*, London: Batsford.

Connor, Steven (1985), *Charles Dickens*, Oxford: Basil Blackwell.

Cottle, Basil (1969), *The Triumph of English 1350–1400*, London: Blandford Press.

Craig, Cairns (1982), *Yeats, Eliot, Pound and the Politics of Poetry*, London: Croom Helm.

Croll, Morris (1921), 'Attic Prose in the Seventeenth Century', *Studies in Philology*, 18, 79–128.

Crombie, Winifred (1984), '"To Enter in These Bonds is to be Free"; Semantic Relations and the Baroque Prose Style of John Donne', *Language and Style*, 17, 123–38.

Crozier, Andrew (1983), 'Thrills and Frills: Poetry as Figures of Empirical Lyricism', in Alan Sinfield (ed.), *Society and Literature 1945–1970*, London: Methuen, 199–233.

Culler, Jonathan (1975), *Structuralist Poetics*, London: Routledge & Kegan Paul.

Culler, Jonathan (1981), *The Pursuit of Signs*, Ithaca: Cornell University Press, Ch. 10.

Culler, Jonathan (1983), *On Deconstruction*, London: Routledge & Kegan Paul.

Delany, Sheila (1974), 'Substructure and Superstructure: The Politics of Allegory in the Fourteenth Century', *Science and Society*, 38, 257–80.

Dollimore, Jonathan and Alan Sinfield (eds) (1985), *Political Shakespeare*, Manchester: Manchester University Press, Ch. 1.

Duncan, Robert (1968), *Bending the Bow*, New York: New Directions.

Ebert, Teresa L. (1985), 'Metaphor, Metonymy and Ideology: Language and Perception in *Mrs. Dalloway*', *Language and Style*, 18, 152–64.

Elam, Keir (1980), *The Semiotics of Theatre and Drama*, London: Methuen.

Engell, James (ed.) (1984), *Johnson and His Age*, Cambridge, Mass.: Harvard University Press.

Flanigan, Beverly Olson (1986), 'Donne's "Holy Sonnet VII" as Speech Act', *Language and Style*, 19, 49–57.

Foucault, Michel (1970), *The Order of Things: An Archaeology of the Human Sciences*, London: Tavistock.

Fowles, John (1986), *A Maggot*, London: Pan Books.

Frow, John (1984), 'Language, Discourse, Ideology', *Language and Style*, 17, 302–15.

Gallagher, Catherine (1980), 'The Failure of Realism: *Felix Holt*', *Nineteenth-Century Fiction*, 35, 372–84.

Garner, Alan (1983), *The Stone Book Quartet*, Glasgow: Collins.

Gibson, Mary Ellis (1981), 'The Poetry of Struggle: Browning's Style and "The Parleying with Gerard de Lairesse"', *Victorian Poetry*, 19, 225–42.

Gilbert, A. J. (1979), *Literary Language from Chaucer to Johnson*, London: Macmillan.

Gilbert, Sandra M. and Susan Gubar (1985), 'Sexual Linguistics:

Gender, Language, Sexuality', *New Literary History*, 16, 515–43.

Gillies, John (1986), 'Shakespeare's Virginian Masque', *English Literary History*, 53, 673–707.

Goodman, Nelson (1981), 'Routes of Reference', *Critical Inquiry*, 8, 121–32.

Gordon, Ian A. (1966), *The Movement of English Prose*, London: Longman.

Greenblatt, Stephen (1985), 'Invisible Bullets: Renaissance Authority and its Subversion', in Jonathan Dollimore and Alan Sinfield (eds), *Political Shakespeare*, Manchester: Manchester University Press, 18–47.

Gutwinski, G. (1976), *Cohesion in Literary Texts*, The Hague: Mouton.

Haggerty, George E. (1984), 'Fact and Fancy in the Gothic Novel', *Nineteenth-Century Fiction*, 39, 379–91.

Hakluyt, Richard (1958 edn), *Voyages and Documents*, selected by Janet Hampden, London: Oxford University Press.

Halliday, M. A. K. and Ruqaiya Hasan (1976), *Cohesion in English*, London: Longman.

Halliday, M. A. K. and Ruqaiya Hasan (1985), *Language, Context, and Text: Aspects of Language in a Social-Semiotic Perspective*, Geelong: Deakin University Press, Ch. 5.

Hansen, Marlene R. (1985), 'Sex and Love, Marriage and Friendship: A Feminist Reading of the Quest for Happiness in *Rasselas*', *English Studies*, 66, 513–25.

Harland, Paul W. (1986), 'Dramatic Technique and Personae in Donne's Sermons', *English Literary History*, 53, 709–26.

Harrison, Bernard (1986), 'The Truth About Metaphor', *Philosophy and Literature*, 10, 38–55.

Hassan, Ihab (1987), 'Making Sense: The Trials of Postmodern Discourse', *New Literary History*, 18, 437–59.

Hill, Jane H. (1988), 'Language, Culture, and World View', in Frederick J. Newmeyer (ed.), *Linguistics: The Cambridge Survey*, Vol. IV, 14–36.

Hofstadter, Douglas R. (1979), *Gödel, Escher, Bach: An Eternal Golden Braid*, Brighton: Harvester Press.

Hrushovski, Benjamin (1984), 'Poetic Metaphor and Frames of Reference', *Poetics Today*, 5, 5–43.

Ihimaera, Witi (1975), *Tangi*, Auckland: Heinemann.

Jakobson, Roman (1971), 'Two Aspects of Language and Two Types of Aphasic Disturbance', in Roman Jakobson and Morris Halle, *Fundamentals of Language*, The Hague: Mouton, 55–82.

Jefferson, D. W. (1982), '"Pitch beyond Ubiquity": Thought and Style in Sir Thomas Browne', in *Approaches to Sir Thomas Browne: the Ann Arbor Tercentenary Lectures and Essays*, ed. C. A. Patrides, Columbia, Mo.: University of Missouri Press, 143–54.

Johnson, Anthony L. (1982), 'Jakobsonian Theory and Literary Semiotics: Toward a Generative Typology of the Text', *New Literary History*, 14, 33–61.

Johnson, Samuel (1773), *A Dictionary of the English Language*, London: W. Strahan.

Jones, John (1969), *Pope's Couplet Art*, Athens: Ohio University Press.

Jones, Nicholas R. (1982), 'Texts and Contexts: Two Languages in George Herbert's Poetry', *Studies in Philology*, 79, 162–76.

Joseph, Gerhard (1985), 'The Echo and the Mirror *en abîme* in Victorian Poetry', *Victorian Poetry*, 23, 403–12.

Joyce, James (1960 edn), *Ulysses*, London: Bodley Head.

Kalstone, David (1965), *Sidney's Poetry: Contexts and Interpretations*, Cambridge, Mass.: Harvard University Press.

Keefe, Robert (1986), 'Literati, Language, and Darwinism', *Language and Style*, 19, 123–37.

Kelly, Gary (1979), '"A Constant Vicissitude of Interesting Passions": Ann Radcliffe's Perplexed Narratives', *Ariel*, 10: 2, 45–64.

Kennedy, Andrew K. (1983), *Dramatic Dialogue*, Cambridge: Cambridge University Press.

Kenner, Hugh (1974), 'Pope's Reasonable Rhymes', *English Literary History*, 41, 74–88.

Knoepflmacher, U. C. (1968), *George Eliot's Early Novels: The Limits of Realism*, Berkeley and Los Angeles: University of California Press.

Kress, Gunther and Robert Hodge (1979), *Language as Ideology*, London: Routledge & Kegan Paul.

Langbaum, Robert (1970), *The Modern Spirit: Essays on the Continuity of Nineteenth- and Twentieth-Century Literature*, London: Chatto & Windus.

Lee, David A. (1984), 'The Language of Literature: A Sociolinguistic Perspective', *Language and Style*, 17, 316–28.

Leech, Geoffrey N. (1969), *A Linguistic Guide to English Poetry*, London: Longman, Ch. 3.

Leech, Geoffrey and Michael Short (1981), *Style in Fiction*, London: Longman.

Leith, Dick (1983), *A Social History of English*, London: Routledge & Kegan Paul.

Lenta, Margaret (1984), 'Capitalism or Patriarchy and Immortal Love: A Study of *Wuthering Heights*', *Theoria*, 62, 63–76.

Levinson, Marjorie (1986), *Wordsworth's Great Period Poems*, Cambridge: Cambridge University Press.

Libby, Anthony (1984), *Mythologies of Nothing*, Urbana and Chicago: University of Illinois Press.

Lipking, Lawrence (1984), 'Johnson and the Meaning of Life', in James Engell (1984), *Johnson and His Age*, Cambridge, Mass.: Harvard University Press, 1–27.

Lodge, David (1966), *Language of Fiction*, London: Routledge & Kegan Paul.

Lodge, David (1981), *Working With Structuralism*, London: Routledge & Kegan Paul.

McArthur, Murray (1986), '"Signs on a White Field": Semiotics and Forgery in the "Proteus" Chapter of *Ulysses*', *English Literary History*, 53, 633–52.

MacCabe, Colin (1978), *James Joyce and the Revolution of the Word*, London: Macmillan.

MacCabe, Colin (1984), 'Towards a Modern Trivium – English Studies Today', *Critical Quarterly*, 26, 69–82.

McConnell-Ginet, Sally (1988), 'Language and Gender', in Frederick J. Newmeyer (ed.) (1988), *Linguistics: The Cambridge Survey*, Vol. IV, 75–99.

McCrea, Brian (1980), 'Style or Styles: the Problem of Johnson's Prose', *Style*, 14, 201–15.

McGann, Jerome J. (1987), 'Contemporary Poetry, Alternate Routes', *Critical Inquiry*, 13, 624–47.

McGowan, John P. (1980), 'The Turn of George Eliot's Realism', *Nineteenth-Century Fiction*, 35, 171–92.

McKee, Patricia (1985), 'Corresponding Freedoms: Language and the Self in *Pamela*', *English Literary History*, 52, 621–48.

McNeil, Helen (1986), *Emily Dickinson*, London: Virago Press.

*Macquarie Thesaurus, The* (1984) ed. J. R. L. Bernard, Sydney: Macquarie Library.

Manning, Peter J. (1979), '*Don Juan* and Byron's Imperceptiveness to the English Word', *Studies in Romanticism*, 18, 207–33.

Marks, Emerson R. (1984), 'The Antinomy of Style in Augustan Poetics', in James Engell (ed.) (1984), *Johnson and His Age*, Cambridge, Mass.: Harvard University Press, 215–32.

Marotti, Arthur F. (1982), '"Love is Not Love": Elizabethan Sonnet Sequences and the Social Order', *English Literary History*, 49, 396–428.

Michels, James (1982), 'The Role of Language in Consciousness: A Structuralist Look at "Proteus" in *Ulysses*', *Language and Style*, 15, 23–32.

Miles, Josephine (1965), *The Continuity of Poetic Language*, New York: Octagon Books.

Miller, Cristanne (1983), 'How "Low Feet" Stagger: Disruptions of Language in Dickinson's Poetry', in Suzanne Juhasz (ed.), *Feminist Critics Read Emily Dickinson*, Bloomington: Indiana University Press, 134–55.

Miller, David Lee (1986), 'Spenser's Poetics: The Poem's Two Bodies', *PMLA*, 101, 170–85.

Miller, J. Hillis (1976), 'Stevens' Rock and Criticism as Cure', *Georgia Review*, 30, 5–31, 330–48.

Milroy, James (1977), *The Language of Gerard Manley Hopkins*, London: Andre Deutsch.

Montrose, Louis Adrian (1977), 'Celebration and Insinuation: Sir Philip Sidney and the Motives of Elizabethan Courtship', *Renaissance Drama*, n.s. 8, 3–35.

Moore, Patrick (1986), 'William Carlos Williams and the Modernist Attack on Logical Syntax', *English Literary History*, 53, 895–916.

Morris, John N. (1983), 'Pope and the Idiom of Art', *Sewanee Review*, 91, 519–50.

Morrison, Blake (1980), *The Movement: English Poetry and Fiction of the 1950s*, London: Oxford University Press.

Mossberg, Barbara (1982), *Emily Dickinson: When a Writer is a Daughter*, Bloomington: Indiana University Press.

Mudge, Bradford K. (1985), 'Song of Himself: Crisis and Selection in *The Prelude*, Books 1 and 7', *Texas Studies in Literature and Language*, 27, 1–24.

Muir, Kenneth (ed.) (1956), *Elizabethan and Jacobean Prose 1550–1620*, Harmondsworth: Penguin.

Neely, Carol Thomas (1988), 'Constructing the Subject: Feminist Practice and the New Renaissance Discourses', *English Literary Renaissance*, 18, 5–18.

Neill, Edward (1987), 'Between Deference and Destruction: "Situations" of Recent Critical Theory and Jane Austen's *Emma*', *Critical Quarterly*, 29:3, 39–54.

Newmeyer, Frederick J. (ed.) (1988), *Linguistics: The Cambridge Survey*, Vols I–IV, Cambridge: Cambridge University Press.

Nichols, Ashton, (1983), '"Will Sprawl" in the "Ugly Actual": The Positive Grotesque in Browning', *Victorian Poetry*, 21, 157–70.

Novak, Maximilian E. (1984), 'Shaping the Augustan Myth: John Dryden and the Politics of Restoration Augustanism', in *Greene Centennial Studies: Essays Presented to Donald Greene in the Centennial Year of the University of Southern California*, ed. Paul J. Korshin and Robert R. Allen, Charlottesville: University Press of Virginia, 1–21.

Page, Norman (1972), *The Language of Jane Austen*, Oxford: Blackwell.

Page, Norman (1973), *Speech in the English Novel*, London: Longman.

Partridge, A. C. (1971), *The Language of Renaissance Poetry*, London: Andre Deutsch.

Patterson, Annabel M. (1979), '"How to load and . . . bend": Syntax and Interpretation in Keats's *To Autumn*', *PMLA*, 94, 449–58.

Pearsall, Derek (1970), *John Lydgate*, London: Routledge & Kegan Paul.

Piper, William Bowman (1985), 'The Scope of Discourse in Berkeley and Swift', *Language and Style*, 18, 334–41.

Porter, David T. (1966), *The Art of Emily Dickinson's Early Poetry*, Cambridge, Mass.: Harvard University Press.

Presley, John W. (1985), 'Strategies for Detemporalizing Language in Modern Literature', *Language and Style*, 18, 293–301.

Prunty, Wyatt (1985), 'Emaciated Poetry', *Sewanee Review*, 93, 78–94.

Richards, Christine (1985), 'Inferential Pragmatics and the Literary Text', *Journal of Pragmatics*, 9, 261–85.

Richardson, Samuel (1962 edn), *Pamela*, ed. M. Kinkead-Weekes, London: Dent.

Ricks, Christopher (1963), *Milton's Grand Style*, Oxford: Clarendon Press.

Rimmon-Kenan, Shlomith (1983), *Narrative Fiction*, London: Methuen.

Roscow, G. H. (1981), *Syntax and Style in Chaucer's Poetry*, Cambridge: D. S. Brewer.

Rose, Mary Beth (1984), 'Moral Conceptions of Sexual Love in Elizabethan Comedy', *Renaissance Drama*, n.s. 15, 1–29.

Rushdie, Salman (1982), *Midnight's Children*, London: Picador.

Ruthven, K. K. (1969), 'The Poet as Etymologist', *Critical Quarterly*, 11, 9–37.

Sacks, Sheldon (ed.) (1979), *On Metaphor*, Chicago: University of Chicago Press.

Said, Edward W. (1978), *Orientalism*, London: Routledge & Kegan Paul.

Scholes, Robert (1972), '*Ulysses*: A Structuralist Approach', *James Joyce Quarterly*, 10, 161–71.

Schuman, Samuel (1978), 'The Widow's Garden – "The Nun's Priest's Tale" and the Great Chain of Being', *Studies in the Humanities*, 6, 12–14.

Scott, Patrick Greig (1980), '"Flowering in A Lonely Word": Tennyson and the Victorian Study of Language', *Victorian Poetry*, 18, 371–81.

Selby, F. G. (ed.) (1956), *Burke's Speech on Conciliation with America*, London: Macmillan.

Sherbo, Arthur (1975), *English Poetic Diction from Chaucer to Wordsworth*, East Lansing, Mich.: Michigan State University Press.

Showalter, Elaine (1982), *A Literature of Their Own*, London: Virago, rev. edn.

Simpson, David (1982), *Wordsworth and the Figurings of the Real*, London: Macmillan.

Sinfield, Alan (1971), *The Language of Tennyson's 'In Memoriam'*, Oxford: Blackwell.

Stephens, John and Ruth Waterhouse (1987), 'Authorial Revision and Constraints on the Role of the Reader: Some Examples from Wilfred Owen', *Poetics Today*, 8, 65–83.

Stephens, John (1988), 'Syntagmatic and Paradigmatic Elaboration, and Middle English Poetic Style', *Parergon*, n.s. 6a (1988), 23–35.

Stoddard, Eve Walsh (1985), 'The Spots of Time: Wordsworth's Semiology of the Self', *Romanticism Past and Present*, 9, 1–24.

Svilpis, J. E. (1982), 'Johnson, Humanism, and "The Last Great Revolution of the Intellectual World"', *Studies in Eighteenth-Century Culture*, 11, 299–310.

Terry, R. C. (1983), *Victorian Popular Fiction, 1860–80*, London: Macmillan.

Toolan, Michael J. (1988), *Narrative: A Critical Linguistic Introduction*, London: Routledge.

Trimpi, Wesley (1962), 'Jonson and the Neo-Latin Authorities for the Plain Style', *PMLA*, 77, 21–6.

Uphaus, Robert W. (1987), 'Jane Austen and Female Reading', *Studies in the Novel*, 19, 334–45.

Waterhouse, Ruth (1988), 'Self-Reflexivity and "Wraetlic Word" in *Bleak House* and *Andreas*', *Journal of Narrative Technique* 18, 211–25.

Welz, Dieter (1973), '"A Winter Landscape in Neutral Colours": Some Notes on Philip Larkin's Vision of Reality', *Theoria*, 39, 61–73.

Whaler, James (1932), 'Animal Simile in *Paradise Lost*', *PMLA*, 47, 534–53.

White, Allon (1984), 'Bakhtin, Sociolinguistics and Deconstruction', in Frank Gloversmith (ed.), *The Theory of Reading*, Brighton: Harvester Press, 123–46.

Williamson, George (1951), *The Senecan Amble: A Study in Prose Form from Bacon to Collier*, Chicago: University of Chicago Press.

Woolf, Virginia (1958 edn), *Mrs Dalloway*, London: Hogarth Press.

Wright, Raymond (ed.) (1956), *Prose of the Romantic Period 1780–1830*, Harmondsworth: Penguin.

Wright, T. R. (1984), '*Middlemarch* as a Religious Novel, or Life Without God', in David Jasper (ed.), *Images of Belief in Literature*, London: Macmillan, 138–52.

# Index